Grieving

with Your Whole Heart

Spiritual Wisdom
and Practice
for Finding Comfort,
Hope and Healing
after Loss

Introduction by Thomas Moore,
author of *Care of the Soul*

Created by the Editors at SkyLight Paths

Walking Together, Finding the Way®

SKYLIGHT PATHS®
PUBLISHING

Woodstock, Vermont

Grieving with Your Whole Heart:
Spiritual Wisdom and Practice for Finding Comfort, Hope and Healing after Loss

2015 Quality Paperback Edition, First Printing
© 2015 by SkyLight Paths Publishing
Introduction © 2015 by Thomas Moore

Library of Congress Cataloging-in-Publication Data
Grieving with your whole heart : spiritual wisdom and practice for finding comfort, hope and healing after loss / Created by the editors at SkyLight Paths. —Paperback edition.
    pages cm
  Includes bibliographical references and index.
    ISBN 978-1-59473-599-8 (pbk.)—ISBN 978-1-59473-605-6 (ebook) 1. Grief. 2. Death—Religious aspects. 3. Loss (Psychology) I. SkyLight Paths Publishing.
  BF575.G7G746 2015
  155.9'37—dc23
                                        2015020743

10   9   8   7   6   5   4   3   2   1

Manufactured in the United States of America
Cover design: Jenny Buono
Interior design: Tim Holtz
Cover art: © Tatiana Kholina / shutterstock.com

SkyLight Paths Publishing is creating a place where people of different spiritual traditions come together for challenge and inspiration, a place where we can help each other understand the mystery that lies at the heart of our existence.
SkyLight Paths sees both believers and seekers as a community that increasingly transcends traditional boundaries of religion and denomination—people wanting to learn from each other, *walking together, finding the way.*

SkyLight Paths, "Walking Together, Finding the Way" and colophon are trademarks of LongHill Partners, Inc., registered in the U.S. Patent and Trademark Office.

Walking Together, Finding the Way
Published by SkyLight Paths Publishing
A Division of LongHill Partners, Inc.
Sunset Farm Offices, Route 4, P.O. Box 237
Woodstock, VT 05091
Tel: (802) 457-4000   Fax: (802) 457-4004
www.skylightpaths.com

Contents

Breathe—Finding a Still Point   43

Remember—Keeping a Connection

Heal—Reaching Out for Comfort and Strength

Reorient—Finding Yourself in an Upside-Down World   161

Index of Practices

Introduction

Grief—A Power of the Soul

Thomas Moore

Though painful and unwanted, grief has unexpected creative and transformative power. It is not just an emotional response to loss but a deep
unsettling of the soul. In grief you realize that you can't go on as before, and
some of the pain comes from losing familiar sources of meaning. You have to
reinvent life, imagine it differently. At the same time grief ties you to the past.
Because of grief your life remains whole, even when events seem to tear it
apart. Grief won't let you forget what life has been like.

As an expression of the soul, grief also has its own purposes and timing.
The pain may be so strong that you don't notice that grief has a positive
impact. You just want it to end, and you may have expectations about how
long it should last. But grief does its own thing, hanging around until its
work is done, and sometimes its work never ends. Real grief rarely goes away.
It may seem to have been absorbed by time, and then unexpectedly one day
it makes another appearance.

To do its work on you, grief has to be accepted, refined, and absorbed. Let
me explain each of those phases, because each one is essential.

First, you allow yourself to feel the grief as purely as possible—no excuses,
no qualifications, no evasions. You speak for it directly, letting people know
the depth of your emotion. If you're embarrassed by it or think that you're
above it, you have to ease up on your defenses and let the grief simply be.

Second, over time you can refine your grief. When you express it directly
and tell the stories that emerge from it, it shifts from being a cloud of emotion to a meaningful collection of images. For example, your grief may lead

you to think about the many good things that came from a person who is no longer in your life. Your grief may be teaching you how to be a more sensitive person, how to be a good friend to others and express your love more openly. This refinement of the plain emotion gives you a task that will transform your pain into relational skill.

Don't overlook this key question in working through your grief: What is it asking you to do? I have met people whose bitter grief told them to start a foundation, make a garden, become a teacher, or build a park. This creative, generous, socially conscious action came directly from the grief, softening the pain and completing the whole experience. I speak of refining grief because, if we take instruction from it, raw emotion can turn into a specific idea and a plan.

Third, you no longer experience grief as coming from outside and making you uncomfortable. Now it has become part of your make-up and personality. You now embody its lessons, redeeming the loss by taking important insights from it. You may value friendship more, or understand the importance of a place or an object. What formerly was a painful emotion weighing you down becomes an aspect of character that helps you live a better life.

When you absorb your grief, it works for you instead of against you. You are relieved, not by having it disappear completely, but by making use of its positive potential. It has gone from being a dominating emotion to a spark of creative action. Notice that certain emotions have us in their power, making us their passive victims. But we can transform those same emotions into creative action, in which we are now the actors and not the receivers.

Interestingly, grief is related to the two words "gravity" and "gravitas." Grief keeps you down to earth with the rest of humanity. It makes you more tenderly human. It also gives you personal weight. If you can carry the grief of many losses, as most of us do, then you will be a person of experience and thoughtfulness. You will have gravitas, and that weight of personality will give substance to your work and your relationships.

You can let grief work for you by responding to it imaginatively. Rituals, prayers, poems, songs, music, drawings and paintings, dancing, and especially gardening can give body to your grief without being excessively personal. They give your emotion an external form that you can contemplate and relate to. Conversations with family members and friends can also help you transform plain grief into a more focused awareness of what is important and how you might change.

Grief may feel overwhelming, but that is only because it is time for you to expand your heart and make it capable of far more love and connection. In this way, grief is a pathway to a more soul-centered life. Grief scoops you out and makes room for deeper experience and increased vitality.

Grief teaches you how to appreciate the bittersweet nature of all that is genuinely human. It takes you beyond romanticism or negativity. Grief teaches you that life is always a blend of the happy and the sad, the easy and the challenging. It shows you how to hold pain without losing pleasure and how to respond to crisis without losing hope.

The ancient Greeks referred to the great god Eros, who held the power to live joyfully and with pleasure, as bittersweet. I don't use this word lightly. If you can live day by day with a full appreciation for the bittersweet nature of your work, your family and your loves, you will find deeper satisfaction in everything you do. And there is no better way to learn about the bittersweet than to go through real grief.

Grief spurs you to grow up into a complete, ripened person. It's a form of initiation, preparing you to be a good teacher, friend, counselor, leader, or spouse. This painful emotion can waken new levels of empathy and compassion. It can prepare you for full engagement with life and raise you to a new level of experience. It is profoundly unsettling, and yet it is your guide.

Surrendering to the Desert

Christine Valters Paintner, PhD, Obl. OSB

The older I get, the more I encounter desert experiences in my life. I seek out the wisdom of the desert fathers and mothers—for courage in staying with my difficult experiences and for hope that these difficult journeys have a bigger purpose. I live the desert way in my ordinary life by making space for silence and solitude, staying present to my experiences, and seeking out elders and wise mentors.

Even while writing [a book on the desert fathers and mothers], I encountered desert times in my life. My mother-in-law, Helen, who had struggled with Alzheimer's for several years, finally entered her last days. There was much relief in her letting go, but also great grief. Her husband did not want his beloved of almost fifty years to leave her body even though she had departed her mind long before; he was left bereft.

As I sat with her in those last few days of her life, I was aware how much this disease had taken from this once beautiful and vibrant woman. I felt wave after wave of grief rise up over how senseless the situation felt. And there, the desert elders met me in my grief, calling me to

> Abba Alonius said, "If I had not destroyed myself completely, I should not have been able to rebuild and shape myself again."[1]
>
> [Abba Nilus] said, "Whatever you have endured out of love of wisdom will bear fruit for you at the time of prayer."[2]

Christine Valters Paintner, PhD, Obl. OSB, a Benedictine oblate, is the online abbess of www.abbeyofhearts.com and frequently leads retreats and teaches on the wisdom of Benedictine, Celtic, and desert ways of praying. She is author of *Desert Fathers and Mothers: Early Christian Wisdom Sayings—Annotated & Explained* (SkyLight Paths), among other books.

not look away, to stay with my experience, to stay with Helen even as she lay dying.

The desert fathers and mothers don't offer up neat and tidy answers for life's struggles. They simply acknowledge that the struggles exist, often mysteriously in the place of our deepest encounters with God. The desert elders embrace mystery and unknowing. The desert strips away all trite and easy explanations for how the world works....

Each of us encounters the power of destruction in our lives: the time when a loved one dies, or we receive a diagnosis of serious illness, or we lose a dream, a job, or an identity. Our temptation is to pretend it doesn't hurt as much as it does. We want to run toward our favorite way to numb the pain.

The paradox in the spiritual life is that this journey through destruction is necessary to reach any kind of resurrection or new life beyond it. We are rebuilt and reshaped through this process. We must fully surrender ourselves to the awfulness of it. We must stay present with how we feel and bring compassion to ourselves in the process. We must learn to no longer feel victim to our suffering, but to instead discover a kind of inner fierceness that allows us to look death in the eye without flinching.

The desert fathers and mothers tell us to do this through practice, day by day, staying with the smaller kinds of grief that arise all the time. We stay with our breath, using it as an anchor in this moment. We allow the fullness of the feelings to move through our bodies.

The only way through grief is to take the journey right into its heart.

Express

The Storm of Emotion

Lament lets pain out of its cage.
—Rev. Dr. Donna Schaper

Grief begs to be named and honored. No matter your loss—a beloved's death, a home left behind, the perhaps foreseen but still wrenching pain of the end of a career or of children growing up and moving away—it's vital to acknowledge what was and express all the layers of emotion surrounding this change.

The laments of others can offer words to explore and fully feel your own emotions, especially when you are numb or overwhelmed. Throughout this part you'll find prayers and poems of mourning, lament, despair, and hope-in-despair. Sit with these songs of sorrow, letting them speak to and unlock your own grief. When words can't express what's inside, perhaps you'll find relief in the embodied practices of "shadow dancing," praying with wordless sounds, the ritual of bowing, or even throwing a tantrum.

All the contributors encourage you toward truth and freedom, honesty with yourself, and the hard but necessary work of honoring your losses by expressing all your pain.

I Cry Out—You Don't Answer

Translated by Rami Shapiro

I cry out—you don't answer!
I stand—you merely look at me!
You turn on me pitilessly;
you hit me with your strong hand.
You grab me and drive me like the wind,
throw me around like the storm.
I know you'll bring me down to death,
to the final dwelling place of all life.
Does one raise a hand against the shattered one,
when in his sorrow he cries to them for help?
Didn't I weep for those whose days are hard?
Didn't my life grieve for the poor?
Yet when I looked for good, evil came;
when I hoped for light, darkness came.
My innards churn endlessly;
days of affliction lie before me.
I am darkened without the sun,
I stand among the crowds and cry for help.
I'm brother to jackals,
companion to the ostrich-brood.
My skin blackens and flakes off;
my bones are heated with fever.
My harp mourns,
my flute wails.

—Job 30:20–31

Rami Shapiro, a renowned teacher of spirituality across faith traditions and a noted theologian, is the award-winning author of *The Sacred Art of Lovingkindness: Preparing to Practice* and *The Book of Job: Annotated & Explained* (both SkyLight Paths), among many other books.

The Sacred Speech of Lament

Rev. Dr. Donna Schaper

When we lament, we let our hair down and let our trouble out. We don't need a response and don't really expect a response so much as we need to speak. Our utterance is holy by its independence! Like unconditional love, a lament is unconditional. It speaks for the sake of speaking.

A lament can be just a whine or a gripe or a "bitch," in politically incorrect language. It becomes a form of sacred speech to the extent that it adds Spirit to the exposure of the trouble. We speak to Spirit, unconditionally. We don't issue commands, such as telling God not to forsake us. We simply acknowledge that we are forsaken or that we feel forsaken. When we risk a lament, we often do so because of spiritual courage. We may back into this courage because we don't know what else to do—or we may take a conscious risk. A lament is sacred because it liberates. Lament lets pain out of its cage in silence. It is like a good cry—we feel better after it, even though nothing has really changed. Lament trusts Spirit enough to show how awful we feel. We admit trouble to ourselves and to Spirit—and to others who may do us the kindness of listening....

A lament differs from a complaint because we don't whine in a lament. We state. We accept. We weep. Complaints are fundamentally despairing kinds of speech. "I can't stand my sister-in-law. Whenever she comes to my house, I get nervous and angry. I can't tell her how I feel—I can't do anything but put up with her unpleasant, judgmental nature. I have no choice." This is a complaint.

A lament ritualizes hope. "I become a person I don't want to be whenever my sister-in-law comes to my house. I become nervous and angry. I have

Rev. Dr. Donna Schaper is widely recognized as one of the most outstanding communicators in her generation of Protestant clergy. Senior minister at Judson Memorial Church in New York City, she is author of *Sacred Speech: A Practical Guide for Keeping Spirit in Your Speech* and coauthor of *Labyrinths from the Outside In: Walking to Spiritual Insight—A Beginner's Guide* (both SkyLight Paths).

to tell someone how I feel about her and the way she makes me feel small. I know I can't tell her not to come. I know she is a part of my family and that my brother would never forgive me for estranging our kids and families from each other. I have to learn to cope with her." Although there is not a lot of hope in a lament that repositions responsibility for a relationship, there is much more hope than despair. Complaints rant, rave, and air distress. Laments rant, rave, and air distress—and then resolve themselves. We take the next step; we manage some kind of action or at least intend some kind of action....

We find ourselves linked and able to cope once we "tell someone" what is bothering us. The yoke becomes easier, the burden lighter. Secrets are often kept precisely because the pain they carry is too horrible to release. Lament occurs when we trust our partner in conversation enough to express the pain that feels inexpressible. Lament breaks down silence and secrets into speech. We may weep when we tell what we have to tell, but we stop the cold, dry internal tears of bearing burdens alone, in secret....

Many people of my generation were raised with the words, "If you can't say anything nice, don't say anything at all." That kind of advice represses speech rather than expresses life. That kind of advice is anti-lament—and therefore against the liberation that the sacred speech of lament offers to people willing to consciously risk it....

Laments often happen for their own sake rather than for the sake of anything else. They are a release of negative energy in order to make room for a new positive. Laments are complaints reaching for and counting on resolution. Their companion is Spirit. They are directed to Spirit more than to anything else. Laments hope. Laments open doors. Laments push for reconciliation with the hard reality they express.

Lament lets out the pain. Lament expresses feeling. Lament is holy speech. Life is not all good—and those who trust Spirit know that truth.

Welcoming and Lamenting with Our Inner Witness

Christine Valters Paintner, PhD, Obl. OSB

As a culture we strongly discourage people who are grieving to stay with their sadness, but instead tell them to "cheer up" or "move on" rather than explore what grief has to teach them. Yet developing the capacity to endure and remain open to difficult feelings is part of the movement toward spiritual maturity.

To help us avoid such resistance, we must cultivate our "inner witness," that part of ourselves that lets us experience what saddens, angers, or challenges us without getting carried away by emotions. The concept of inner witness or internal observer goes by different names in different spiritual traditions.... The twentieth-century monk and poet Thomas Merton drew from the Sufis to describe the *point vierge*—the "virgin point" of the soul—the part of ourselves deep within the heart that is untouched by our daily fears and anxieties, the place in which God dwells. This inner witness is our calm core, the place within us of infinite compassion and curiosity about our experience. When we move into silence and we begin to notice the inner voices rising up, it is our inner witness that can observe this dialogue without getting caught up in the emotional drama of it. Cultivating an awareness of this dimension takes practice. We enter into contemplative ways of praying to access this brilliance within us, to rest into our own hearts and discover there the heart of God. When making the space within ourselves to experience the full range of what wants to move and open, we also make room for the difficult and challenging aspects of our humanity.

Christine Valters Paintner, PhD, Obl. OSB, a Benedictine oblate, is the online abbess of www.abbeyofthearts.com and frequently leads retreats and teaches on the wisdom of Benedictine, Celtic, and desert ways of praying. She is author of *Lectio Divina—The Sacred Art: Transforming Words & Images into Heart-Centered Prayer* (SkyLight Paths), among other books.

The Rule of Benedict instructs that all are to welcome in the stranger at the door and greet that stranger knowing that Christ is present. There is deep wisdom here for us to ponder. In our meditation practice, we are similarly called upon to welcome the strangers knocking at the inner door of our hearts and see the presence of the Holy there. We are able to do this because we have within us an inner witness, a virgin point, that remains steadfast and is not carried away by emotions. We have the capacity to allow in the full spectrum of our emotions and thereby grow in wisdom by staying present to them.

A Place for Praise and Lament

The practice of *meditatio*[1] calls us to welcome in and make room for the full spectrum of who we are. Through this process we remember all the parts of ourselves; we are made whole again. We make this kind of space to explore difficult feelings to bring the wholeness of who we are into prayer. Prayer is not just about finding happiness—although certainly joy is often a fruit of prayer—but also about allowing the full range of ourselves to have voice. We often resist our grief and may find freedom in the sacred tradition of lament.

The book of Lamentations is traditionally ascribed to the prophet Jeremiah following the destruction of Jerusalem and the Temple in 586 BCE. In the Hebrew Bible it is called *Ekah*, meaning "How," which is the first word of the text and the formula to begin a song of wailing: "How lonely sits the city that was once full of people!" The Hebrew scriptures are filled with these songs of wailing—deep expressions of grief, anger, and helplessness. As you pray with difficult texts, notice the feelings that stir in you and make space for them. Remember that emotions are a form of energy that will move through the body when we welcome them in and breathe deeply. From the perspective of the inner witness we can be present to the landscape of grief and "know sorrow as the deepest thing," as the poet Naomi Shihab Nye writes, without being swept away by it.[2] We grow in compassion when we can honor the song of wailing that dwells within each of us....

The prayer of lament is first and foremost truth telling. *This* pain, *this* suffering should not be. It helps us name the lies we have been living and participating in. Lament opens us up to a new vision of how God is present to our suffering. We call on the God who weeps with us, whose groans are our own, and we express our hope in God's tender care. These biblical texts offer us a sacred container within which we can experience the full range of our humanness. We are called upon in *lectio divina* to both pray with texts that seem difficult and allow the difficult emotions to rise up within us, even when we weren't expecting them—perhaps especially so.

Lectio Divina: Praying with the Senses and with Sorrow

Suggested Texts

> How lonely sits the city
> that once was full of people!
> How like a widow she has become,
> she that was great among the nations!
> She that was a princess among the provinces
> has become a vassal.
>
> She weeps bitterly in the night,
> with tears on her cheeks;
> among all her lovers
> she has no one to comfort her;
> all her friends have dealt treacherously with her,
> they have become her enemies.
>
> Judah has gone into exile with suffering
> and hard servitude;
> she lives now among the nations,
> and finds no resting-place;
> her pursuers have all overtaken her
> in the midst of her distress.
>
> —Lamentations 1:1–3
>
> I am poured out like water,
> and all my bones are out of joint;
> my heart is like wax;
> it is melted within my breast;
> my mouth is dried up like a potsherd,
> and my tongue sticks to my jaws;
> you lay me in the dust of death.
>
> —Psalm 22:14–15

Cry aloud to the Lord! O wall of daughter Zion!
Let tears stream down like a torrent day and night!
Give yourself no rest, your eyes no respite!
Arise, cry out in the night, at the beginning of the watches!
Pour out your heart like water before the presence of God!
—Lamentations 2:18–19

Settling and Shimmering

Begin your practice ... settling into your body and breath. Allow your breath to embrace the presence of God in this moment and release whatever stands in the way, such as your personal expectations or judgments. Allow your awareness to descend from your head into your heart and open yourself up to the experience of reverential listening and receiving the words of a sacred text as a gift. Read through the passage twice, identifying the word or phrase that shimmers today. Then rest for a few moments with it, gently repeating it to yourself.

Savoring

Once you have allowed the word or phrase to choose you, sink into the experience of allowing it to unfold in your imagination. What images are you aware of? Savoring the sacred text means tending to its sights, smells, sounds, tastes, and touch. With each breath, open yourself to the experience being offered to you. Imagine the word or phrase as a tiny sacred seed being planted in the rich and fertile soil of your heart, and this unfolding as a process of beholding what emerges. Allow each inhale to create more inner space within your heart for your intuition and imagination to have freedom.

As you become aware of thoughts, judgments, or expectations, gently release them with your breath. You may find that as images rise up, your thinking mind wants to either dismiss them as unimportant or analyze them to figure out their meaning. Release these tendencies when they come up. Remember that savoring takes time, and you are allowing the full spectrum of possibility to bloom. Allow some silence to surround the images that are forming.

Notice if a memory is beginning to stir, and allow yourself to tend to the experience it evokes. What do you remember about the sense experience of this moment? Allow some silence around the act of remembering.

Stirring

As you continue to be present to images and memories, notice what you are feeling right now. Using your breath, create some space within you to pay attention to whatever it is that is stirring in you. If the experience feels uncomfortable, allow the breath to deepen as a way of relaxing your body into the feeling. Imagine that within you is this virgin point, this inner witness, and when you are in touch with this part of yourself you can be fully present to whatever it is you are feeling right now, but from a place of calmness, curiosity, and compassion. As you notice resistance to feelings, return to the breath again, and imagine your breath dissolving the wall within you. Remember the monastic practice of stability. See if you can stay with the stirrings of your heart and soul. Allow as much time as you need. Continue to be aware of the images, feelings, and memories that rise up in you.

Sound Prayer

Cait Johnson

Prayer does not have to be just the rote repetition of words you have been taught. As poet Elizabeth Cunningham reminds us, "You can only pray what's in your heart."

Take a little time now to close your eyes and go deeper. Bring your energy down from your head into your heart-center. Allow yourself to feel whatever it is you are feeling right now. What is in your heart at this moment? Peace? Stress? Grief? Anger? When I go to my heart, I am often aware of sadness, mixed with a hope of hope. What is the truth in your heart?

Open your mouth now, take in a deep breath, and, keeping your heart-truth in mind, allow a sound to come out. It can be any sound—a groan, a giggle, a howl, a long, true note—whatever wants to sing through you, allow the sound to flow. Imagine that the great spirit permeating all is carrying your sound on its wings, accepting it, transforming it. If your sound wants to shift and change, allow this to happen. If feelings come up, let them.

Julia Cameron tells a very moving story in *Vein of Gold* about doing a meditation like this one: "I began to 'sing' my dead mother, whom I miss but seldom weep for. Within minutes, tears were rolling freely down my face. I was contacting and healing a grief that I had carried, frozen, for a decade and a half."

Sound has the magical ability to unlock, to release, to heal. While I was in the painful midst of my relationship breakup, I began playing Beethoven's Ninth Symphony over and over at top volume whenever I was alone. That magnificent music released huge feelings in me—feelings I had to suppress when I was with other people—and I was finally able to weep and wail and

Cait Johnson, author of *Earth, Water, Fire and Air: Essential Ways of Connecting to Spirit* (SkyLight Paths), teaches workshops on connecting to Spirit, seasonal elemental approaches to self-healing, poetry writing, and conscious eating.

rage. It was the most cathartic thing I have ever done; I like to think that Beethoven was my ally in getting through the ordeal. As the poet John Dryden said, "What passion cannot music raise and quell?"

Confucius on True Expression in Mourning

Translated and Annotated by Rodney L. Taylor, PhD

Lin Fang asked what was the first thing to be attended to in ritual. The Master said, "A great question indeed! In *festive* rituals it is better to be sparing than extravagant. In rituals of mourning, it is better that there be deep sorrow than a minute attention to detail."

—Confucius, *Analects* III:4

Confucius suggests that in mourning rituals it is easy to be swept away with attention to detail and to use such attention as a way of diverting or hiding your true feelings. Yet the true meaning of a mourning ritual has nothing to do with detail. It is instead about feelings of profound sorrow.

Frankly, a number of rituals presented in our own time, either through extravagant displays of wealth or through elaborate performances, convey only a perfunctory sense of inner feeling. Suppose we ourselves consider the relation between all the ritual moments that make up our lives and attempt to see them in the light of propriety—true feelings representing inner feelings of goodness. Does such an insight change the nature of our performances?

Rodney L. Taylor, PhD, the foremost American researcher of Confucius as a religious and spiritual figure, is author of *Confucius, the Analects: The Path of the Sage—Selections Annotated & Explained* (SkyLight Paths) and professor emeritus of religious studies at the University of Colorado at Boulder.

Dancing with Our Shadows

Cynthia Winton-Henry

Casting a shadow is physically unavoidable. Yet when it comes to our "emotional or moral shadows"—anything deemed opposite of our lighter, loving selves; anything too emotional, weird, or dangerous—we do everything in our power to hide them. Those who value love and joy are often shocked by their feelings of hate, doubt, or rage....

What if emotions are actually movement? What if resisting "e-motion" is to resist healing itself? Some healers suggest that our bodies are designed to move emotional energy in the most efficient way possible. If we are anxious, for example, shaking and quaking can be helpful. If we are angry, then muscular thrusting is a natural release. If we are fearful, then breathing keeps us from becoming overly rigid. If we feel love, then our flowing, free, open movements distribute these energies throughout our bodies and out into the world....

Our shadows often stem from repressing emotions. Over my piano is a small collection of masks from Africa, Asia, and Latin America. None are "pretty," but I like them because, frankly, I'm jealous that masked dancers get to wear fear, anger, and lust on their faces as they forage for fruit in humanity's shadow lands.

A mask can be a kind of creative "confessional" for emotions. Rather than analyzing our shadow, if we play with our shadow side in creative tasks, we can more easily light the way for aspects of shadow to emerge before they take us down. Dancing with your "evil twin" playfully releases repressed energy and can help you enjoy the natural aspects of human wholeness.

Masked Dances

1. Hold your face in a frozen position, then moosh it around.
2. Squirm your mouth into a weird shape.

Cynthia Winton-Henry teaches people to unlock the wisdom of the body through movement and creativity. She is author of *Dance—The Sacred Art: The Joy of Movement as a Spiritual Practice* (SkyLight Paths) and is cofounder of InterPlay, an international not-for-profit organization with locations in over fifty cities on five continents.

3. Let your body mold into a "mask" to match the expression on your face.

4. Taking a few steps in any direction, move your body with the energy and feeling of the mask.

5. Take a deep breath and shake out the mask.

6. Let your face assume another "mask." Exaggerate it as much as possible.

7. Mold your body into the shape of this mask and move with that dynamic.

8. Add a little wiggling of your hips, even though it may not match the character of the mask.

9. Add a little dance, shaking a pointer finger at the world.

10. Relax this mask, take a deep breath, and let it out with a sigh.

11. "Put on" one more mask. Exaggerate it, as you mold your body to match and move.

12. Speak a repetitive syllable or sound to accompany your movement.

13. To end, take some deep breaths and shake everything out.

Take some time to journal and notice anything about these masked parts of you. What or who do they remind you of? Did you enjoy or resist the idea of playing with your masks? Either way is fine.

We don't have to become our shadows, but if we invite them out and play with them, they're less likely to hide in the balcony and take potshots at us when we're not looking. More importantly, shadow dancing can be liberating. Besides giving us much-needed laughs, we're less likely to erupt in anger when we confront the shadows of other people. Wise people call this "doing your work."

There is no better way to be introduced to your spiritual shadow than through silliness. It may feel corny, but in the spirit of grace, creativity, and fun-loving, if you let yourself be transformed by the alchemy of a new behavior, you'll unleash all the pressure it took to hold yourself back. If you let go of the worry about "dancing well," you will get an energy boost and a dose of integration. And you'll get clued in to some mysterious, ridiculous, and often heartbreakingly beautiful truths.

No-No! Dances

What are some things you're not supposed to do? Turn a few of these behaviors into ten-second spiritual "No-No!" dances. The Divine knows and accepts you any way you are, so why not give a few of these a try?

- "You should be peaceful." No-No! Do a ten-second ranting dance. Stomp around and punch the air.

- "You should be sober." No-No! Do a drunken, blurry, flop-and-drop-dead dance.

- "You should be prim and proper." No-No! Dance for ten seconds with your butt sticking out.

- "You should be reserved!" No-No! Shake parts that you shouldn't shake.

- "You should be demure!" No-No! Dance sassy, hands on your hips or thrusting your pelvis.

Raging at God

Marcia Ford

In situations where no human being can be held responsible for a tragedy, victims need a place to direct their anger. God becomes a convenient and logical target—especially when an "act of God" takes a loved one's life. Who else is there to blame for an avalanche, an earthquake, a tsunami?

Sometimes the line between God and a person's loss is even more direct. A young boy falls from a tree and snaps his neck. A toddler manages to crawl through a fence and drowns in the pool on the other side. A young pastor and fellow author is electrocuted when he unthinkingly reaches for a microphone as he's performing a baptism. Couldn't God have prevented Kyle Lake from grabbing an electrical cord while standing in shoulder-high water? How could God allow him to suffer electrocution in front of eight hundred people, including his wife and the brand-new believer he was about to baptize?

How can we possibly make sense out of tragedies like that? We can't. All we can do, if we're somewhat distanced from the situation, is acknowledge that there are some things that we'll never understand.

But for the survivors—that's another story entirely. I don't know if Kyle's wife ever had a moment when she gen-

For reflection: How do you make sense of the senseless tragedies you either have experienced or have heard about? Do you believe that God is really in control? Do you tend to blame God when bad things happen and there's no one else to blame? How has that affected your relationship with God?

uinely "blamed" God, but I'm guessing that more than once Jen questioned why God allowed such a horrible thing to happen. The survivors of tragic accidents like Kyle's have no human being to blame, no one they can vent

Marcia Ford is author of many books on spirituality, including *The Sacred Art of Forgiveness: Forgiving Ourselves and Others Through God's Grace* and *Finding Hope: Cultivating God's Gift of a Hopeful Spirit* (both SkyLight Paths).

their anger on. They run the very real risk of sinking into clinical depression, one of the results of bottling up all that anger. I have a feeling God would rather be blamed than see that happen.

One thing I know for sure—God is big enough to take your blame, your rage, your outrage. I've duked it out with him so many times that it's a wonder we're on speaking terms these days. It has never occurred to me to forgive God, though; I seem to always end up asking God to forgive me for blaming him for all my troubles, most of which are of my own making.

But blaming God poses another problem—estrangement. As long as you are blaming God, the two of you can't very well have a healthy relationship. Only through forgiveness can you be reconciled to God again.... Once you've enjoyed a healthy, loving relationship with God, alienation from him is never fun. It's much better to vent your anger over a horrible loss than to live with the frustration and misery of trying to go it alone. Forgive God and get over it. Living apart from the Spirit is just not worth it.

Clearing the Air

Maybe you're like me—the thought of "forgiving God" just doesn't sit well with you. Still, you have unresolved issues with God that you'd like to get cleared up. Do what I do—let him have it. Vent your anger to God. Be specific—very specific. Make this one an encounter with God of epic proportions. Hold nothing back. Just be prepared to be humbled. Ask God's forgiveness for yelling so loud, trust that you will eventually get the answers you feel you deserve, and get on with your life and your relationship with the Spirit.

Life and Death Are in Thine Hand

Annotated by Paul Wesley Chilcote, PhD

Life and death are in thine hand;
In thine hand our child we see
Waiting thy benign command,
Less beloved by us than thee.
Need we then his life request?
Jesus understands our fears,
Reads a mother's panting breast,
Knows the meaning of her tears.

Human tears may freely flow
Authorized by tears divine,
'Till thine awful will we know,
Comprehend thy whole design.
Jesus wept! And so may we;
Jesus suffering all thy will,
Felt the soft infirmity,
Feels his creature's sorrow still.

Jesus blends them with his own,
Mindful of his suffering days.
Father, hear thy pleading Son,
Son of man for us he prays.
What for us he asks, bestow;
Ours he makes his own request;
Send us life or death, we know,
Life or death from thee is best.

—Charles Wesley, "For a Child in the Small-Pox"

Paul Wesley Chilcote, PhD, is an academic dean, a professor, and a Benedictine oblate at Mt. Angel Abbey in Oregon. He is author of *The Imitation of Christ: Selections Annotated & Explained* and *John & Charles Wesley: Selections from Their Writings and Hymns—Annotated & Explained* (both SkyLight Paths).

Smallpox devastated families and communities in the eighteenth century. In this hymn, "For a Child in the Small-Pox," Charles pours out his heart to God in prayer on behalf of his son. No hymn expresses human pathos more profoundly than this one. Charles, unlike his older brother, enjoyed an idyllic marriage and the joys and agonies of parenthood. Like most families of that time, he and Sally grieved the loss of children to death, and this experience in life deepened Charles's capacity for compassion. The child of whom he sings here, a musical prodigy by all accounts, did not survive this ordeal.

In the two concluding stanzas of the hymn, Charles plumbs the depths of the mystery of human suffering. Rather than providing an answer to the question of theodicy—the attempt to understand and explain God's goodness in the face of evil—Charles points to a God who stands alongside us and suffers with us in life. Because God sojourned among us in this broken world in the person of Jesus, God knows what suffering means to us. The images that Charles creates in these lines are staggering. Jesus weeps with us in our sorrow. Jesus blends our tears with his own. The hymn concludes not with a stoic resignation to the pain and agony of life, but with an affirmation that the One who has stood with us will never abandon us and loves every person with an undying love.

Acknowledging Large and Little Losses in Caregiving

Marty Richards, MSW, LCSW

Grief and loss—and the resulting sadness—are constant companions in caregiving. Even if they are not spoken about, these feelings are present. Our society tends to think of grief only as it relates to death, dying, and bereavement. And while it is true that many care partners face these "large" losses in the future, there are many "little" losses in the present that can create large concerns.

Knowing how grief and sadness affect everyone in the caresharing setting will not only help assuage the intensity of grief but will also go a long way toward helping everyone cope. Be aware of *all* the losses involved, and don't be afraid to speak about them. It is also important to remember that grief is a normal response to any kind of loss, at any age....

Facing Transitions

Transitions and losses of many kinds are part and parcel of our middle and later years. Going from full-time work to retiree status, downsizing from a large house to a small apartment, or watching children move to other cities are just a few common examples.

As a caregiver, you are also likely to be facing transitions in your priorities, your daily living routines, and your emotions. One of the things I often suggest to caregivers, and I offer this to you as well, is to sit for a few moments with these three questions to clarify exactly what it is you are facing.

Marty Richards, MSW, LCSW, is a clinical social worker, an affiliate assistant professor at the University of Washington School of Social Work, and a popular speaker on the topics of chronic illness, Alzheimer's disease, elder care, and spirituality and aging. She is author of *Caresharing: A Reciprocal Approach to Caregiving and Care Receiving in the Complexities of Aging, Illness or Disability* (SkyLight Paths).

To whom are the changes happening? The first and most obvious answer is that your care partner is the one experiencing changes. Yet the changes that are happening to them are affecting you as well. For example, if your care partner has suffered a paralyzing stroke, you may feel the stress of a change in lifestyle as intensely as, or sometimes more than, they do.

How are the changes affecting you or your care partner? Although it is natural to look ahead and think about what may happen, to ask "What if?" and "How will I ... ?," take some time to focus on what is happening now. What are the day-to-day changes—in functioning, in emotions, in spirits, in physical changes? Be sure to consider the changes that both you and your care partner are experiencing.

How have you or your care partner dealt with change in the past? Under the stress of a caresharing situation, it is easy to forget that you and your care partner have used your strengths in the past to "get through" difficult situations. It is good to remind yourselves that these strengths have gotten you to where you are now. Are any of these ways that you could employ to get through this time? Talking with others—especially in a caregiver support group or in one-to-one counseling or with a spiritual advisor—and reflecting on what you have done in the past may help you find strength to deal with the present situation.

The transitions of change and loss can be bumpy. You or your care partner may have times of feeling really "up," when you experience something good. Then there may be "down times" of sadness, times of trying to find out the meaning (the why) of what you are going through. And there also may be times when one or the other of you gets "stuck" in one place for a while.

There is no "rule" about the transitions of grief, nor is there any precise way to experience grief. Most people go through some "normal" grief stages, including shock and denial, emerging awareness and intense emotion, and then a reengagement in life or some resolution to the losses. The important thing to know is that there is no particular way that you and your care part-ner *should* do this, and that you will bounce back and forth in your feelings. As you walk the grief road, you will likely encounter griefs from the past and anticipate future griefs, but the journey of facing losses starts with where you and your care partner are right *now*.

Facing Losses

When someone dies, we all understand and respond to this "big loss." We recognize it as an important event, and we have proscribed rituals that help us deal with the grief. We sit shivah, we go to a wake, we attend a memorial or funeral. We are used to sharing the grief of death with those who are hurting—whether it's with casseroles or hugs or flowers—and we do what we can to help.

But when a person is aging or dealing with chronic illness, there are many transitions and "little losses" that often go unrecognized or unnamed. Because there are no rituals for these times, many people don't know how to respond to these sadnesses in a helpful way. Even those who are attempting to offer support may say or do something that has just the opposite effect. Many people have recounted how comments offered by someone trying to comfort them felt hurtful. (If this happens in your situation, try to understand that the person is not being deliberately mean; rather, their response likely comes out of not knowing what to say.)

In a caresharing scenario, what might seem like a "little loss" to an outside observer may be a very big loss for the person who is experiencing it. One of the loving things you can do for your care partner is to honor and recognize that each loss is uniquely theirs. "Little losses" can have a cumulative effect, and the person you are caring for is suffering the emotional and spiritual consequences. Each loss is real and painful for them, no matter how "small" it might seem in the face of other, more serious concerns....

Anticipatory Grief

A common aspect of grieving is not about what someone has *already* lost, but what they *expect* to lose. Anticipatory grieving arises from future losses your care partner expects, and it can surface in many areas.

Your care partner, for example, may be having trouble keeping up with work around the house, and they know that they will soon need to leave their beloved home. Long before moving day arrives, they may start mourning the upcoming loss. Each painful disposition of a possession or memento of meaning may be a catalyst for another round of grieving. Actually, the giving away of treasured things can be a double-edged sword. If a person gives a book, for example, to someone they know will enjoy it, this gift giving may make them happy, knowing that the book will continue to be valuable to someone. But if the reason they are giving up the book is that the print is too small and they cannot read it, this may be very sad indeed.

Or perhaps your care partner is scheduled for an upcoming surgery where they expect to lose a body part, such as a breast because of cancer or a foot because of diabetes. Or, if they are going though chemotherapy, they may dread losing their hair. Some women and men deeply mourn this loss long before it actually happens.

If you are caring for someone who has Alzheimer's, you and your care partner may experience pre-loss grieving about the massive changes that will inevitably come and the resulting loss of relationship ahead, as memory loss becomes more and more acute. Some have called living with Alzheimer's a "funeral with no ending." As each of you tries to cope with the present, you are already grieving the next effects of the illness.

Similarly, if you are caring for someone who is inch by inch losing their physical abilities due to extreme old age or illness, either or both of you may experience times of being overwhelmed by anticipatory grief. I have heard this gradual failing called "the dwindles," and each noticeable loss can cause sadness for the present as well as grief for what is yet to come.

An especially difficult anticipatory grief comes when you know you are losing a care partner to a terminal illness. Either or both of you may have periods when you are flooded with a sense of loss about what is to come. It is important to recognize that, because each person deals with grief in their own way, your way of grieving and your care partner's way of grieving may look totally different. One of you may be weepy, while the other is more reserved, but that does not mean that the reserved one is not grieving. As Elisabeth Kübler-Ross explained in her groundbreaking work about death and dying, people tend to die "in character." In other words, people die in much the same way as they live. For example, if a person has always been introspective and kept their own counsel, they may not display or disclose the "expected" signs of grief. Others in the family may feel as if the one who is dying is not realistically facing up to their situation. In truth, both the family and the person dying are grieving; the one who is dying is simply experiencing grief in character with who they are.

I had a clear example of this in my own life with my father-in-law, who, when he was told he did not have much time to live, made appointments with his accountant and lawyer and set up all the paperwork for his wife's benefit. Then he went to the basement and labeled all his tools. He was not a person who would communicate with us about his dying, even though we wanted to talk through our loss and grief at losing him. He had been a stoic person in life, so indeed he died "in character." Though this was difficult for those involved in his care in his last days, his way of anticipatory grieving was to take care of his business to ease life for his family after his death. And it did give us some comfort in the days that followed.

The methods of helping and coping with anticipatory grief are much the same as dealing with "normal" grief, but I want to point out a few ideas here that could be especially helpful for you and your care partner in dealing with anticipatory grieving.

- Plan a farewell celebration for a much-loved house before you start packing. If possible, invite people who have memories associated with that house to join you. Include time for your care partner, guests, and yourself to describe your most memorable events in the house.

- Go shopping with your care partner for an assistive device, such as a walker or wheelchair, before they need it. Help them get used to it, even to view it as a reassuring friend.

- Go wig or hat shopping with your care partner if they are going to lose their hair. Talk about what their hair means to them, and what part of themselves they feel they will be losing with their hair. One of my friends asked for her care network to lend her their favorite "chapeaus" when she started her treatments.

- Make a "LifeStory" book with a person who is grieving the expected loss of their memory. You could work on this with your partner, making it a shared endeavor as you anticipate what's to come.

- Help a person who is terminally ill write a "loving letter" or an "ethical will" for their loved ones.[1]

Intimate with Suffering

Andi Young

The floor is cold under my bare feet as I stand, palms pressed together and centered at my heart. Incense drifts in faint wisps across the dharma room, and I can smell its sandalwood and juniper smoke. Outside, the half-light of predawn gives the rows of cushions blue shadows. It is 5:00 a.m., and the residents of the New Haven Zen Center—myself included—are up for morning practice.

We begin with the Four Great Vows:

> Sentient beings are numberless; we vow to save them all.
> Delusions are endless; we vow to cut through them all.
> The teachings are infinite; we vow to learn them all.
> The Buddha Way is inconceivable; we vow to attain it.

After the recitation, we do a half-bow from the waist. Then we begin our daily practice of one hundred and eight bows.... We do this together, in silence and synchronicity, one hundred and eight times in the chill blue light.

Daily, across America and across the world, people begin their day by bowing. Christians kneel for morning prayers, Muslims turn east to Mecca for the first *salat* (prayer) of the day, Jews *daven* (pray), and Buddhists prostrate themselves. Over the course of the day, many more people will find time to pause and, bending their body toward the earth, bow as part of their spiritual practice....

Because bowing is physical, it is *beyond* words and thoughts. Often, when we are unable to articulate our feelings, we turn to movement to express ourselves. The words for our feelings—joy, despair, gratitude, or sorrow—are only words. How we express these emotions is the great question of ritual and worship. Bowing is one answer to the question of how we can express

Andi Young is a member of the Kwan Um School of Zen (founding teacher Zen Master Seung Sahn) and author of *The Sacred Art of Bowing: Preparing to Practice* (SkyLight Paths).

our spiritual aspirations; yet, even among spiritual practices, bowing stands alone in its sheer physical nature. Our movement becomes its own purpose, and, at times, our need to articulate drops away and we can make our bow itself a prayer and an aspiration....

Suffering, embracing suffering, letting suffering go, and attaining great wisdom and compassion—this is bowing too.

I've often been told by people who know a little about Buddhism, but who haven't ever really practiced it, that it seems like a pessimistic spirituality. "Life is suffering?" they say to me. "How depressing." But the flip side of suffering is the release from suffering. Intimacy with suffering doesn't mean to suffer but to let go of our fears of suffering so that we can awaken great compassion. That's not depressing or pessimistic. Jesus suffered terribly on the cross, and yet in his suffering was the release of all Christians from their suffering. Is that depressing? Intimacy with suffering doesn't mean that we walk around feeling down, upset, always weeping because the world is full of war and sickness. To be intimate with suffering is to let go of even our sadness and our joy, to do just what must be done to help everyone around us. I find this teaching of helping others, of compassion, in all the world spiritual traditions.

Bowing is a form of being intimate with suffering. And bowing is just bowing, suffering is just suffering. We put it down, and we just do it. The marrow of practice is doing it. In these confusing times, full of distractions and world events and all the ordinary stuff of everyday life—friends, work, cooking dinner, doing laundry—we need to give our actions and lives direction. Spiritual practice helps us with our direction. Bowing helps us attain our direction....

Bowing as a Spiritual Practice

In the Zen tradition, we begin our bows standing, with our feet firmly planted on the floor and our hands at our hearts. This is a strong stance, and it's one that allows us to both stretch and ground our bodies.

Before we begin our first bow, we should take a deep breath and really wake up our bodies. Our breath should go all the way down into our bellies, so that we feel our stomachs and chests rise with our breathing. As we wake up our bodies, we can start to wake up our mind. Be aware of your body. How does it feel? Are your legs tight, is your back stiff, or are you tired? Maybe you feel refreshed and alert. Whatever your physical state, be aware of it. Don't make anything out of it, though—you don't need to think that a stiff back is bad and feeling limber is good. When you're beginning your practice, you just want to be aware. Awareness is without judgment, because it comes before thinking.

After you've maintained an awareness of your body for about ten deep breaths, then you can shift your awareness to your inner state. How do you feel? Are you sad about something? Are you joyful? Whatever your mood, just be aware of it. Again, you don't need to make anything of it, such as being sad is bad.... Just be aware. This awareness takes time to develop. It's difficult not to get involved in our emotions....

We should try to keep a sharp and strong awareness of our inner state for another ten deep breaths. Then we can set an intention, either spoken or not. The Four Great Vows of Zen are the intention I set before I bow: "Sentient beings are numberless, I vow to save them all; delusions are endless, I vow to cut through them all; the teachings are infinite, I vow to learn them all; the Buddha Way is inconceivable, I vow to attain it." These vows remind all Zen students of their direction: to attain enlightenment and save all sentient beings from suffering, no matter how difficult or impossible the task seems. Muslims also set an intention before they perform their daily prayers, but the intention is silent. We should have an intention before practice, because it clarifies our actions and our direction. Anything that connects you to your greater purpose is helpful: "May I practice patience," "May I bring peace to the world," "May I come closer to God."

When we bow, we can hold our intention in our heart. If we have a specific prayer, then we should say that, either aloud or silently. If we have no specific prayer, then we should hold our intention in our heart and keep our awareness on our actions. Staying aware of our actions and our inner state is challenging— if it weren't, we'd all be Buddhas already! Keeping aware is helpful, though, no matter what our tradition or practice. When we act mindlessly or carelessly, we lose the power of bowing. Bowing is an opportunity to reorient our lives. Spiritual practice gives us many bridges between intention and action. Bowing is one of them.

When we bow, we can put down whatever baggage we have. Our baggage isn't just "bad" baggage, such as a rough day at work or a fight with a friend. We have "good" baggage too, and this can impede us if we get too attached to the good things in our life. We want only the good things and none of the bad things, and we carry around the fear of losing the good. When we bow, we can put all of it down, good and bad. We have our intention, and we just bow.

If your spiritual practice is one that can incorporate Zen-style bowing, that is, formal and repeated bows, then I would encourage you to try it.... Whatever form we use, the important part of the physical bow is to make sure we engage our entire body. If our knees allow it, we should also make sure our head touches the floor. If we need to be kind to our knees, then we can bow from the waist, making sure that we lower our heads, so that we remember humility as we bow. We can bring awareness to any tradition and any practice, and we will benefit....

The most important thing is to be awake, one hundred percent, as we bow. This one hundred percent focus is enlightenment, faith in God, union with the Divine—everything that spiritual traditions have pointed to throughout the ages as the ultimate goal or direction of human spiritual endeavors. These are not the same and they are not different—if we are one hundred percent awake when we bow. Then, we are just bowing and our direction is clear, whether it's saving all beings, serving God, or understanding the Divine.

With Me in Pain—
In Times of Anguish

William Cleary

Are you with us in every pain and anxiety,
Evolutionary Spirit,
Holy God of magnificence beyond our knowing?
For all your majesty and bewildering otherness,
still you are a compassionate and caring creator
for the best human parents and friends
were each your inventions too,
given to this world to be your paradigms, your agents,
your incarnations.
We feel your closeness,
dear Mystery,
in times of anguish, and rejoice nevertheless
in your continuing gift of life and time.
Amen.

William Cleary was a Jesuit priest for over twenty years, a filmmaker, and a composer. He is author of many books on spirituality, including *Prayers to an Evolutionary God* (SkyLight Paths). His musical *Chun Hyang Song* was performed at the Seoul Olympics.

Mourning the Loss of Physical Well-Being

Dr. Nancy Copeland-Payton

"It's a roller coaster. I didn't buy a ticket, never wanted a ride. First they say everything is okay, surgery removed the tumor. Later they say everything isn't totally okay, that I need chemotherapy—just a precaution. But in those months of chemo, I receive a gift of sorts. I learn I'm not indispensable at work. It's freeing, actually, as so much of my identity came from work. But now who am I? I yearn to meet the self who is defined neither by work nor by a brush with cancer."

Mariam talks openly about her fearful encounter with a potentially fatal illness. Her taken-for-granted health is shattered and her professional image is turned inside out. When she looks in the mirror, the face staring back is not the person her mind's eye expects to see. Who is she now? Her cancer demands that she look deep for an unexplored identity hidden beneath her previous mental image.

> The roller coaster careens downward. Years later, lung nodules show up on my scan.
>
> I'm scared. Angry. This isn't fair—everything was supposed to be okay. Oh, I can keep taking chemotherapy, hopeful for remissions. But the cancer will keep recurring. I will die of it.
>
> Who am I? I still refuse to be defined by my disease or by my losses. I'm no longer the person who used to be in control, who had energy to take care of tasks and other people. Rather I'm the one who needs care. I'm the one who is vulnerable. This is not an identity I choose. Buried

Dr. Nancy Copeland-Payton, a pastor, hospital chaplain, and physician who practiced medicine for twenty years, leads retreats at church centers, monasteries, and with church groups to help people explore their experiences of loss. She is author of *The Losses of Our Lives: The Sacred Gifts of Renewal in Everyday Loss* (SkyLight Paths).

inside are losses that need to be cried out. This is a long mourning process.

Loss of physical well-being steals our identity built on being physically strong, on feeling good, and being full of energy. We watch this previous self slip through our fingers inside the EMI scanner and drain out as chemotherapy drips through an IV tube into our veins.

But even worse, fatal illness steals our future. We must venture into this unknown terrain bereft of the tomorrows that we assumed would be ours.

> I finally let go of my control and let myself be vulnerable and cared for by others. When I learn to receive their care with profound gratitude, I receive the greatest gift. I realize how much I am loved. It's extraordinary. This love lets me be even more vulnerable. It finally lets me release little concerns and being so busy with work. I don't have to row so hard every day.
>
> My advice? Relish the goodness in every day. Delight in the smell of green grass and the warmth of sun, laugh with your friends, let go of everything else. I'm in solidarity now with others through this experience of love—with those who hurt and with creation as I'm aware of being part of God's natural rhythm of ebb and flow.

It is agonizingly difficult to let go—to name and mourn our loss of control and health at a much-too-early age. We peer into a dark abyss where we cannot see the bottom or the way ahead. But once we let go, a different way of seeing is given. With less time left, the time that remains is priceless. The sense of each day's treasure is heightened and perfected to let us relish the glorious taste, sight, sound, and feel of each moment's gifts. Something in us breaks open as we begin to savor this ordinary, extraordinary life that bestows such extravagant presents as green grass, sunlight, and laughter.

After a life-changing accident, middle-aged Benjamin talked with me:

> One moment I'm driving. The next thing I know, I wake up in the ICU, days later. I know it's bad, really bad. I've never been taken care of before. But there's no choice—I have to just accept it, to accept what is. Others clean me, feed me, change my gown, and make decisions for me. Later, at home, people help me dress, drive me to appointments, and fix my food.

But in my devastating loss, I am also given a gift. When I allow others to support, love, and care for me, when I gratefully embrace their presence, there is an unexpected sweetness. I feel their fierce love. God's love is vibrant in their love. And God's presence is in the moment-to-moment goodness, beauty, and magnificence of this world. An intense awareness of the blessing of life fills me. When I'm so depleted and weak, I'm also most intensely aware of the blessings given to me. I receive gifts—I can breathe, see, hear, and speak. In attending to the gifts of the moment, I'm overwhelmed with gratitude, particularly for small things—very small things—such as a sandwich for lunch.

This is the key to recovery, to "heart" recovery. My being "fine" is not tied to the external physical markers of being okay. The accident gives me clarity that the gift of life is so great, there's no time to be petty, small, or negative. Rather, we're to live into the largess of God's astounding gift of life.

To lose physical health, abilities, and self-image is a grievous loss that we must name and mourn. Such overwhelming loss challenges us to search for a more profound identity, which is not defined by our physical well-being—or by its loss. It is a paradox that when we are vulnerable, we can more fully receive life's greatest gift—the astonishing gift of love. Our masks, protective barriers, illusions of "having it together," and our false sense of self-sufficiency keep love from penetrating our deepest being. But tangible expressions of human love, like help with dressing, a sandwich, a get-well card, or a ride to the doctor's office—gifts bestowed on us when we're most helpless—can awaken us to the love that binds us all together at our most exposed level, beneath all our surface bravado.

Human love lets us glimpse divine love, that birthright love for which we yearn. Being vulnerable breaks us open to our most profound being, the self created by and loved by God. We are fiercely loved because we were created in sacred love. Period. In tearful acceptance, we can let the love of God and others gently rain on us and soak into our driest, most thirsty depths. We who are created in the image of God can love one another and be loved with sacred intensity. We experience a larger identity, one of solidarity, as Mariam so beautifully puts it, "with others through this experience of love; with those who hurt and with creation" as we are part of nature's endless ebb and flow.

Loss of Well-Being

The loss of physical well-being shatters our illusion of control and invincibility. This is a sobering, difficult place for us. The following exercise invites you to sit with this disillusionment and to explore your thoughts and emotions.

- Settle into a quiet, peaceful place. Give yourself the gift of time. Recall concerns and tasks that await you, hold them one by one, then put them aside.

- Be aware of the details and textures and colors around you. Notice the silence and the sounds.

- Do you grieve the loss of anything physical? Have you yearned for well-being or physical wholeness from childhood? Has illness or accident taken something from you?

- What emotions or thoughts surface?

- Have other people ever taken care of you? How did they help you? What did you think or feel at the time? What about now?

- How did this loss affect your self-image? Who were you before? Who are you now?

Tagore on Beauty and Tragedy

Annotated by Swami Adiswarananda

"Trust love even if it brings sorrow. Do not close up your heart."
"Ah no, my friend, your words are dark, I cannot understand
    them."

"The heart is only for giving away with a tear and a song, my love."
"Ah no, my friend, your words are dark, I cannot understand
    them."

"Pleasure is frail like a dewdrop, while it laughs it dies.
But sorrow is strong and abiding. Let sorrowful love wake in your
    eyes."
"Ah no, my friend, your words are dark, I cannot understand them."

"The lotus blooms in the sight of the sun, and loses all that it has.
It would not remain in bud in the eternal winter mist."
"Ah no, my friend, your words are dark, I cannot understand
    them...."

—Rabindranath Tagore, from "The Gardener," in
Tagore: The Mystic Poets

The inner-seeking spirituality of India infused all of Tagore's writing. He wrote in many genres of the deep religious milieu of Hinduism. This passage from his novel *The Home and the World*, for instance, offers a domesticated version of the devotion so common in the spiritual feelings and actions of the Indian people:

I know, from my childhood's experience, how devotion is beauty itself,
in its inner aspect. When my mother arranged the different fruits,

Swami Adiswarananda, former senior monk of the Ramakrishna Order of India, was minister and spiritual leader of the Ramakrishna-Vivekananda Center of New York and annotator of *Tagore: The Mystic Poets* (SkyLight Paths).

carefully peeled by her own loving hands, on the white stone plate, and gently waved her fan to drive away the flies while my father sat down to his meals, her service would lose itself in a beauty which passed beyond outward forms. Even in my infancy I could feel its power. It transcended all debates, or doubts, or calculations: it was pure music....[1]

Tagore's mystical approach to living was also fed by tremendous sorrow in his personal life. Over the space of only five years, in the middle of the first decade of the twentieth century, Rabindranath's wife and two of his children, a boy and a girl, each thirteen years old, died. His three other children moved away from the family home; two daughters married and his other son went off to college in America. Tagore turned these tragedies and the resulting loneliness into great depths of spiritual insight. He saw these happenings in a much broader context than his own life; his own life, in fact, had no boundaries. "He sought God not merely in the privacy of his soul," writes one critic who worked with Tagore for several years, "but in every manifestation of [God's] play in the outside world."[2] Sadness and gaiety, beauty and tragedy, all were held in the life of God among us, according to Tagore's mystical perspective....

> I plucked your flower, O world!
> I pressed it to my heart and the thorn pricked.
> When the day waned and it darkened,
> I found that the flower had faded,
> but the pain remained.
>
> More flowers will come to you with
> perfume and pride, O world!
> But my time for flower gathering is over,
> and through the dark night I have not my rose,
> only the pain remains.
>
> —Rabindranath Tagore, from "The Gardener," in
> *Tagore: The Mystic Poets*

Becoming Whole

Rev. Timothy J. Mooney

Wholeness is a biblical word found in the Gospel of Matthew. When Jesus says, "Be perfect as your heavenly Father is perfect" (5:48), he is instructing us to be whole. The Greek word *teleios*, usually translated as "perfect," is a much more complex word, meaning completeness, wholeness, fullness, maturity, oneness. Becoming whole is the result of becoming aware of all the emotions, thoughts, and desires playing within us and bringing them into God's gracious presence in prayer. We need to admit to all our desires and emotions: (1) admit, as in confess and acknowledge to ourselves, and God, what is real in us; and (2) admit, as in allow those desires and emotions entrance into our awareness. As we admit all these aspects of ourselves to God, we find God healing us, honing our desires down to the deepest, truest desires within us, making us whole.

Embracing Our Emotions Willingly Rather Than Willfully

Just *expressing* anger or hurt or grief isn't enough. Some psychologists have encouraged the expression of everything one feels: Don't hold back, just let it out. But this can cause a great deal of hurt and pain. There is a profound difference between expressing every emotion and desire and *being aware of*, feeling, and praying with and through our emotions and longings.

Becoming aware of our emotions, observing them in contemplation without acting on them, offers a profound freedom. "In the experience of quiet," writes Gerald May, "one begins to observe that there is always a space between feeling and response, between the impulse and the action. Within this space there is a great freedom for choice."[1] Within that space, God is very present.

Rev. Timothy J. Mooney, a Presbyterian minister, reatreat leader, visual artist, and spiritual director, is author of *Like a Child: Restoring the Awe, Wonder, Joy and Resiliency of the Human Spirit* (SkyLight Paths). A pastor for over twenty-five years, he currently leads Community of ONE, a worshipping community in the heart of urban Denver.

Children admit everything about their world and experience. When they are hungry, they cry out. When they are hurt or sad, they feel it, show the expression on their faces, let tears come. When they are happy, they embody it, dancing with delight. So, too, as adults we are invited to admit internally, feel bodily, all that is real within us.

How do we do this without pushing people away with childish—not child-like—volcanic emotional eruptions? Gerald May, in his book *Will and Spirit*, provides a helpful distinction: We must be willing, rather than willful, to embrace our emotions and desires. What would it mean for us to attend to all our desires and emotions willingly rather than willfully, with our whole selves?

Jesus practices this in the Garden of Gethsemane, as he struggles with the knowledge of his pending death and the cruel and violent manner in which it will be played out (Matthew 26:36–56). In his prayer he lays bare all his desires and emotions. He pleads, asks if there is any other way, sweats drops of blood, according to some manuscripts. Every desire and emotion is brought to awareness, admitted, allowed to exist, voiced, brought to God. Due to the length and anguished nature of this prayer, I do not hesitate to call it a tantrum of sorts. But in this place of prayer, where Jesus acknowledges all his desires and emotions, he finds the freedom to respond, not willfully, but willingly.

Throw a Fit

Set aside at least thirty minutes when you are alone. Think of something that really bothers you or has disappointed or angered you and give yourself permission to throw a fit. Even if you don't feel like you have something to throw a fit about, begin acting and see what emotions or memories surface.

Involving your body in this exercise helps access feelings that might not emerge if it were just an intellectual exercise. It is important to do this in such a way that you, others, and property will be protected and safe. For example, you might close the door to your bedroom and throw or punch pillows as you vocalize your feelings.

Once you have allowed yourself to say, feel, and embody what you usually keep below the surface, take the time to journal or record your experience and your reflections on it.

Throwing a fit may feel awkward, if not childish, but it provides a way for you to recognize and experience the myriad complaints, disappointments, and laments that exist within you, as well as the underlying and often conflicting desires and longings. The key is becoming aware of what lies within you, and prayerfully reflecting on what you find.

What Do You Want Me to Do for You?

Jesus is portrayed in the Gospels as asking others, "What do you want me to do for you?" Ignatius of Loyola, the founder of the Society of Jesus (better known as the Jesuits), made this a key component of spiritual formation and prayers of discernment.

Set aside thirty minutes in a comfortable place where you will not be interrupted. Prayerfully imagine God asking you, "What do you want me to do for you?" After your initial response, keep responding to this question and delve more deeply into the heart of your desires and longings. What is it that you *really* want?

When you have allowed your true self to open up and express these desires, be gentle in your response. Don't criticize or judge but simply treasure any realizations or new knowledge of your deepest self. Hold them quietly in your heart as you go about your daily life, and see what they might blossom into.

Not All Tears Are Equal

Imam Jamal Rahman

"It is He who has created for you hearing, sight, feeling, and understanding," says the Qur'an (23:78; 32:9), from which Sufi teachers conclude that our feelings are from God and are therefore sacred, whether joyous or sorrowful. Happy feelings are easy to accept as gifts, but what about difficult ones, such as suffering or rage? Teachers from many traditions say that these feelings are simply energies begging to be acknowledged, healed, and integrated. We become more developed as humans when we embrace not only our joys but also our sorrows. If we avoid the latter, we do so at our peril. One day those shunned feelings will rise and revolt. Thus, it is essential to embrace, little by little and with compassion for self, the sharp-edged feelings we tend to deny or circumvent.

There are gifts and teachings in moments of pain and suffering, but we can realize these divine favors only when we embrace and integrate the unhappy feelings that they evoke. If we are willing to do that hard spiritual work, we will experience an inner spaciousness and a sense of freedom because, as Rumi says, "Something opens and lifts my wings." The tears we weep in our difficult moments are the subject of poetic metaphor in Sufi literature. Wherever water flows, life flourishes. Thus our tears are sacred, watering rose gardens in the invisible realms and attracting divine mercy. "Weep like the waterwheel," says Rumi, "so that sweet herbs may grow in the courtyard of your soul."

The Mulla fully agrees,[1] but cautions us that that not all tears are equal.... Tears lose their sacredness when we get attached to them. While it is absolutely paramount to acknowledge our pain and suffering and do the work

---

Imam Jamal Rahman, beloved teacher and retreat leader, is author of *Spiritual Gems of Islam: Insights & Practices from the Qur'an, Hadith, Rumi & Muslim Teaching Stories to Enlighten the Heart & Mind* and *Sacred Laughter of the Sufis: Awakening the Soul with the Mulla's Comic Teaching Stories & Other Islamic Wisdom* (both SkyLight Paths), among other books.

of healing and integration, it is also critical not to be devoted to our tears because they have secondary benefits. At a certain point we have to let go. Don't be sad any longer, pleads Rumi, "for your sadness is blasphemy against the Hand of Splendor pouring you joy." In another utterance, he teaches us that in prolonged periods of grief, we need to say to ourselves at the right time, "Enough is enough!" and that "it is time now to speak of roses and pomegranates and of the oceans where pearls are made of language and vision ..."

Just as it is sacred to spend time with our suffering, it is equally sacred to spend time with our blessings. Don't neglect moments of joy in your life. Consciously acknowledge and celebrate them. Feel gratitude for them. Sufi teachers exhort us to do practices where we honor the happy moments in our life and the blessings that come our way....

A Sense of Balance

The Mulla was apprenticed to a teacher who complained that he wasted time and energy repeating tasks that he should have been able to consolidate more efficiently. For example, rather than going to the market three times to buy one egg each time, the smarter approach would be to go to the market only once and buy three eggs. The Mulla took the lesson to heart. When his teacher became ill and dispatched the Mulla to fetch a doctor, the Mulla returned with four people: two doctors for the sake of a second opinion, an imam who would offer fervent prayers in case the medical treatment did not work, and an undertaker in case nothing worked and the teacher died!

What the Mulla really needed was a lesson not in efficiency but in balance and proportion. We humans often tend to overdo it, whether in thoughts, feelings, words, or deeds. We don't know when to stop, and end up drawing legs on a snake, to quote a Zen metaphor. The Qur'an advises us to pay attention to the divine sense of proportion in the universe. "In true proportions God created the Heavens and the Earth," says a typical verse. "Truly, in that is a sign for those who have faith" (29:44).

We display our lack of balance in many ways, and the Qur'an offers appropriate corrective advice. For example, we easily become attached to our joys and sometimes even to our sorrows, so that we don't make room in our hearts for opposing emotions, but the Qur'an tells us that both laughter and tears are sacred and each should be experienced with equanimity. "Don't despair over things that pass you by nor exult over blessings that come to you" (Qur'an 57:23). If we insist on laughing all the time, even in times of pain and suffering, we miss out on the holiness of tears that water our inner growth. Similarly, if we are overly attached to our tears and regrets, we are, in the words of the poet Tagore, like someone who cries all night long for the daylight and misses out on the beauty of the stars. And if we persist in tasting the bitterness of life in the hope of one day tasting the sweet, we are like the Mulla, who bought some exotic-looking fruits and couldn't stop eating them, even though his tongue felt a painful sting and his eyes began to water. A passerby told him that the fruits were hot chilies native to India and he should stop eating them immediately if he didn't wish to suffer. The Mulla replied that he was actually eating his spent money, and surely at least one of those peppers might turn out to be sweet!

Finding Balance

In what areas of your life are you feeling unbalanced or overstepping bounds? Make a list and with compassion for self, reflect on them. What are some small changes you could make immediately?

If you are engaging in obsessive thoughts or feelings, do some self-talk whenever you become aware of it. Tell yourself with mercy but firmness, "Stop! I choose to stop. Cancel. Delete." Select words that work for you. Then, take that thought or feeling, place it in your heart, and say, "I release you to Spirit."

If you have a loving and trustworthy circle of friends, or a partner you can be vulnerable with, ask frankly if you tend to exaggerate, are overly critical in your opinions and judgments, or are overstepping limits in any way. If possible, ask them for helpful suggestions. You might be surprised how healing and creative the counsel can be from caring friends and family members.

Breathe

Finding a Still Point

> The power of silence gives us breathing
> room. There is wisdom in the silence.
>
> —Kay Lindahl

There are times in the grief spiral when the best thing to do is just breathe. What you need most right now might be simply to find a quiet place inside your heart, learning to be present with what is.

Through prayers, meditations, and embodied practices, the contributors in this section invite you into a haven of stillness. Though it is natural to fear what memories and emotions you might encounter, sitting with the pain is what begins to loosen its grip on you. There will be time to express, remember, and reorient, and you will do all of those things. But in the midst of the journey, let your soul rest a while; let the healing of silence and stillness sink into your heart.

Give Ear to My Prayer

M. Basil Pennington, OCSO

Give ear to my prayer, O God, and hide not yourself from my supplication.
Pay attention to me and hear me. I am overcome with troubles and
    distraught
because of the shouts of the enemy,
because of the oppression of the wicked,
for they heap invectives upon me and in their anger they hate me.
My heart is sorely pained within me
and the terrors of death come upon me.
Fearfulness and trembling have come upon me
and horror overwhelms me.
I cry, "Oh, that I had wings like a dove!
For then would I fly away and be at rest.
Yes, I would fly far away and settle in the wilderness;
I would hasten my escape from the raging storm and the tempest."
Confound them, Lord, divide their speech!
for I see violence and strife in the city.
Day and night they go about upon its walls;
evil and sorrow are in its midst.
Wickedness is in its midst;
deceit and guile depart not from its streets....
Cast your burden upon the Lord and he shall sustain you.
God shall never allow a good person to be overcome.
You, O God, shall bring them down into the pit of destruction;
bloody and deceitful men shall not live out half their days.
But I will trust in you.

—Psalm 55:1–23 (author's translation)

M. Basil Pennington, OCSO, was a monk for more than fifty years. He lived at St.
Joseph's Abbey in Spencer, Massachusetts, and was the author of many modern spiri-
tual classics, including *Finding Grace at the Center: The Beginning of Centering Prayer* and
Psalms: A Spiritual Commentary (both SkyLight Paths).

We all have had moments when we wished we could get away from it all. Our thoughts might not have been as poetic as our Psalmist's: "Oh, that I had wings like a dove," but we did want to "fly away and be at rest."

We are rightly horrified by the pictures of the terrible sufferings of our sisters and brothers that enter our homes and our hearts. We will never forget the devastation of the tsunami of December 2004, the terrorism of 9/11, or the daily horrors being wrought upon the victims of terrorism around the world. But we do not have to go so far or into the past. In our own affluent society, the rich get richer and the poor get poorer; children suffer malnutrition and abuse; the old are warehoused; the victims of war are left in veterans' hospitals to wait out whatever remains of their lives. Some corporate crime is uncovered and mildly punished, but for the most part such crime mocks the adage, crime does not pay. Political and corporate dishonesty is so prevalent that it is almost accepted as the norm and doesn't disturb the perpetrators' consciences, while migrants work like slaves and others cannot find employment.

But sometimes even all this pain and suffering and human misery gets blocked out by our own personal sufferings. Sickness, poverty, and insecurity are bad enough, but they can perhaps be more easily measured by the plight of others. It is when personal venom, even betrayal, are heaped upon us that our spirit is crushed: "the terrors of death come upon me."

Yes, we would like to get away from it all. "I am overcome with trouble and distraught.... My heart is sorely pained within me.... Yes, I would fly away and settle in the wilderness."

How wonderful it would be to have great wings and be able to rise above it all and fly far away. But, in truth, can I really get away from it? No matter what solitude I find, I bring with me my own troubled spirit. I am woven into the fabric of humanity. I cannot cut myself off from the sorrows and pains in my own life or anyone else's.

It is fanciful to think of having great wings—even the wings of a peaceful dove who knows how to settle in the crags in the rocks and welcome the day with its peaceful cooing. Yet, we can—and if we are wise, we will—take refuge in meditation regularly, in the morning and evening, cooing our prayer word, resting in the Divine Love. "Be still and know that I am God." In these moments of restful communion we do "fly away and ... rest."

Still Life—Stepping Back

Linda Novick

Stepping back can mean getting a better view by standing further away from the situation at hand and taking time to breathe. It can also mean taking our egos out of the equation and becoming more silent by detaching slightly from—but not denying—the events in our lives and our ever-present emotions and thoughts. By detaching and simply witnessing each moment, we are practicing what enlightened masters have been talking about since the first word was uttered....

Painting is an activity that can bring each of us back into direct experience and the peace of the present moment. It helps us to let go of the past and the future and allows our minds to dwell in the beautiful present moment of creation....

The first step is to practice watching the conversations in your mind without judging them. As you engage in the pastel activity at the end of this chapter, try to observe the voices that comment on your experience.

For example, after painting a stroke on your paper, if you notice the thought "I made a mistake," or perhaps "I love this!" simply notice the thought and keep going. Don't let discouraging thoughts stop your process, and don't let encouraging thoughts make you take yourself too seriously. Observe the fullness of your experience and be present to it all.

The second step in this process is to keep noticing your breathing. Stay focused on your breath while making your painting. Breathing keeps the flow of life force moving and keeps supplying you with energy. Use the breath as a source of energy and be conscious of the breath flowing into your painting. Breath brings *prana* to your body, and this is transmitted into your painting.

Linda Novick leads painting and yoga retreats in the United States and abroad and is author of *The Painting Path: Embodying Spiritual Discovery through Yoga, Brush and Color* (SkyLight Paths).

The third step is to drink in all the aspects of your experience, including the sights, sounds, smells, and physical sensations. These will include feeling your heart beating, the warmth on your skin, and the weight of your body. As you move your body, feel the movements your arm is making. Pay attention to the texture of the materials you are using, such as the grittiness or softness of the pastels and the roughness of the sandpaper....

Prepare your art space before practicing meditation so that you can flow right into the pastel project. You may even want to read through the first few steps of the art project to prepare your paper surface ahead of time. Be sure that you have your pastel supplies nearby so that you can go to them when you're finished meditating.

Observing the Breath Through *Anapanasati*

Our yoga-inspired exercise is a simple but effective form of meditation called *anapanasati*, a technique taught by the Buddha in which breathing is used to develop a serene and concentrated mind. By consciously focusing on the minute details of our breath, our mind begins to see into itself and discovers a unique freedom. This form of meditation is said to be the form that brought the Buddha to full awakening.

Note: This meditation is best experienced without referring to the book. Please read through instructions before you begin the practice, or record the instructions and play them back to yourself, making sure to leave enough space between instructions so they will be timed correctly when you play them back.

As you focus your attention on your breathing, you'll be allowing your mind to move as it will, without becoming involved in the thoughts. You will be witnessing your thoughts without paying attention to them but simply being aware that they are "saying something." You'll simply be the observer, not a participant, in the mind's conversation.

In this process of observing your breath and disregarding your thoughts, you are training yourself to release your identification with your thoughts and even discover who you are behind your thoughts. You become present, watching your breath. Thoughts will come and go, and you'll let them go without attaching to them. This is a powerful way to develop witness consciousness....

1. Set a kitchen timer or other alarm for five to ten minutes. (If you find you like this meditation technique and want to continue with it, you can slowly increase the amount of time you practice.)

2. Sit on a chair or couch and place your feet firmly on the ground. Let your body relax into the chair. Rest your hands in your lap and let your elbows fall against the side of your body. Consciously relax your shoulders, belly, and any part of your body that feels tense.

3. Lengthen your spine by pressing the very top of your head toward the ceiling. Keep your spine straight but not rigid, as this keeps energy flowing freely throughout your body and prevents sleepiness.

4. When you feel relaxed and centered, close your eyes, or if you prefer, keep your eyes slightly open with a soft gaze toward a spot on the floor. Bring your awareness to your breath, feeling it flow in and out of your body. Let your breath be natural and steady.

5. Notice where you feel your breath the most. If you feel your breath strongly in your chest, then focus on your chest rising and falling, over and over. If you feel your breath in your nostrils, focus there. Notice all the sensations involved in your breathing, such as the temperature of the air as you inhale and exhale. Let yourself become involved in these sensations until your breath becomes your whole world.

6. If your mind wanders, bring your attention back to your breath with compassion and gentleness. It is natural for your attention to be drawn away from the breath, because the mind tends to be restless. Noticing this and gently turning your awareness back to your breath is part of witness consciousness.

7. If you notice yourself thinking, don't cling to the content of the thought. Instead, let the thoughts float by like clouds in a clear sky, drifting away gently. Continue to observe your breath; maintain a straight spine and allow your body to relax even more.

8. Simply stay with your breath. Let the sensations of breathing calm and focus your mind. Watch your breath flow in and out like waves on the shore. Keep your mind on your breath.

When the bell on your timer rings, slowly open your eyes. Gently allow your awareness to return to the room you are in and let go of the meditation. Allow yourself some transition time before beginning the painting project.

Painting a Still Life Using Pastels

Things You Will Need

- Variety of objects to arrange in a still-life composition

- Box of soft pastels (not oil pastels), at least 36 colors

- Vine charcoal

- 5 or more sheets of sandpaper, 9 by 11 inches, in two types:

  - 413Q 3M 600 wet or dry sandpaper (grayish black in color)

  - 413Q 220 wet or dry sandpaper (grayish black in color)

- 2 or 3 sheets of toned pastel paper, assorted colors (at least 11 by 14 inches)

- Sheet of foam core or corrugated cardboard, 20 by 26 inches or larger

- Roll of masking tape

- Newspaper to cover your worktable

- Workable fixative

- Colorful tablecloth and table

Tip: I recommend affixing your sandpaper and pastel paper to a cushioned surface before drawing because pastels work best when the drawing surface has some give to it. Taping your papers to a piece of foam core works well, as does simply spreading a layer of news-papers on your table as a cushion.

Optional

- Desk lamp or other source of direct light

- Small box of hard pastels, at least 24 colors

- Tortillon or blending stump

- Colored construction paper

- Larger artist's sandpaper, colored or white

- Latex gloves

- Baby wipes

- Stiff bristle brush

Tip: Since all paints are made from pigments that may contain tox-ins, many artists use latex gloves while painting with pastels to avoid prolonged contact with the skin. I especially recommend that students with sensitive skin wear gloves. I do not wear gloves, but I do use baby wipes to frequently remove pigments from my hands.

Still lifes are a good subject because they can remain in place for the time it takes to complete your work. You can choose objects that may have meaning, such as a special doll or a prized vase or statue.... As you gather objects for your still life, you may be aware of witnessing this activity. What are your thoughts and feelings as you look for the objects you will paint? Simply observe your experience without judging or evaluating it....

Consider using a light source such as a spotlight or a lamp. Placing a light source on the side of the still life will throw the objects into sharp contrast and will emphasize the light and dark areas.

1. Cover a table with a colorful tablecloth.
2. Choose several everyday objects that appeal to you and that are diverse in shape, size, texture, and color. Arrange them on the tablecloth in a composition that pleases your eye. Use your imagination and play with it until you feel good about the way your objects look....
3. Prepare a piece of paper, either taping it to a piece of foam core or placing it on top of a layer of newspapers on the table.
4. Gather the rest of your supplies and take a moment to sit still in front of the still life you've created. Witness your thoughts and your feelings as you approach your project. Are you anxious? Excited?
5. Take the vine charcoal and, using light linear strokes, sketch the outline of the objects of your still life. (Don't use the soft pastels yet.) Look at the outside contour of the objects. Note their placement, their relative sizes, their shapes. Observe carefully, but don't worry about getting the details absolutely correct.
6. After you've sketched in the object or objects, you are ready to begin adding colors with the soft pastels....
7. Start by carefully noting the colors you see in your objects. If you are painting a red apple, what various tones of red do

Tip: There are many different ways to apply pastels, and they are fun to play with on a wide variety of surfaces, from smooth paper to fine sandpaper.... My favorite surface is the grayish-black sandpaper sold in hardware stores. I recommend a 600-grit surface, which is finely ground and feels like you are stroking a fine suede coat. It is a luscious color too, and every color you apply to it looks good, from subtle earth tones to brilliant high-key colors. When you lay the pastels on their side and stroke them across the page, the sensation is satisfying and sensuous.

you see in the apple? Are there other colors, perhaps green or yellow, mixed in with the red?

8. Find the colored pastels you will need to paint your still life and remove them from the box. One by one, use them to make strokes on your paper to color in the outlines. Notice your reaction to the feel of the paper and the feel of the pastels in your hand. If at any time you feel nervous or anxious, return your attention to your breathing, the way you did during meditation.

9. Try to follow the form or the contour of the object you're painting. For example, if your object is round, use rounded linear strokes to mimic the shape as you fill in the color. Where there are shadows, consider using cross-hatching or side strokes. If you want to smooth out an area, use the blending technique.

10. Is there reflected light on any of the objects? For example, a red apple sitting on a yellow satin cloth will create an orange glow on the cloth. The yellow might even be reflected on the surface of the apple. As you notice these lovely tricks of the light, you will be able to see why artists such as Cézanne and French painter Chardin have delighted in painting still lifes over the centuries—there is always more there than at first meets the eye.

11. From time to time, you may find that you have built up layers of pastel so thickly that the paper no long has any tooth to it and additional layers won't adhere. If this happens, take a stiff bristle brush, like an old toothbrush, and brush off the excess pastel and restore some tooth to the paper.

12. Keep working on your still life until you are happy with it or at least satisfied with your attempt. If tension arises, return your attention to your breath and focus on slow, steady breathing.... As the witness, all you need to do is watch and observe your experience.

13. When you are done, shake the can of fixative well, hold it twelve to sixteen inches from the surface of your pastel painting, and spray a light layer over the entire surface of the page. (Spray outdoors or in a well-ventilated place.) Later, if you want to, you can continue painting with pastels over the layer of fixative.

Painting still lifes is terrific because it encourages you to look ever deeper into details.... As you develop your powers of observation without judgment, you may notice your experiences becoming more vivid and infused with life. Whatever you notice, it's okay. Nothing needs to be any different than it is.

The Healing Art of Living in the Present

Imam Jamal Rahman

Will you not see? Will you not listen?
Will you not pay attention?
—Qur'an 54:17, 7:204

Theoretically, we know how important it is to live in the present, but the truth is that our awareness is often interrupted because our minds are busily flitting back and forth between past regrets and future anxieties. Living in those worlds of past and future, we miss out on the opportunities and gifts of the present moment, what Sufis call the divine party that is always happening in the now....

Does the commitment to living in the moment mean that we should forget the past and ignore the future? Of course not! We need to learn from our past experiences and plan for future needs. The problem comes when we allow ourselves to flit from one tense to another without being conscious of where we are right now. Our minds are everywhere and nowhere—a psychological displacement that is both physically and spiritually exhausting. What is called for is a clear intention to focus consciously on the issue at hand and give ourselves permission to dwell on it for a specific amount of time.

For example, whenever I catch my mind continually veering away from the present moment to dwell on some past regret, I tell myself compassionately, "Brother Jamal, I notice that something is bothering you and you are not present. Let's resolve this now. I give you permission to think and feel

---

Imam Jamal Rahman, beloved teacher and retreat leader, is author of *Spiritual Gems of Islam: Insights & Practices from the Qur'an, Hadith, Rumi & Muslim Teaching Stories to Enlighten the Heart & Mind* and *Sacred Laughter of the Sufis: Awakening the Soul with the Mulla's Comic Teaching Stories & Other Islamic Wisdom* (both SkyLight Paths), among other books.

your past regrets fully and freely for, say, the next twenty minutes." This "allowing" makes me present with my past regrets. The past becomes graced with energies of the present, and often I glean useful insights from the past. I use the same technique of self-talk to be present with my anxieties about the future. I might say, "Brother Jamal, I give you twenty minutes to worry as much as you want to about this issue." When the allotted time is over, I return myself gently but firmly to the present moment....

Some of the most powerful lessons I have learned about the art of being present have occurred while visiting friends who were terminally ill. I particularly remember my good friend Janet Turner, who lived for a number of years on borrowed time with a transplanted kidney. Filled with gratitude and intensely mindful about time, she constantly asked herself, "What is it that I would truly like to accomplish, experience, and express to others?" She traveled extensively, took countless classes, volunteered to help complete innumerable projects, and tended her relationships with family and friends. Eventually, the transplanted kidney began to fail, and Janet felt her life force ebbing away. Although disabled by pain and weakness, she continued to nourish her soul by listening to chants and music and by reflecting on verses of insight and beauty from sacred texts and sublime poetry. Two weeks before she died, she softly held my hands in hers and said with utmost honesty and clarity, "Thank you from the core of my heart for your words and chants, but what I really need from you is for you to be present. That is your best gift to me." I asked her to tell me more. She explained, "If you feel awkward, feel awkward. That is healing to me. If you feel like crying, cry. That is healing to me. If you are speechless, don't say anything. Be silent. That is healing to me. If you feel you really want to tell me something, talk to me. Your words are healing to me." She said many more words along the same lines, and in that moment I began to grasp something of what it means to be present and authentic. Thanks to Janet, I am blessed with a slight knowing of the mystery that the present moment is suffused with, the fragrance of the divine.

Grounding Yourself in the Present Moment

The Sufis have a saying, "A Sufi is a son or daughter of the present moment." Whenever you realize you have strayed unconsciously into the past or future, immediately intervene with compassionate self-talk. "Dear one," you might say, "will you not see? Will you not listen? Will you not pay attention?" And then remind yourself of that Sufi saying, that you are a son or daughter of the present moment.

To help build your ability to stay grounded in the present moment, try these two meditations:

- Close your eyes and bring your attention to rest on your heart. Go deeper into that space, and begin to connect with your heart. Listen to your heartbeat and repeat a life-affirming word or verse with gratitude for the present moment. Stay with this for a few minutes.

- With your eyes closed, focus on the lowest part of the spine, the sacrum area, and from there intend to send a beautiful cord of light deep into the earth. Take the light even deeper and feel this shaft of light connecting you to the womb of Mother Earth. Feel a sense of rootedness and grounding. Spend some time here. Shift your focus now to the crown of your head. From there, send out a cord of light traveling upward, piercing the mysterious realms and connecting you to the heart of heaven. Feel a protective bonding with the dimensions of Mystery. Again, spend some time just savoring this connection. If you wish, chant or repeat sacred verses into that space, and use those same chants to remind yourself to stay centered and mindful throughout the day.

The Heart of a Moment

Margaret D. McGee

Images that evoke complex feelings often touch more than one sense (sight, sound, smell, taste, and touch), as well as other aspects of consciousness, such as the sense of balance and the sense of movement. This practice is designed to help you be fully present to all your senses and develop mindfulness in the moment at hand.

Now and Then Haiku

You will need paper and pencil, and at least twenty minutes of quiet time. Give yourself the time you need....

- First, look over the whole practice; then go through the steps one by one.
- Start with a grid using these seven headings: Scent, Taste, Sound, Touch, Balance, Movement, and Sight. You can either use the grid below or draw your own on a fresh piece of paper, leaving room under each heading for a sentence or two. Allow some extra room under Sight.

Scent	Taste
Sound	Touch
Balance (in or out of balance)	Sight
Movement (moving or still)	

Margaret D. McGee, a writer, teacher, and leader of spiritual workshops and retreats, is author of *Sacred Attention: A Spiritual Practice for Finding God in the Moment* and *Haiku—The Sacred Art: A Spiritual Practice in Three Lines* (both SkyLight Paths).

- If it is practical, go outside and find a place to sit comfortably. If that's not practical, get comfortable where you are.

- Relax, breathe, and look around. Start with the first heading, Scent. Can you smell anything right now? Or do you see something that has a scent— maybe lavender in bloom? (Or even a pile of dog poop!) Write down the first thing you notice with a distinct scent. Do not spend much time describing the smell; let the image do the work. For example, "Rover's old pillow" carries a scent that needs no description.

- Now close your eyes, relax, and let your mind wander. Go back in memory, focusing on your sense of smell. Let the memory of a particular scent come to you, possibly something from childhood, or something from last week. For example, one scent image from my memory is "campfire wienie roast." Open your eyes and, under the Scent heading, jot down a few words that evoke the scent from your memory.

- If no memory comes in a moment or two, that's okay. Instead of jotting down a scent memory, just look around right now and jot down, under the heading for Sight, the first thing you notice.

- Repeat the process for each heading, including an immediate sense and one from your memory. When you come to Balance, look for something in this moment that feels to you either in balance or out of balance. Then look for the same kind of dynamic in your memory. When you come to Movement, look for something that is either moving or particularly still. Some of your images may evoke more than one sense and fit under more than one category. You may also have many entries under Sight, and that is okay.

> *Tip:* If you find yourself obsessing over the placement of commas, dashes, or semicolons, try eliminating all punctuation marks and let the images themselves do the work. Then add only the punctuation you really need.

- Once you have an image or two under each category, stop and look them over....

- Now that you have a number of images full of sensory feeling, it is time to make connections. On a fresh sheet of paper, write down two images from your list that resonate with each other. You can choose two images that rise up and appeal to you right now. They may come from the present moment or from your memory. They may come from the same sense category or from different categories. You may have a distinct idea of how they are related, or you may only sense a relationship between them.

Tip: If you are accustomed to writing haiku with a 5-7-5 syllable count, feel free to use that form in your haiku. Or, if you are new to haiku writing, you may want to give that approach a try. Your shorter image will contain five syllables, and your longer image will contain twelve, broken into two lines of seven and five syllables. Just be careful not to let counting syllables take over the experience of the moment. Give yourself permission to pay more attention to the image than to the number of syllables in a line.

- Condense one of the images down to a single short phrase. Find the essence of the image and include only what's needed.

- Condense the second image down to its essentials in a longer phrase or sentence, still including only what's needed.

- Put your two images together in a three-line haiku. Make the shorter image either the first or the last line, and spread the longer image over the other two lines.

- Finished? Take a moment to enjoy what you've written. Congratulations on your haiku!...

Mindfulness has been called a state of calm awareness in the moment. How did noting and jotting down your sensory impressions change your awareness of each passing moment? Did you find the practice calming, inspiring, or both?

In the coming week, you may want to delve into the images from this practice to write more haiku. You can also repeat the practice anytime and anywhere you have twenty minutes or so to reconnect with all your senses.

From Deserts of Loneliness to Gardens of Solitude

Rev. Jane E. Vennard

"Our language has wisely sensed the two sides of being alone," writes theologian Paul Tillich. "It has created the word *loneliness* to express the pain of being alone. And it has created the word *solitude* to express the glory of being alone."[1]

Loneliness is a human condition; it will never leave us. We can embrace this reality, or we can fight against it. When we encounter this existential loneliness, we often have feelings of sadness and a sense of isolation and seek to find ways to feel better. If we are able to accept that we are simply alone, that nothing is wrong and there is nothing to fix, we are on our way to embracing solitude.

In our religious and secular cultures, we usually defend against loneliness by seeking others to fill the void we are experiencing or by distracting ourselves with busyness. If this has been your pattern of coping with loneliness, you know that it may work for a while, but never for long. We are disappointed when the new friend or lover doesn't make the loneliness go away. We find a new community and join it wholeheartedly, hoping it will ease our pain, and we become disillusioned when we find we are still lonely in the midst of gatherings. A host of new activities might mask our loneliness, but soon we realize that what we are doing is purposeless and is just making us tired. We may then realize that the only way to ease our loneliness is to face it and experience the feelings, as difficult as that may seem.

When we don't run away from our loneliness, we may find in it a clue to what we truly are longing for. When we embrace our loneliness, we may

---

Rev. Jane E. Vennard, a popular teacher on prayer and spiritual practice, is ordained in the United Church of Christ to a ministry of teaching and spiritual direction. She is author of *Fully Awake and Truly Alive: Spiritual Practices to Nurture Your Soul* and *Teaching—The Sacred Art: The Joy of Opening Minds and Hearts* (both SkyLight Paths).

discover possibilities for new life. To live life fully "we must first find the courage to enter into the desert of our loneliness and to change it by gentle and persistent effort into a garden of solitude," writes spiritual teacher Henri J. M. Nouwen.[2]

I believe the persistent effort he calls us to is not striving to solve the problem of our loneliness, not trying to figure out why we are lonely, and not running away. Rather, it is the practice of staying still, sitting with the feelings, listening attentively to our own struggles so we are able to find answers in our own hearts....

The good news is, there is great relief in facing what we have been afraid of or hiding from. With things out in the open, new ways of being and behaving appear. New possibilities often give birth to liveliness and a lightness of spirit. Our deserts of loneliness may turn slowly into gardens of solitude as we develop the capacity to be alone....

A Furnace of Transformation

The Desert Fathers and Mothers of third- and fourth-century Christianity can be our guides for this practice. They were called into the Egyptian desert to come face-to-face with God and with themselves, thus testing and studying what it meant to be fully human. They aimed to live a life that reflected a reversal of all the ordinary social values and expectations of their time.

For these early hermits, the desert was a barren place. Vegetation was scarce and the environment challenging. They were alone, with no place to hide and no one to blame; there was no room for lying or deceit. The Desert Fathers and Mothers could only face up to themselves—their temptations, their attachments, their deepest desires, and their own deaths. This brutally honest accounting smashed old beliefs and old ways of seeing—everything they knew and thought was true.

Many of the stories from this period tell of the abundance of tears shed in the desert. The hermits understood their tears to signify a softening of the soul, clarity of the mind, and an opening to new life. Tears confirmed their readiness to allow their hearts to be broken and their lives to come apart, so as to be free to be reborn into a world of healing.[3]

This desert practice of the early centuries is not likely one that we aspire to. However, many of us have been through a desert, those times when we find ourselves alone, with no place to hide and with nothing to do except wait, watch, and listen while we face ourselves. I think of my divorce and how I felt set apart and lonely; how I silenced myself in my pain. I had to face the end of all I had believed to be true and look closely at my participation in the ending of my marriage and my attachment to cultural expectations. Facing my demons made new life possible.

When my father died suddenly at age sixty, I was pulled through another desert. My world turned upside down, there was no firm place to stand, and nothing seemed real. My heart was broken, but my soul was softened. After a long time of grieving, I was able to face the future with a new understanding of the amazing gift of every moment. Right now I am in the middle of a different kind of desert.... I am realizing that although I still claim my Christian roots and identity, I have let go of many of the teachings of traditional Christianity. I have had to look carefully at each belief, sorting through what is true for me and what needs to be discarded. My old images of God have disappeared, and my habitual ways of seeing the world have changed. It is a lonely place to be, but at the same time I feel deeply connected. I see options before unrecognized, and I feel the promise of liberation.

We do not need to seek out the desert. The desert will come to us. Our smaller, quieter, less dramatic practices of silence and solitude will help us navigate the journey through the wasteland: knowing how to be still and listen, knowing how to face our own loneliness. Welcoming our tears, knowing they will cleanse our minds and hearts and will soften our souls, will give us the strength to go on to new life. Transformation does not only happen in one journey to the desert—in one large furnace. The possibility of transformation is present in every moment.

Exploring Your Experiences of Loneliness

Find a place where you can be alone for about thirty minutes. You may wish to have a journal with you or some other writing material.

Take a moment to quiet yourself, using your breath and paying attention to your body, feelings, and mind.

When you are ready, bring into mind and heart a time of loneliness in your life. It might be in your childhood, or you might be in the middle of it now.

Remember and experience the context of that time. Where were you? What was going on in your life? Who was with you, and who was absent?

As you experience the loneliness of that time, see if you can locate the feeling in your body. What other feelings were part of the lonely experience—grief, physical pain, fear?

Remember what you did with those lonely feelings. Are you willing to accept the ways you responded to loneliness at that time of your life?

Imagine now that the man or woman you are today can reach out and embrace your lonely self. How does that feel? What words of comfort or assurance might you offer to the lonely child, adolescent, or young adult?

If you are experiencing loneliness in your life right now, imagine you have a wise and loving self within who can embrace you. Hear and receive the words of assurance that you are given.

When you have experienced all you need at this moment in time, allow the images to fade, and bring your attention back to the present.

Reflect on, and maybe write about, what it would mean in your life to not run from your loneliness or try to fix it, but rather to accept your loneliness so that it might turn into a garden of solitude.

The Chant of the Heart

Ana Hernández

S ound can open us up and sound can close us down. For years, I would jump at the sound of a slamming door. Why? Because I had a cellular memory of an experience that was traumatic. It took me a long time to figure out that now it was simply the sound of a slamming door. It wasn't the shadow of a bad experience, unless I chose to keep reliving the experience.

Sound opens me up to the world in ways that are mostly inexpressible, yet it moves me to the core. I'm pretty sure that our paths in life are connected to the things that move our hearts, and I've realized that chant is the type of sound that has the capacity to move and transform me more than any other kind of sound....

For this exercise, you don't need anything except an intention to be present with your own heart and an openness to what it can teach you about love. Random thoughts tend to arise as soon as we turn the corner and head for quietness, but don't be discouraged. Just take note of them and let them depart.... Take the time now to sit with your heart. Listen closely to where it is leading you, and follow its pulse through the meditation.

Heartbeat Meditation and Chant

Find a quiet place. Sit in a comfortable position, either on a chair or on a cushion on the floor. If you choose a chair, sit up straight and place both feet on the floor (posture matters). Place one hand palm up on your lap. Using your other hand, try to find your pulse. Start with your radial pulse. It's usually pretty easy to find, just below your thumb. Take your second and third fingers and place them in the groove toward the outside of your wrist. If you can't find it, don't worry, you're not dead yet. You can try to find your carotid pulse, which supplies blood to your neck and head, by running your fingers along the outside edge of your windpipe. The lub-dub sound your heart makes represents the closing of the

---

Ana Hernández, a composer, arranger, and performer of sacred music, is author of *The Sacred Art of Chant: Preparing to Practice* (SkyLight Paths).

valves behind the blood. Once you find your pulse, sit with it for a minute or two, breathing regularly and feeling the pump, pump, pump. Each and every one of us holds this small beat in common. Note how fragile we are. Life is precarious and random, and we are easily broken.

When you feel comfortable enough and secure in the knowledge that you know your own heartbeat, the time comes to join the community. Listen. We must know our own heart before we can share it with others. Listen again to the driving rhythm of your heart; take all the time you need. When you feel ready, use your voice to replicate it. Try it on an AH or OH sound, one sound per beat, one beat at a time. Don't forget to breathe. Make a nice sound, not just a grunting noise, but more like the kind of sound you'd like to make so that the people you love can recognize you and your heart. The kind of sound you might make if you thought it was safe enough to be on familiar terms with the rest of God's people. This can be tricky, because most of God's people are not trouble-free. The point is that this is about you and your heart, and about your taking the time you need to get to know yourself so that you can be comfortable trusting the presence of God in you—enough to be able to live life with an open heart. This is not about believing in God, or even about God believing in you. Rev. William Sloane Coffin once said that "faith is being seized by love."[1] Imagine your heart opening like a flower, naturally reaching toward the source of love.

Find your pulse again. Sit with it while you breathe regularly and picture what it is like to open your heart to the people you love the most in the world, both known to you and unknown; those who have made it possible for you to be here now; all who have come before you. Sit with them for a moment, allow yourself to feel their support, and thank them for it by letting them hear your heart sound. Then, when you feel ready, and a little more comfortable and sure of your heart sound, enlarge your field of vision to include your neighbors, your favorite teachers, the people on line at the grocery store, the people who make you laugh, the people whose hearts are closed to you, the people your heart is closed to, the ones who've caused you pain, and the ones you've caused pain. This part can be hard. I sometimes do it in the shower so there's a steady stream of water to wash away the tears. Return often to your pulse and your heart sound, to check in with yourself. Take it easy. Even the people who have hurt us are fragile and broken in places. As for your heart, I once read that when a heart is broken open, it can hold the whole world.

Waiting for Light

Karyn D. Kedar

The story is told of the ancient Israelites wandering in the vastness of the desert not knowing which way to go. God told them that they would be guided by the Divine Presence. They should follow a pillar of cloud by day and a pillar of fire by night. When the cloud descended upon the people, it would be a sign to camp, not to journey on until it lifted.

As I explore the vast possibilities that life brings, I am at times confused, as if I am in a cloud and unable to see the way. During those moments, I know I should pause and reflect and have patience. It is uncomfortable being in a cloud, in a haze of thought. But these moments are when I can shift into new directions, bring new dimensions into my life. If I run, I will be lost. If I wait and let the confusion and anxiety settle, then the cloud lifts, pointing toward a way that is clear. It is possible that confusion just may be an unrecognized moment of clarity. Suddenly, my eyes open and I see that all is possible and that life is filled with endless variety. In this moment of clarity, I know that the future holds a thousand renditions of what might be and a million possibilities of what may never be. As my mind races through these, my eyes cloud, my stomach tightens, my head enters a dense fog. I squint and try to focus on all the "maybes" and "why nots" and "what ifs." Anything is possible, and I am confused as to what is fundamental, essential, right.

A student in my adult education class asked me to lunch recently. We chatted about our children, our husbands, our work. There was a pause. I took a long sip of my raspberry iced tea, thinking how clever it was to combine fruit flavor and tea and ice. I looked up at my companion. Her face seemed relaxed in deep thought. "You know," she said softly, "of all the lessons you taught last year, the one about the cloud has really helped me. When I do not

---

Karyn D. Kedar is senior rabbi at Congregation B'nai Jehoshua Beth Elohim in the Chicago area and the inspiring author of *Our Dance with God: Finding Prayer, Perspective and Meaning in the Stories of Our Lives* and *God Whispers: Stories of the Soul, Lessons of the Heart* (both Jewish Lights).

know what to do or where to go, I see the cloud of God surround me, and I simply wait." It was her turn to sip tea, as I quietly thanked God for moments of calm and faith.

When the cloud descends, still your instinct to run or flee. Stay quiet and make no decisions while you are in the cloud. Be patient and know that as you squint and toss and turn, God is with you in the cloud. And when it lifts, you may journey on.

Build Yourself an Ark

There are times that I am truly lost and overwhelmed and seem to be incapable of knowing the way to joy. It is as if a strong wave has sent me tumbling to the ocean floor. "Don't panic," I remember my swimming teacher saying. "If you don't panic, you will float to the top." How can I be patient when I feel as though I am drowning?…

There are times when you feel as if you are under a deep dark ocean. You must learn to build an ark to protect yourself from drowning. Just as in the story [of Noah], this ark is made with the specifications of wisdom, to be an ark that will float and not leak. And God said, "Make a window so the daylight can come through." Always have an opening, a window, however small, where the light can shine through. And know, from within your ark, that there will be a moment when you must emerge. You may need help knowing when to come out. Have patience. Send a white dove to find

> God said to Noah, "Build yourself an Ark. Make an opening for daylight to come through."
> —Genesis 6:13–14, 16
> (author's translation)

green peacefulness. Have a friend who will search for dry ground for you. She may come back with nothing at first. Life is a process. It takes time. But she will come back and beckon you through that small window toward the door. It's okay to be shaken. You have been floating awhile, but know that every rainbow shines with the many colors of survival.

Heart-Centered Prayer

Christine Valters Paintner, PhD, Obl. OSB

When the heart is hard and parched up,
come upon me with a shower of mercy.
—Rabindranath Tagore

I invite you into a very simple heart-centered practice. It takes less than five minutes and can be done almost anywhere, but can completely shift your grounding and awareness so you respond to the world from a more heart-centered place....

1. Begin by becoming aware of your body. Notice how your body is feeling, simply being present to sensations you are experiencing. Welcome in both the body's delight and the body's discomfort. If there are any areas of tension, see if you can soften into those places.

    Shift your focus to your breath, deepening it gently. As you inhale, imagine God breathing life into you. As you exhale, allow yourself to experience a moment of release and surrender into this time and place, becoming fully aware. Take several cycles of breath and simply notice this life-sustaining rhythm that continues, moment by moment, even when you are unaware of it.

2. In your imagination, gently allow your breath to carry your awareness from your head—your thinking, analyzing, judging center—down to your heart, a place of greater integration, feeling, and intuition. This movement is not forced, but more of a permission. Imagine your heart as a great magnetic force drawing your energy into your center.

    Place your hand on your chest, over your heart, to experience a physical connection with your heart center and help draw your awareness to

Christine Valters Paintner, PhD, Obl. OSB, a Benedictine oblate, is the online abbess of www.abbeyofthearts.com and frequently leads retreats and teaches on the wisdom of Benedictine, Celtic, and desert ways of praying. She is author of *Lectio Divina—The Sacred Art: Transforming Words & Images into Heart-Centered Prayer* (SkyLight Paths), among other books.

this place. Rest in this heart-centered space for a while. Release expectations of what the experience will be, staying open to the surprising ways of God.

3. Imagine drawing your breath down into your heart center as you inhale. Begin to notice what you are feeling right now in this moment, without judging or trying to change it. Allow your breath to soften the space around your heart. Take a few moments to be present to whatever it is you are feeling. Make room within yourself for this experience—whether grief, anger, boredom, joy, anxiety, serenity—without pushing it away. Welcome in the full spectrum of who you are.

4. Taking another breath, call to mind the spark of God that the ancient monks and mystics tell us dwells in our heart. Bring the infinite compassion of God that lives within you to whatever you are feeling right now. You are not trying to change anything, but just gently hold yourself in this space. As you experience yourself filling with compassion for your own experience, imagine breathing that compassion out into the world and connecting to other hearts—both human and animal—beating across the world in a rhythm of love. Allow that love to expand within you with each inhale. As you exhale, imagine allowing it to expand into the space around you, getting wider with each breath. Fill with gratitude for whatever your experience has been and for the gift of a holy pause in which to simply rest in what is.

5. Gently allow your breath to bring your awareness back to the room and take a moment to name what you noticed in this experience.

This practice is especially powerful when you find yourself feeling tenderhearted, anxious, sad, or any emotion that is uncomfortable or confusing. The idea is not to resolve the emotion or figure it out, but to simply allow it to have a moment of space within you. When you need to make a decision about something, try grounding yourself in this way first, connecting with your heart center to access the wisdom of compassion within you.

Listening for a Still Point

Kay Lindahl

Have you ever noticed the discomfort with silence in our culture? Think about the last time someone called for a moment of silence in a public gathering. The first ten to fifteen seconds are usually comfortable. After that, people tend to get restless and cough, rustle paper, cross and uncross their legs, clear their throats.

Notice what happens in daily conversation. It's as though there is an unwritten rule that whenever there's a hint of silence, someone must fill the vacuum with a rush of words. We start to talk faster and faster. Listening quickly takes a backseat to talking.

The power of silence gives us breathing room. There is wisdom in the silence. It can alter our perceptions and ability to see what is happening. It can give clarity in the midst of apparent chaos. One way to practice silence is to get centered within yourself. Take a few deep breaths before speaking. Ask what wants to be said next.

Another practice is to turn off the car radio, CD, or tapes and drive in the silence. See what it's like to be centered in the midst of traffic.

One thing you might begin to notice with these practices is all of the background noises that permeate our lives. After a while you will learn to simply let them be and enjoy your own interior silence.

The power of silence is the power to slow things down, to give us a chance to reflect on what is happening, to listen to the collective wisdom, and to be present.

We are used to being present in our heads, our minds, our intellect, so the innermost self may take a while to surface. Take the time. Being present in

Kay Lindahl teaches the sacred art of listening to a variety of groups all over the world. She is author of *The Sacred Art of Listening: Forty Reflections for Cultivating a Spiritual Practice*, cofounder of Women of Spirit and Faith, and founder of The Listening Center in Long Beach, California.

our hearts leads to compassion, love, and service. Imagine listening to silence as a global behavior!...

Reflection can teach us to be better listeners—to ourselves, to God, and to others. Wisdom tells me there's something very important about taking time to acknowledge what happens each day. This is a part of my listening practice. It can take the form of a journal, a walk on the beach, a conversation with a close friend, or some quiet time with myself.

I've learned to ask myself questions in order to become a more reflective listener to myself and others. Try asking these questions in your own practice:

- What just happened?
- What did I learn from that?
- How did I grow from that?
- What's next for me?
- How did this impact others in my life?
- How does it relate to patterns in my past?
- What learning can I share with others?

Taking the time to explore these questions opens us up to the creative possibilities in listening. The key is to give ourselves permission to "do nothing"—to value our experience enough to honor it with silence, to daydream without feeling guilty. When we do, we will approach our listening with others renewed and refreshed and with a sense of awe and wonder. New possibilities will show themselves when we listen this way.

Running as Sanctuary

Dr. Warren A. Kay

Running is not a religion, it is a place.[1]
—George Sheehan

The late runner, doctor, and philosopher George Sheehan was internationally known for the columns and short articles on running that he wrote during his twenty-five years as a contributing writer and medical editor for *Runner's World* magazine. He also traveled all over the world spreading the gospel of running. In one of his essays, he wrote about a lecture tour that included a trip to Alaska. Upon his arrival in Anchorage, he was asked by a reporter, "Is it true that you have called running a religion?" He had, on occasion, made comments about running and religion. They were sometimes jokes, such as when he repeated a story about a woman who said that her husband "used to be a Methodist, but now he's a runner." But sometimes his comments about running and religion were more serious....

George Sheehan was able to say that running, for him, was like a monastery. It is "a place to commune with God and yourself, a place for psychological renewal." This is a basic principle of the spirituality of running. Running is a place. It is a place you can go to be alone—even when there are other people around. It is a place to think. Running helps you concentrate because it takes you out of the often mind-numbing cycle of the everyday routine of going to work, going home, going to bed, getting up, and going to work. Most important, running is a place that you can go to regardless of where you are. Whether you are on a business trip, on vacation, or visiting family, you can still go for a run. The scenery might

---

Dr. Warren A. Kay, an avid runner, is associate professor and former chair of religious and theological studies at Merrimack College in North Andover, Massachusetts. He teaches a popular course called "The Spirituality of Running" and is author of *Running—The Sacred Art: Preparing to Practice* (SkyLight Paths).

change, but when you go for a run, that is your special place. Your run can be your own sanctuary.

Running in London

One of my former students, an avid runner himself, told me a story of a time when his girlfriend broke up with him while he was studying in London. To deal with the pain of this breakup, he went out for a run through the streets of the city. The only unusual thing about this particular run was that he left the college where he was staying at about two in the morning. Initially, he went for this run to tire himself out so that he could go to sleep. As he ran the four-mile circuit around Regent's Park, he reached a point where, as he put it, "it was almost like my mind was blank, just sitting in neutral, while my legs churned along."[2] By the time he completed his run, all his feelings of hurt and anger had disappeared and were replaced by a feeling of calmness. As he later described it,

> On this particular run, I finally received a taste of the true spiritual power of running.... I believe that through running I was able to have a meeting with God, who calmed my aching heart and allowed me to momentarily forget my aching legs.... Though it was never my intention to find God that night or seek his healing, I believe that I experienced it nonetheless during this run.

Running around Regent's Park in London became for him a sanctuary—a place where he could go to deal with his feelings and, as he stated it, feel the presence of God.

In a now-famous passage, philosopher and mathematician Alfred North Whitehead once remarked that religion "is what the individual does with his own solitariness."[3] Years later, the great twentieth-century theologian and Jewish spiritual writer Abraham Joshua Heschel observed, "Religion is not 'what man does with his solitariness.' Religion is what man does with the presence of God. And the spirit of God is present whenever we are willing to accept it."[4] That young man, running by himself in the streets of London, was open to the presence of God on his run. And the activity of running in his time of anger and sadness brought him to his special place, his sanctuary, where he could realize that, in the end, he was not alone. Going to your sanctuary doesn't guarantee an experience of God, but it helps you be open to God.

Making Your Own Running Ritual

The key to transforming your run into your own personal sanctuary is to develop your own rituals, and that, in turn, means you need to be intentional about it. There are a number of things you can do for this.

Select a special time to run. Although I recognize that every run has the potential to be a spiritual run, begin by selecting a special time once per week for a run that will include the ritual elements. This may or may not be a time that already has spiritual meaning for you, but it might be best to select a day you are not working or don't have any pressing responsibilities. Also, pick a time of day that is comfortable for you and when you will not encounter a lot of distractions.

Select a special place to run. Pick a route that is pleasant for you to run. It can be hard or easy, as long as it is not something that you will dread. And depending on your fitness level, pick a reasonably long distance. If it is too short, you will spend most of your time warming up. If it is too long, you will grow too tired before it is finished, and this will detract from the experience and also potentially give the run negative associations.

Play music. In the worship services of organized religions like Judaism and Christianity, the service may begin with music and readings from scripture. In a similar way, you can prepare for your run by listening to music, but this is entirely optional. If you decide to play music before your run, you should select music you like. It can be any genre, and perhaps even be a song with a specific message. Take your time and experiment with different kinds of music, and remember that the music should be motivational for your spiritual mind-set. You are using this music to set off regular time from your sacred time and regular space from your sanctuary.

Try other activities. Read scripture, say a prayer, or meditate.

Read your journal. This may be an appropriate time to read sections of your journal that you find particularly meaningful in a spiritual sense.

Run at a good pace—but not too fast. What you are about to do is neither a race nor a typical training run. You want it to be your spiritual time. So keep your pace deliberate but not hard. You shouldn't run so hard that you could not carry on a conversation with someone else, but not so easy that you hesitate to call it a run and want to call it a jog. Maybe you will find it helpful to read the following lines from *Running and Being* by George Sheehan before you start your run: "I take the universe around me and wrap myself in it and become one with it, moving at a pace which makes me part of it."[5]

Focus your mind. During your run you can recite poems or sing songs that you have found to be spiritually significant (sing the songs in your imagination if you don't wish to sing them out loud). There may even be phrases that you can repeat to the rhythm of your stride. Concentrate on the words and the message of the poem, song, or phrase that you are taking with you. This practice will help focus your mind as you run.

Write in your journal. Just as you stretch before and after a run, don't forget to write down in your journal the things you experienced on your run. The writings of the saints have become inspirational spiritual reading for many people in traditional religions, and your spiritual journal should become inspirational reading for you.

The Grace of the Present Moment

Rami Shapiro

Grace is to life as current is to ocean. Grace is the dynamic nature of things. It is the flow, the dance, the turning of the universe. Without grace nothing happens, for grace is what happens. Hence the prophet Isaiah taught that God's throne is founded in grace (Isaiah 16:5). The Rabbis agreed: "From the beginning the earth was built only upon grace" (*Mekilta*, Vol. II, p. 69). To be in touch with the world at its most true is to be graceful, literally filled with grace....

Cultivating grace is a bit of a paradox. You cannot get what you always and already have. There is nothing you can or need do to merit grace. All you need do is accept grace. The reason this is so difficult for us is that our hands are full. We are burdened by carrying the past and future around with us wherever we go and have no room for the grace of the present moment. Cultivating grace means putting down the burden of time and opening our hands to the timeless now....

How do we practice letting go and cultivating grace? By making Sabbath. We can drop all that we carry for one day each week and live as if we trust God's grace. In this way narrow mind learns the power of trust and grace. It stops worrying so much. It realizes that it can function more effectively without having to carry the past and future around on its shoulders. It begins to understand that it has a role to play in the present that has nothing to do with the role it imagines for itself based on past memory and future fantasy. Its role is to open to the wisdom of spacious mind and channel it into acts of lovingkindness in this and every moment.

Rami Shapiro, a renowned teacher of spirituality across faith traditions and a noted theologian, is the award-winning author of *The Sacred Art of Lovingkindness: Preparing to Practice* and *Perennial Wisdom for the Spiritually Independent: Sacred Teachings—Annotated & Explained* (both SkyLight Paths), among many other books.

Teaching this concept to teenagers in Miami, I would sometimes hold classes on the beach. I would give each student a plastic bucket and spoon and ask them to fill the bucket with seawater using the spoon. As they raced to fill their buckets they did not notice that I had sliced small holes in the bucket bottoms. Theoretically, if they raced back and forth quickly enough, they could keep a bit of water in the bucket, but if they stopped for even a moment, the water would seep out the bottom.

It soon became obvious that the buckets could not be filled this way. "Alternatives?" I would ask, and watch happily as someone tossed his bucket into the sea and let it fill up of its own accord. "That is Shabbos," I would say. "Now how can we make it on land?"...

Shabbos is more than a day of rest; it is a day of grace. It is a day devoted to celebrating what is, rather than frantically trying to create what might be.... The Sabbath is the end of craving. The Sabbath is tossing the bucket of narrow mind into the sea of spacious mind and allowing your original divine nature to put an end to fear, anxiety, and craving.

Living Grace Through Sabbath Keeping

Grace is living with radical trust, and the Sabbath is a day devoted to doing just that. For observant Jews, of course, there is a huge body of law and lore regarding the Sabbath, but for most of us, Jew and Gentile alike, the legal aspects of Sabbath observance are beside the point. In fact, they may even obscure the point. So let me suggest ways for making Shabbos that draw on Jewish tradition without necessarily imitating it.

Open and close your Sabbath with the lighting of candles. Even if the only Sabbath you can muster at this point in your life is just a few hours long, begin with the lighting of candles. Jewish tradition sets a minimum but no maximum to the number of candles you can light. The minimum is two—symbolizing the state of duality that usually precedes Shabbos. You come to the Sabbath with a split mind, maybe even a fractured heart. The week has been grueling, and you feel alienated from others and perhaps even from yourself. So you light multiple candles to honor where you are. Yet notice that the candles offer singular light. So you are beginning with two and aiming at one.

Offer a blessing. Begin your Sabbath with something like this: "May this Sabbath be a time for deepest surrender that I might discover the grace of

God's living in me and as me." Adjust the pronouns if you are making Shabbos with family and friends.

Prepare a simple meal and offer thanks before eating it. For guidance in reciting a prayer before meals, look to Psalm 22:27: "The humble ate and were satisfied" (author's translation). Say something like, "Let this Sabbath meal be for us a time of humbling, of returning to our simple selves as the image and likeness of God. And, eating this way, may we be satisfied."

Bless children, loved ones, and friends. If you are sharing your Sabbath meal, make time for people to bless one another. If you are alone on Shabbos, offer blessings to those you love who are not present. You can use a variation on the *metta* prayer for this: "May you be blessed with simplicity; may you be blessed with humility; may you be blessed with grace."

Take a walk. Make time during your Shabbos to walk outdoors. "Walk like a camel," as Henry David Thoreau says in his timeless classic *Walking*. Thoreau says a camel thinks as it walks, so let your mind wander along with your body. Become what Thoreau calls a saunterer from the French *Sainte-Terrer*, a Holy Land pilgrim who wanders *sans terre*, without a specific home, for she is at home wherever her feet touch the ground.

Go slow. There is no rushing on Shabbos. You can't be late and there is no early. Do whatever you do with attention and care, and you will find a rhythm that is your Shabbos speed.

Pamper yourself. Take a long bath. Take a long nap. Surround yourself with fragrances you love, and books you want to read, and people with whom you really want to converse. Make love and give pleasure.

Make a to-do list for Shabbos. Put only one word on it: "Nothing."

Get off the grid. Don't bother with email, web surfing, TV, or radio. Listen to music that soothes you. Or better yet, learn to play some yourself.

Close your Shabbos with candles. Judaism has a ceremony for closing Shabbos called *Havdallah*, meaning distinction. It marks the return to the week. What I love most about *Havdallah* and what I suggest you try is closing the Sabbath with a different kind of candle. A *Havdallah* candle is a single braided candle composed of wicks. While you began the Sabbath with two candles, honoring diversity even as you move toward unity, you end the Sabbath with a single candle that speaks of unity blossoming into diversity. The

Havdallah candle reminds you not to mistake unity for uniformity and to open yourself to the complexity of the coming week without complicating it by wishing it were other than it is.

Havdallah Prayer for the Week

Light your candle and offer the following prayer for the week:

> May this be a week of faith:
> Faith in truth, faith in love, faith in friendship, and faith in You who manifests all things and their opposite.
> May my labors hasten the perfection of the world, and may kindness awaken those deadened by despair.
> May this week arrive with gentleness, good fortune, blessing, success, good health, prosperity, justice, and peace.
> May it be a week for uplifting the children and honoring the aged.
> May this be a week of constructive purpose for me, for my loved ones, and for all who dwell upon this good earth.
> Amen.

Living Awake to What Is

Kent Ira Groff

Days pass, years vanish, and we walk
sightless among miracles.

—Hebrew prayer

Living awake means cultivating awareness: being with what is changes what was and what will be.... When you hear people say, "It is what it is," the expression sounds fatalistic, resigned. But "being with what is changes what was and what will be"—this calls you to see something more.... What would it mean to "be with" what's going on in your world—so that you don't walk sightless among miracles?

A Daily Prayer of Reflection and Examen

Imagine you invite the Sacred Light of the world to walk with you, scanning over the past twenty-four hours (or recent period). Breathe deeply: in ... out.... Gently sift through events and encounters.... Imagine scenes unfolding as from a slow-moving train.

1. **Gift** (Wow!) *As you reflect on your day, notice and give thanks for specific gift(s).* Celebrate God's empowering love at a time or times when you felt loved or loving.
2. **Struggle** (Whoa.) *Notice times when you struggled to feel loved or loving.* Observe any unrest or unresolved tension in your soul. Celebrate God's undefeated love and hear: "You are my beloved."
3. **Invitation** (What now?) *Ask: What grace do I need to name and claim to be more whole today?* Allow a word or phrase—an image or metaphor—to

Kent Ira Groff, a spiritual companion for journeyers and leaders, retreat leader, and writer-poet, is founding mentor of Oasis Ministries in Pennsylvania. He is author of *Honest to God Prayer: Spirituality as Awareness, Empowerment, Relinquishment and Paradox* (SkyLight Paths).

come to mind. Begin to repeat it, slowly with your breathing, or picture it if it's an image (silence)....

Meditative Thanks with Your Body

Sit in silence, and slow down your breathing. Allow a centering word or phrase to arise (like "Here I am," or *hineini* in Hebrew), or a quieting image, such as a babbling brook. Repeat it slowly if it's a word, or visualize it if it's an image. In many spiritual streams, the body is the temple of the Spirit, and genuine worship begins by presenting one's body. Inhale lovingly ... meditate ... exhale thankfully.... Begin inhaling while tensing your left foot, then release it when exhaling ... right foot ... left ankle ... each area of the body up through your abdomen ... to your heart ... then each shoulder, arm, hand ... return to your larynx ... parts of the face ... to the top of your head.... Gratefully bask in an aura of peace. When you finish, use your journal to write reflections from the experience.

Option: Using your journal, doodle a pencil sketch of your body, noting areas that need attention.

Remember

Keeping a Connection

> Honoring memories ... is a way of paying tribute to the presence of the lost loved one.... We neither idealize nor demonize the person, but remember her just as she was—a human mixture of light and shadow.
>
> —Linda Douty

> "The task," whispers the Spirit, "is to re-member who you are ..."
>
> —Caren Goldman

The things, people, places, and identities that you lose shape you just as much as the ones that are still in your life. This section contains embodied and meditative practices to strengthen you as you sort through the memories. You might try making a pilgrimage to reconnect with places associated with your broken heart or creating a memory quilt or listening for words of blessing through a guided visualization.

Whatever ways you decide to honor your loss and keep a connection to it, may the wisdom and practices here offer companionship and affirmation in your process.

The Circle of Life

Michael J. Caduto

In the full leaf of late summer, when I walk through our herb garden, I often circle it sunwise, moving in the direction in which our home star arches across the sky. In the garden's center, which represents the nexus of the cosmos, stand the erect stems of the lofty joe-pye weed, whose flowers are so tall I must look up at them.... Weeding the corn, I enjoy seeing the sturdy stalks arrayed atop each mound to the points of the compass, a planting pattern symbolic of wholeness and of giving thanks to the four directions, a practice I learned from a Wampanoag healer many years ago. I think of that dear friend, who was once alive and vibrant with enthusiasm for his culture and ancient traditions. He has now made the long journey to the spirit world, as these herbs and cornstalks will do later in the autumn, as we all will do when it is our time to close the circle and return to the cosmic center. The memories of friends and family who have gone before inspired me to slightly turn the biblical passage 2 Samuel 12:23 and hold it up to reflect their light:

> It is a small consolation to know,
> that one day we will go to join them.
> But our hearts ache with the truth—
> that they can no longer come to see us.

Life and Death

There is a peace that comes from being so close to the garden's symbolic center of the cosmos, so alive with a palpable sense that here the circle of life and death turns each day as freely as bees gather nectar for the hive. It is no wonder that traditional Islamic gardens, especially those in Persia and Muslim India, have long been the final resting place for those who lovingly watered the roots and tended the seeds and shoots of their green brothers and sisters.

Michael J. Caduto is a renowned ecologist, educator, and storyteller, and author of *Everyday Herbs in Spiritual Life: A Guide to Many Practices* (SkyLight Paths). He is founder of Programs for Environmental Awareness and Cultural Exchange.

There they began the long journey between earth and heaven. Perhaps this juxtaposition of cosmic realms inspired two Islamic words for garden, *firdaus* and *rauda*, which mean, respectively, "paradise" and "mausoleum."...

Grief and Renewal

One reason that so many of us live our daily lives feeling emotionally wounded is that the contemporary way of life does not allow us time to properly resolve our grief. From the Italian family I was raised in to a number of Native American cultures I have come to know, the traditional period of mourning after losing a beloved was at least one year. Nowadays, we are given a day or two off from work, then we're expected to put grief behind us, to "move on." But as we resume our daily routine, we are aware of a dull pain, an elegiac veil over our heart that can become a constant companion if we do not allow ourselves the time, energy, and space to pass through the stages of loss. For a time, we are suspended between these two poles of human experience. Then, after our grief, there comes a renewal.... The days and nights of loss start to lose their hold on us. Once again we notice the sweet songs of birds, the scents and colors of herbs and flowers, the beauty of a butterfly's wing. The face of a child sends rays of light into our heart. A loved one takes our hand, and we feel the warmth and spark of old. The power of connection, the essence of life, beckons, and we rejoin the dance of the living.

Herbal Memorial: Lustral Water

Materials

Fresh sprigs of hyssop	Small ornate vessel with cap
Large glass bottle of water	

Blessing with hyssop is an ancient tradition after the passing of a loved one. Hyssop cleanses the spirit and sanctifies whomever and whatever it touches. Preparing and using lustral water is a way to honor the loss of someone you love.[1]

1. Soak sprigs of hyssop in a glass bottle full of water for several days.
2. Pour this water into a small, ornate vessel, cap it off, and take it with you to the burial service. Bring a fresh sprig of hyssop as well.
3. During the burial service, when there is an opportunity for those present to share, say your words of remembrance and blessing, then sprinkle the earth, urn, or casket with the lustral water.

Bereavement Bouquet

Materials

Dried herbs of your choice that are still on the stems (rose, rue, eucalyptus, betony, and rosemary)

Pruning clippers

Brightly colored wrapping that measures 12 by 6 inches (paper, piece of felt cloth, or the like)

Yarn

Scissors

Ribbon

Vase

Photograph or other memento of the person you wish to remember

1. Here are some herbs that can be included in a bereavement bouquet to help you honor and heal your relationship with the deceased: rose and rue (forgiveness), eucalyptus (spiritual healing), betony (healing of the whole person), and rosemary (remembrance and revitalization of love for that person).
2. Use these herbs to create an arrangement.... The stems of dried herbs only need to be tied together with yarn.
3. Wrap the bouquet in paper and tie with ribbon. Put this bouquet in a dry vase and keep it in a special place in your living space to honor the loved one you have lost. If you like, keep a favorite photograph of your loved one by the bouquet. Whenever you miss your loved one, or have something you want to share or say, go to that place and speak to her or him, or simply visit in silence and listen for that person's voice.

Joy in the Memories

Margaret D. McGee

When my mother was a girl in the 1930s, she spent summers at her grandparents' farm near Lancaster, Ohio. The two-story farmhouse, big barn, and other outbuildings that formed the heart of Myrtle and Ira Cave's homestead were joined to a wheat field, a corn field, a hay field, and a little woods in back—all tucked into thirty acres of Ohio flatland. The farm provided most of Myrtle and Ira's sustenance, with a bit left over for sale or barter.

According to my mother, chicken had more flavor back then. "The chickens Grandmother raised and fried in her cast-iron skillet make the chickens we buy in the store today taste like almost nothing," she laments.

Myrtle and Ira Cave lived long enough to know all their great-grandchildren. I remember them both, but my mind's eye holds only a few faint sketches of their life on the farm: Myrtle's hand slipping between a roosting hen and its nest, then reemerging with two eggs cradled in her palm. The deep-throated smell in the outhouse, two dark holes for seats. A sleepover in their guest room, roses on the wallpaper, handmade quilts on the bed. That's about it.

I don't remember how the chicken tasted.

Nowadays, standing at the supermarket, looking over the packages of boneless, skinless breasts, the rows and rows of identical square thighs, I sometimes hear a powerful call from the Cave family farm, and the call feels like an echo from a world that exists outside the treadmills of time....

"What I remember best about Grandmother was her big, soft bosom. It was like resting your head on a pillow," says my mother. "I could run all over that farm. I didn't have to be afraid of anything. It was freedom."

Margaret D. McGee, a writer, teacher, and leader of spiritual workshops and retreats, is author of *Sacred Attention: A Spiritual Practice for Finding God in the Moment* and *Haiku—The Sacred Art: A Spiritual Practice in Three Lines* (SkyLight Paths).

Though I don't remember much of the farm myself, I do hold clear memories of the two who made it their home. It's true that my Great-granddad Cave didn't say much. And I, too, rested my young head on my great-grandmother's big, soft bosom, a warm pillow that came with arms to hold me.

So every once in a while, instead of buying my standard big package of thighs for barbecuing, I pick out a whole chicken at the supermarket, take it home, cut it up, and use every part. Cutting up a chicken forces me to pay attention and reminds me that the chicken I eat was once a living creature, made by the same God that made me....

Every time I cut up a chicken, I think of Great-grandmother Myrtle. It feels good to share this basic task with her across the century. Though memory is a creative companion and capable of distorting the truth, at the same time, memory has the power to draw out essence and pass it down through generations.

Real life on a farm in the 1930s was, in many ways, much harder than life is today. After all, this was the heart of the Great Depression. Myrtle and Ira worked long and hard just to feed their livestock and themselves. Even so, my mother's memories of that time focus on abundant life: ripening blackberries, just-hatched chicks, blooming flowers, sweet corn, heavenly fried chicken, and a sense of freedom that defines a place and time for her. Though the farm was enclosed on all sides by a society in a state of economic collapse, still, in my mother's memory, that sense of freedom and plenty is all that matters.

For reflection: Describe a place where you've felt safe and free. How did that place and its freedom affect the rest of your life? What do you do now that connects you to freedom-giving events from the past?

Share a Visit to Freedom

This week, make a date with a friend, letting your friend know that you'd like to share stories about the experience of freedom in your lives. When you get together, ask your friend to tell you a personal story of freedom or release from fear, deprivation, or self-doubt. Listen and ask questions. Pay attention.

Then tell your friend about your own time or place of freedom. How are your stories different from each other? What do they hold in common?

Seeing God in Memories and Lasting Love

Carolyn Jane Bohler

> Soon we shall die and all memory of those five will have left the earth, and we ourselves shall be loved for a while and forgotten. But the love will have been enough; all those impulses of love return to the love that made them. Even memory is not necessary for love. There is a land of the living and a land of the dead and the bridge is love, the only survival, the only meaning.
>
> —The abbess in Thornton Wilder's *Bridge of San Luis Rey*

When our son, Stephen, died, one of my biggest fears was that I would lose some memories of him. At first I worked tenaciously to remember, to hold on to remembering. A year later, my experience matched the abbess's "thoughts passing in the back of the mind"[1]: love is a bridge, what survives, what has meaning. Of course I regret deeply that we do not have current events to share as a family with Stephen, but I no longer feel that I have to hold tightly to memories. Love is enough.

For me, it is enough for God to be and to have the power of Dynamic Love. Instead of thinking of God's power as similar to the physical force of the moon's pull on the tides or the power of a command or a thunderbolt, I find it more helpful to consider God's power as consistent, dependable Love. I have come to see God's Love not only as important, but also as sufficient.

Carolyn Jane Bohler is former professor of pastoral theology and counseling at United Theological Seminary in Dayton, Ohio, and author of *God the* What? *What Metaphors for God Reveal about Our Beliefs in God* (SkyLight Paths).

The Power of Transformation: God as Persistent Life

Many years ago, when our daughter was in second grade, she had an assignment to find a caterpillar. That seemed a difficult task, but lo and behold, we found two while biking on a gorgeous path that always reminded me of a Louisiana bayou, even though it was along a river in Dayton, Ohio. We put each caterpillar in a jar with twigs, grass, and water. This occurred in October. Alexandra took one jar to school, to stay in the classroom, and we put the other on top of our refrigerator at home. To my surprise, the caterpillar did indeed cuddle up to the twig and turn into a cocoon. Then, nothing happened.

The caterpillar that went to school also turned into a cocoon, and nothing happened.

Early in February, the second-grade teacher threw away the dead cocoon, but we were not so tidy at home, forgetting about the jar amid the refrigerator clutter. Then, on exactly the first day of spring, something moving caught my attention. Things actually worked as they were supposed to! A butterfly emerged! We took it outside where it flew away, presumably happy.

We speak about life, death, and resurrection. We experience the life and the death of loved ones. We experience dormant times and bursts of joy or blooming. Yet, sometimes we daringly wonder whether we are just pacifying ourselves, persuading ourselves that there is more to life or that life has a continuity that is not visible. I had doubted that the caterpillar would really become a cocoon, then had given almost no thought to the cocoon actually becoming a butterfly.

Maybe one of God's important powers is the power to transform living things. Most creatures undergo spectacular transformations. We humans are not only transformed in our bodies, in each new life stage, but also in our minds and emotions and spirit. These transformations take place in many people so many times and sometimes so dramatically that we are truly more authentically named as *changing* than as *staying the same*. We could claim that God as Persistent Life not only fosters transformation but also enables us to "hold on" or "carry on" when we have given up on life, or forgotten the possibility that newness can emerge out of what seems like only death.

Quite a few times in seminary classes or churches, I have explained one idea of God's power as envisioned by the philosopher, mathematician, and theologian Alfred North Whitehead. He presented the idea that God encourages "the best that can happen" to come into being every moment, even after a tragedy. This theologian did not think that God is in control of every event, but did think that, in every event, God is persuasively trying to urge the best possibility to be born.

After the tragedy with our son, the one scripture passage that came to me as a kind of comfort was the one from the Gospel of John in which Jesus encourages his mother to consider his friend John as her son, and for his friend John to consider Mary as his own mother (John 19:26–27). I thought of this passage as prescribing a way to carry on. Yes, Jesus would die, but his family would carry on in a modified, adapted manner.

Two young women, lifelong friends of our children, spoke at our son's first memorial service in Irvine, California. They flew across the country to be with us and informed our daughter, Alexandra, that they were now her sisters. I concluded that they were my daughters. Since I had known them and shared so much time with them over the course of their lives, I was glad to be considered their mother and they my extra daughters. When I informed them that this new relationship meant they would now be the recipients of chocolate chip cookies from time to time, they said they could stand that consequence.

I thought of Jesus telling Mary and John that they were now family, of Jesus essentially giving them to each other. They might have found each other anyway, but maybe Jesus was not so sure they would take that step. I took this message to heart: "Carolyn, you can carry on, with family and adopted family members."

This message is only comforting if there is something meaningful to carry on. A new young woman friend, who lived on the same floor as our son in the college dorm, told a story at the second memorial service, which was held in Dayton, Ohio. When she and Stephen went to a climbing wall to get some exercise, she asked him if he could climb to the top. His answer was, "Probably." They started up together, and in two seconds he had reached the top, while she was only two feet up. He came back down to guide her and encourage her. This young woman said that when she returned to the university, she would seriously try to climb to the top of that wall on her own.

I think this young woman was saying much more than her words may have conveyed. She was saying she would carry on, and carry on with some of Stephen's values incorporated into her life. Later, other people told me they had admired Stephen's conscientious-objection stance. They realized that they had not acted, as he had, on their views.

Whether it was our son's incredible warmth, his in-your-face frankness, his devotion, or his tendency to relate to strangers and break down barriers, the values Stephen brought to our lives are worthy of carrying on. In the face of grief, we don't carry on because life is lousy and we must put one foot in front of another, barely moving. We carry on because there is meaning and value in living, and people have shown us this. For me, I realized that I carry on with family and adopted family because I still have hope for a meaningful future, because life is persistent.

As much as I have gulped in grief and truly wondered whether tear ducts could run dry, the God of Persistent Life keeps transforming me, helping me to carry on, in part because my relationship with Stephen prods me to be part of the continuity of his being. We all have to envision a very different future than we would have enjoyed with him, a transformed future. Those who had a relationship with him continue, as I do, to have that relationship "inside." Meanwhile, since life is so persistent, though filled with startling transformations, Stephen himself probably continues his being in some transformed manner—beyond our understanding, but congruent with the persistence we observe about life.

Like the amazing butterfly emerging from the forgotten cocoon, nothing is lost in God, but instead undergoes surprising re-creations. Just when we think that nothing is happening, or when something or someone has died, we realize in an amazing way that the God of Persistent Life fosters some continuity with a twist.

The Gifts of Blessing Another

Rabbi Elie Kaplan Spitz

Exchanging blessings can be a powerful exercise in expressing long-held emotions in times of crisis. I recall visiting my colleague Rabbi Allen Krause when he was dying of cancer at his home. Every fifteen minutes he pressed a button on a pump to relieve his pain with medication. Fortunately, his mind was clear. My friend had served as a caring pastor until the age of seventy. His preaching and scholarship had emphasized social justice. Like the prophets, he accepted even rejection by some of his constituents. Sitting before him, I wanted to express my gratitude for his mentorship and to pray for his gentle passing. But it felt presumptuous to initiate a blessing upon an elder of such wisdom and goodness. Instead, I asked him to bless me. He closed his eyes and spoke slowly and haltingly. At times the pauses were so long that I was unsure if he had fallen asleep. I listened patiently as words emerged. I experienced his expression of care and affection as a precious gift. I then took his hand in mine and, in the context of addressing God, shared his importance to me and my most deeply held wishes for him and his family.

Ten days later my colleague passed. I led a memorial service on one of the nights of mourning in his home. Before we began, I privately asked his wife, Sherri, if she had any requests, and she asked me to guide the group in a visualization meditation. I readily agreed. Toward the end of the traditional prayers, I described how Allen and I had exchanged blessings. I invited anyone who wished to participate in a guided visualization of blessing to do so. I then led them in the following exercise, "Receiving and Giving a Blessing."

At the close of the guided imagery offered on behalf of Allen, I opened my eyes and scanned the quiet room. As others opened their eyes, many wiped away tears. Participating in such a guided visualization of blessing had

Rabbi Elie Kaplan Spitz is a spiritual leader, scholar, author, and speaker to a wide range of audiences. He is author of *Increasing Wholeness: Jewish Wisdom and Guided Meditations to Strengthen and Calm Body, Heart, Mind and Spirit* (Jewish Lights) and rabbi of Congregation B'nai Israel in Tustin, California.

allowed those present to access and experience profound emotions that they may not even have had the words to fully articulate.

Receiving and Giving a Blessing

Please follow this link for a video of this guided visualization.

http://youtu.be/
Wv2MyD5EkYc

Sit comfortably with your back straight, feet flat on the ground. Close your eyes and breathe out tension. Breathe in calm.

See before you a person whose blessing you seek. Become sensually aware of his or her presence. Notice the color and texture of your loved one's hair, the color of the eyes, the shape of the face. Take your loved one's hand in yours.

Now listen. Your loved one has words of blessing to give to you. Listen to the blessing spoken to God on your behalf. Allow yourself to be surprised by the words that arise spontaneously.

Now, still holding hands, bless your loved one.

Pause and feel the goodness of your loved one's presence. Share an embrace. Let go and allow him or her as a lit figure to slowly fade away. Linger for a moment, feeling the goodness of having had this relationship and recalling the words that you exchanged.

Hold on to the words of the exchange. Remember your loved one's blessing and recall what you spoke as well. Feel the goodness of the heartfelt words. These words will endure for you as a gift. Breathe out and open your eyes.

Keeping a Soul Connection as Your Loved One's Mind Fails

Marty Richards, MSW, LCSW

Despite all the debilitating changes that accompany the progression of dementia, there is one truth that you can hang on to: No matter how extensive your care partner's memory loss is, no matter how difficult their behavior becomes, the core of the person is still there; the spiritual remains. And you can build many connections on this spiritual base. The spiritual is one facet of a person's life that does not totally depend on cognitive abilities. You can access your care partner's soul when other avenues seem blocked. Even when people do not understand things on a cognitive level, I am convinced that they comprehend in their heart, and it is in the heart and soul that most of us experience the spiritual throughout our lives. I believe that connecting soul to soul is the root of sharing between care partners when one of them has a memory loss. When you can access the soul, and not worry so much about the mental limitations, a whole world opens up....

Donald McKim's excellent book of essays, *God Never Forgets: Faith, Hope, and Alzheimer's Disease*, makes the important point that God never forgets us, even when we might not remember important facts. God remembers even when a person forgets who they are or who the people in their care network are. The community around them may not know how best to talk with them, yet God stays with them. When other people stop interacting with them, the Presence of Love is constant. Even with their limitations, people with dementia are always much loved by God. Through love and relationships, the sense of being cared for and the connection "soul to soul" happens.

Marty Richards, MSW, LCSW, is a clinical social worker, an affiliate assistant professor at the University of Washington School of Social Work, and a popular speaker on the topics of chronic illness, Alzheimer's disease, elder care, and spirituality and aging. She is author of *Caresharing: A Reciprocal Approach to Caregiving and Care Receiving in the Complexities of Aging, Illness or Disability* (SkyLight Paths).

A chaplain in an assisted-living center shared an illustration that captures this truth. Ruby, a former missionary, entered the dining room in her church-related center wearing an odd mix of clothing. As often happened, this garish ensemble elicited loud negative comments from her peers. Understandably upset by these remarks, she left in tears. A chaplain who visited with her later that day gently encouraged Ruby to ask the staff for assistance in dressing. Ruby agreed that maybe she was beginning to need that help.

Then Ruby sadly asked the chaplain, "Will I eventually forget even my name?" The minister honestly responded, "You might ... but I will not forget your name, and more importantly, God will not forget your name."

You may need to emphasize this reassurance over and over for the person you are caring for, and for other people in the network of care. There are many things you can do to share the spiritual together, even into the latter stages of dementia. Since long-term memory remains well into cognitive decline, your care partner can still access liturgies and rituals, prayers, and music that they learned early in life. I've listed some ideas below for keeping this soul-to-soul connection alive, but I also urge you to be open to holy moments that can emerge spontaneously. The simplicity of your care partner's faith may lead you to a new understanding of your own spiritual truths.

Liturgies and Rituals

Although mental ability may be needed to understand the commandments and tenets of religions, it does not take full cognition or speech to experience liturgies and rituals. Your care partner may welcome hearing or participating in liturgies and rituals that they learned as a younger person. It is best to use the versions and the language that they are familiar with. You may also need to simplify more complex rituals. Remember, even if your care partner's response is slightly unusual, the rituals still have meaning for them.

I think of a woman named Nicole, whose pastor brought her the sacrament of Communion. He spoke the traditional words over the bread and wine and gave her the wafer. When he handed her the small Communion cup, she held it delicately in her hand like a glass of fine wine. She asked, "Is this wine?" He responded, "Well, yes, Nicole, it is," to which she answered, "Well, here's to you and to me."

Although her response to the Eucharist was unorthodox, from the pastor's liturgical tradition, he did not try to correct her. He later made the comment,

"Maybe Nicole understood the Communion of all believers better than my parishioners on Sunday mornings!" At a deeper level, the pastor understood Nicole's connection to the sacred, and he was leaving it to the Spirit to make whatever adjustments needed to be made.

Prayers

The ability to pray is something that remains with people even in the advanced stages of dementia, and their prayers often get to the heart of the matter quite quickly. You may need to pray aloud to help rekindle their memories. Or you may need to encourage them by doing whatever they are familiar with to create an ambience for prayer, such as folding your hands, bowing your head, or kneeling, so they will mirror your behavior. Using familiar prayers from their tradition, such as the Lord's Prayer in the Christian tradition, can be a good place to start. A meditation chant that they might have used in the past can be comforting to a person who has practiced an Eastern religious tradition. The *Shema* (the foundational prayer in Judaism proclaiming faith in one God) might be significant for someone of Jewish faith. Blessings over a meal or table grace are also easy prayers to share.

Over and over again, I have been amazed by the fervency of the prayers shared by persons with dementia, as were my friend Linda's. In her women's prayer group, Linda's prayers for the world and social concerns were as strong as they had ever been. Despite the fact that her dementia was encroaching into other areas of her life, her prayer life was still very real and alive and gave her a good deal of comfort....

Familiar Teachings

One wife found another way to share the spiritual with her husband, who had been a teacher in their church's adult Sunday school classes. She encouraged him to "teach" her Sunday school lessons that were still deep in his early memory. He found a sense of meaning and purpose in something he had always enjoyed, and together they reflected on biblical passages. This sharing kept a strong connection between them. Though the discussions were not as cognitively satisfying as they might once have been, they were still very important for both partners.

Again, learning about your care partner's spiritual teachings may take a little research on your part, if you have not grown up in the same religious tradition. You may need to consult a rabbi or imam or priest from your care partner's tradition for ideas on what might be most meaningful to them. A Jewish person might welcome hearing a recitation of the Shema; a Muslim, *al-Fatihah*; a Christian, Psalm 23 or John 3:16.

The Faith Community

Helping your faith community understand what is happening with your care partner can go a long way toward their acceptance of your care partner in formalized worship. Keep in mind, however, that there is a delicate balance between informing the congregation of any special concerns and maintaining respect for your care partner as they were and are. You will want to be careful to avoid revealing any confidential medical information. You will also need to be careful to convey that you are sharing information so your care partner can remain an active participant in the community of faith, not that they are in some ways weak or "less than" others.

I think of Edith, who came to church with her carer. As a longtime member of her church, she was much loved as a teacher in the community and as a Sunday school teacher, by young and old alike. Even though she would often mix up parts of the service, there was a general feeling of acceptance of her limits among her congregation, and she appeared comfortable in these familiar surroundings.

One day after church, she greeted me and asked, "Are you still working at the Lutheran home?" I answered, "Yes, I am." Then she responded, "God bless your ministry!" Only a moment later she was standing at the church door, clearly confused about what she was supposed to do next. That blessing, offered in a rare moment of lucidity, strengthened me. It is always good to be open to such grace-filled moments and celebrate them when they occur. They can provide a lot of encouragement when things are not going well.

Creative Arts

In my years of practice, I have found that the creative arts offer a broad avenue of soul-to-soul connection that is closely linked to the spiritual. Even for people who don't think of themselves as creative or artistic, the arts convey a life force so powerful that many have written about creativity as being an expression of God in us. New research shows the connection between the arts and improving the brain's function. (See the National Center for Creative

Aging, www.creativeaging.org, for more information.) Even in people who have limited language or expression, there is still something that responds to the beauty and joy of the arts. The arts can greatly enhance the communication and relationship between you and your care partner and enable you to share in meaningful ways despite their cognitive limits....

When I write group poetry with people with dementia, we pick a topic and talk about it, using pictures and props to get some discussion flowing. Then each person shares an image for the poem we're going to create. In one group, where summer was the general topic for the poem, the participants offered the following images: "Hot hot it's too dang hot ... running through the dewy grass in the morning ... ice cream holidays." We then fashioned these images into a group poem that we shared together and later posted for family and staff to see. Wonderful word pictures came alive for these people who had severe memory deficits. And their spirits were touched as well....

Connecting soul to soul is possible and will go a long way toward affirming the one you are caring for. With a little imagination and a lot of patience, both of you can still be in a meaningful relationship, despite, and maybe even because of, the dementia. Connecting in this way enables the dance of caresharing to continue.

As you strive to have the most meaningful relationship you can with your loved one, keep these ideas in mind:

- Learn as much as you can about where your loved one is in the disease process so you can understand and communicate in supportive ways.
- Use nonverbal communication to get through when words do not....
- Validate your care partner's stories and feelings, even if they are not totally "realistic."
- Affirm your care partner's abilities and build on what they can still do.
- Remember that behaviors, though difficult, are challenges that can be worked through.
- Utilize the creative arts to connect you and your loved one in new ways.
- Connect soul to soul, remembering that you and your loved one are precious children of God.

Childhood Losses

Caren Goldman

We were both born in Brooklyn, New York. Bernard, who was always called Junior, was the second son of first- and second-generation Italian-American Roman Catholics. I was the first daughter and eldest of three born to second-generation Eastern European Jews. Although our parents always encouraged our close friendship, they also made it clear that a lifelong interfaith alliance would never be kosher. Such concern was unnecessary. In 1959 the school bells that rang for junior high, puppy love, and forging new friendships took us to the earliest parting intersection. Junior, who suddenly preferred to be called either Bernie or Bernard, traveled by bus to a boys' school in downtown Brooklyn. I traveled by foot to PS 285 four blocks away. No longer playmates, classmates, or the blood sister and brother we swore to forever be, Junior and I found ourselves living on different sides of imaginary tracks. Moreover, it seemed not to matter. In fact, when my parents gave me two weeks' notice that we were moving to northern New Jersey, I never told him. Maybe my indifference was due to the shock of sudden uprooting. Maybe it was about something else. All I remember is that ten days before my sophomore year, I walked down my stoop for the last time, got in the car, and as my father headed west, I glanced back tearfully and then looked ahead angrily.

The German philosopher Arthur Schopenhauer said that "every parting gives a foretaste of death; every coming together again a foretaste of the resurrection."[1] Moving to Jersey made me feel dead. Numerous pieces belonging to an unfinished jigsaw puzzle picturing my life suddenly disappeared. My fears of never finding and replacing them grew. Looking out the window of our mountaintop home, I saw a rural wilderness that mirrored my loneliness

---

Caren Goldman is an award-winning journalist, spiritual retreat leader, and conflict-resolution consultant to churches, synagogues, and not-for-profit organizations. She is author of *Restoring Life's Missing Pieces: The Spiritual Power of Remembering and Reuniting with People, Places, Things and Self* (SkyLight Paths).

and sadness. Sad because I was homesick and friendless. Lonely because I no longer had classmates down the block. The closest lived more than a mile away. My abrupt uprooting meant I had left a gap in my circle of friends. I cried whenever I visualized someone else—possibly a stranger—filling it. Strangers, I realized, would soon take over everything in Brooklyn. They would occupy and place their stuff in the empty house that I loved. Someone else would sleep behind the closed door to *my* bedroom. My faraway friends would still walk on the New York sidewalks to the Jewish deli, soda fountain, double feature, Hebrew school, public school, and parties....

I lost a part of my way and part of my soul when my parents whisked me to a far country called New Jersey against my will. Childhood, adolescence, and other developmental stages passed by decades before I realized the impact of these losses on the life stories I told others and myself. By knocking, steadfastly, the Spirit of Re-union awakened me to the extraordinary task of setting my heart to edit and rewrite many chapters with new eyes, revealing enhanced truths. The Spirit helped me see that I would find more healing and truth every time I joined old pieces of my personal puzzle with newer ones. "The task," whispers the Spirit, "is to re-member who you are. Find who you were before vital parts of your original self disappeared, withered, and went to sleep for a long, long time. Find a missing piece named Junior and join his stories of Caren to yours. See, hear, feel, and acknowledge the Caren he saw. See the Caren he sees."

At last I did. Now, nestled in my heart and soul where I don't fear losing those pieces again, I look forward to finding other pieces of myself. Their presence has become a constant reminder never to take the Spirit of Re-union's persistent knocking, lessons, and healing gifts for granted. I say and I pray that I won't, because in the remembering and re-union, I am coming to believe that I've been abundantly blessed.

Reuniting with a Childhood Friend

At different points in our life's journey, circumstances and geography separate us from someone who has played an important role in how, what, where, when, and why we are whomever we've become. If the time is right, the Spirit of Re-union's reminders of those people generate pervasive visceral and spiritual feelings. For example, feelings of joy, love, and gratitude may make us rejoice that we were blessed to share common ground along the way. Other feelings—such as loss, abandonment, and guilt—may cause despair, depression, shame, and great sorrow. In either case and in others like them, desires for antidotes to quell waves of tears, nostalgia, loneliness, curiosity, and mystery manifest. For many of us, reunions have been and can be one of those remedies.

In this exercise allow your special childhood friends to come to mind. Pick an early friend with whom you've had no contact yet feel sincere longings for reunion.

Why was this particular person so special back then?

What may be special about this particular person now?...

In your mind's eye see this person as you remember her or him the last time you were together.

Where are you?

What are you doing?

What are you saying to each other?

What are you saying to yourself?

Do you know or sense it will be the last time you are together? Or has something happened earlier or during this encounter that is causing you to part ways?

Note any voices and images within you that evoke feelings about this person. Explore and give content to what your feelings of joy, anger, sadness, guilt, longing, grief, relief, or other emotion say to you about this relationship.

Are you discovering anything new or different about yourself then and now?

Do you sense or feel something missing in your life that this person might help you find or give to you?

Imagine that for the first time in so many years you are now face-to-face with this person.

What do you hear yourself saying?

What do you hope or expect to hear back?

Although the other person is not physically present, you have just reunited. Was it only with another person? Or has something in you been reunited also?

Is there a next step? If so, where is it already taking you? ...

Putting Places in Their Place

When have you felt complex nostalgic tugs from the Spirit of Re-union that went coursing through your body and psyche to enliven yearnings for places past and home? The essayist Akiko Busch, who writes for the *New York Times* about design and culture, focused on this question in her book *Geography of Home: Writings on Where We Live....* Busch refers to a survey by *Metropolis* magazine. To help people ponder the meaning of home, the survey asked readers to identify what room they most fondly remembered from childhood and why. The largest percentage said the bedroom. Busch observed that the kitchen came in second for physical and psycho-

> It may be that places exist in order that memory itself has a home.
>
> —David St. John

logical reasons such as memories of cooking with mothers or grandmothers. As for the basement and the garage, Busch found that these quiet places with all the junk they contain "are an infallible combination, it seems, to ignite the creative spark in children and adults as well." Busch concluded that as long as the places we live have the bedroom, the kitchen, and the basement—"the private and necessary sanctuary, the place of nourishment and community, and the area where things get made," that particular place "might be called home."[2]...

On his first journey back home as a college student in Cincinnati, Rabbi Lawrence Kushner had an encounter with the Spirit of Re-union. As he writes in his book *Invisible Lines of Connection: Sacred Stories of the Ordinary*, at the time he didn't understand the simple power of going away and coming back: "I now realize that this setting out and returning home again is a kind of dance we do with our Source and our Destiny.... If we learn it right, when our time comes to die we are not afraid."[3]

Discerning the Power of Place

For the Aboriginal people in Australia, the concept of home is multidimensional and holistic. So-called songlines produced in a state referred to as "the Dream-time" reunite them with not just a building, a backyard, or a town, but with a more expansive and inclusive home found in their ancestral origins and original ground of being. The travel writer Bruce Chatwin has described songlines as invisible and intuitively understood "maps" that "meander all over Australia." They are the "footprints of the ancestors" or the "way of the law." In his book

The Songlines, Chatwin writes of their origins: "Aboriginal Creation myths tell of the legendary totemic beings who had wandered over the continent in the Dreamtime, singing out the name of everything that crossed their path—birds, animals, plants, rocks, waterholes—and so singing the world into existence."[4]...

Bring to mind the home you associate most with childhood, family, and your "songlines."

> When over the years have you felt tugs and pulls to physically return to that place for a day, a year, or a lifetime? Are there predictable times, such as holidays and holy days? Or do you find yourself blindsided by sudden, unforeseen yearnings?
>
> If you decided to return, how might the Spirit of Re-union have influenced your decision? Was it because you felt called or heard someone calling? Was it to know that place again or to know it for the first time? Was it to restore missing pieces or to find peace? Did remembering begin a process of re-membering?
>
> If you chose not to go back, what were the thoughts, memories, or feelings about reuniting that said, "Not now" or "Not ever"?

Honoring Memories

Linda Douty

"Tell me if I've already told you this," my friend insisted as she began her story. It's a phrase that creeps into casual conversations as we grow older. To be sure, declining memory is the butt of jokes among our peers and derision from the young. We know all too well the panic of flipping through a mental filing cabinet in search of the right word or a familiar name, only to have it pop into our heads two hours later.

Better to laugh than to lament, but why not find ways to honor memory, to cherish it for the gift it is? Though we are familiar with the downside of memory, many seniors are finding ways to emphasize the upside by intentionally sharing their memories with family and friends.

Emotional or Ethical Wills. This kind of will carries no dollar signs; values are bequeathed, not valuables. It is designed as a way for you to share your thoughts, values, lessons in life, passions, hopes, and dreams with your family and friends. You don't want to leave this life with things left unsaid.[1]...

Video and Tape Recordings. Use whatever technology is available to simply speak your remembrances in your own words, adding whatever commentary and advice that comes from your heart.

Photo Scrapbooks. Marian gathered pictures reflecting her life with each child, grandchild, or family unit as a way of honoring their presence in her life. She personalized each collection of photos with messages and memories. "Who knows," she said with a smile, "one fine day, it may find its way into some grandson's treasure chest!"

Linda Douty, a leading speaker on the topics of meaningful aging, personal growth, and spiritual formation, is author of *How Did I Get to Be 70 When I'm 35 Inside? Spiritual Surprises of Later Life* (SkyLight Paths), a spiritual director, and a contributor to *Presence* (the journal of Spiritual Directors International).

Trips to Yesteryear. Each spring my sisters and I take our two aunts (now ages eighty-nine and ninety-nine) on an annual "Cemetery Tour" in west Tennessee. With a station wagon brimming with flowers, we visit the graves of dozens of extended family members, decorating the gravesites and tracing the lineage as far back as we can. Sharing stories of saints and rascals under the family tree produces misty eyes, as well as gales of laughter.

Honoring memories has its place in the grieving process also. It's a way of paying tribute to the presence of the lost loved one and focusing on the meaningful intersections of her life with ours. Grief, love, and sometimes even anger can be simultaneously present when we neither idealize nor demonize the person, but remember her just as she was—a human mixture of light and shadow.

The Ritual of the Rose contains significant symbolism as a means of honoring the life of someone who has died. It goes like this: Purchase a long-stemmed rose, complete with thorns. Standing beside a lake or river, pull a petal from the rose as you recall each good memory and toss it in the water. When unpleasant or irritating memories arise, pluck a thorn from the stem and throw it in also. As the rose becomes free of all its petals and thorns, toss the whole thing in the water to symbolize your release of that person. It's a beautiful ceremony of letting go that affirms the reality of relationships; they are all a "mixed bag."

Fragments of Life

Louise Silk

When my partner, Heath, died, we were in the midst of a struggle. My late beloved was an obsessive collector.... Heath collected books, scripts, playbills, videos, audios, props, costumes, uniforms, hats, walking sticks, religious artifacts, and toy soldiers. Separate from the formal collections, he kept every contract, review, and photo related to his long and prestigious career. He also kept every artifact related to our eight-year relationship, but that's a whole different story. He titled his collections "an embarrassment of riches."

To give you a very small example, when sorting his videos I found nineteen different years of the Queen of England's birthday parade. That's right, nineteen unique videos on one very specific theme. Heath was consistently over the top. He did everything in full flower, acquiring each and every—and then some—object related to the various subjects that caught his interest.

After two years of my following him around the world, we discovered that he had an incurable case of prostate cancer. To have regular treatment, he relinquished his vagabond life to stay with me in Pittsburgh. As we acknowledged the ending of his life, it became imperative to me that he dispose of all the items in storage, not leaving them in my reluctant hands. Getting Heath to face this reality wasn't a pretty picture. By the time he had unloaded, as he called it, his entire ego wagon from storage, our loft was overflowing with hundreds of carefully packaged and labeled boxes housing his multiple collections.

I have done quite a bit of sorting and purging, but it will take years to disperse his collections. The only thing I can be sure of is that his fibers will eventually make their way into quilts. The first of these was a Birds-in-Air T-shirt quilt made from Heath's beloved T-shirt collection. To accent the T-shirts, I included his special compilation of red dharma cloth pieces and a kid's twin bed blanket from his childhood. Because he and I had a mutual connection to birds,

Louise Silk is a spiritual teacher, integrated kabbalistic healer, and professional quilter. She is author of *The Quilting Path: A Guide to Spiritual Discovery Through Fabric, Thread and Kabbalah* (SkyLight Paths).

I picked the Birds-in-Air patchwork pattern. Everything contained within the quilt—every stitch and patch, the pattern and the backing—allows me to be in his presence even though he is no longer alive. He inadvertently collected the shirts for me rather than for himself, as I am the one using the quilt.

How does one deal with the loss of a loved one? Being a quilt maker, I always knew about the great tradition of remembrance quilts. A remembrance quilt is any quilt created to remember something of significance. It can be a person, an event, or a realization—any important life experience the quilt maker wants to immortalize in fabric. Creating these quilts opens a space to reflect, recall, weep, lament, sigh, smile, and laugh....

Well-versed quilters know about the most distinctive historical memory quilt to survive today. It is Elizabeth Roseberry Mitchell's Graveyard Quilt. It has a central medallion that is a fenced graveyard with four named coffins. The bulk of the quilt, surrounding the graveyard, is alternating star and solid block, with an outside fence-like border with a dozen or so more named coffins.

Elizabeth produced the quilt in the 1830s to help her grieve the loss of her son, John Vannatta. He was two years and eight months old when he died. At that time, a good housekeeper saved every fabric fragment so that nothing was wasted. Patchwork was one example of this economy. For this quilt, she stitched together tiny remnants from the shirts and dresses of her children. Every bit was precious. The quilt became the only record of her son as there were no death records kept at that time in Ohio, where she was living.

After my parents died, I produced over twenty pieces using their clothing and textiles. I made embroideries, a linen jacket, a poncho, table runners, photo-transfer books, and a range of pieces big and small. I even transformed the scraps into usable squares and strips to make traditional patterned bed covers, one for each of the seven grandchildren.

I cleaned out my parents' belongings twice, once to move both of them to an assisted-living facility and the final time after my dad's death. Both times, along with photos and special mementos, I was overwhelmed with the array of memories I carted back to my studio. I specifically selected clothing and textiles that I hoped would be quilt worthy. There were numerous cross-stitched tablecloths, all kinds of knitted sweaters, fancy formal wear, brightly colored golf attire, and heavy Turkish towels. The fabric piles were unruly, requiring continual sorting, ripping, and discarding, and I had trouble throwing any of the precious cloth away.

The strongest memory I have of the actual quilting experience is the first time I cut and ripped off one of the pant legs from my dad's tux. Ripping that leg gave me a powerful, direct understanding of his death, the clear reality that I had no choice but to destroy these pants. He had no more use for them. It became my responsibility to make them over into something new. I was letting go of Dad and transforming the pants to a different and useful existence....

Crazy Quilt Table Runner

This quilting project is a direct opportunity to transform the unhelpful need to control into being with and accepting what is. Begin by choosing some material with deep-seated memory and meaning—something that is very precious to you. By giving it up, letting it go, and transforming it, you will have the true heart of victory....

Each of us has a bag of memories associated with our clothing and textiles. Life's constant change leaves tangible tactile surfaces as a handy reminder. Our project is a table runner that will be 12 inches wide and multiples of 12 inches in length. You can put as many squares as necessary in a line to fit the length of your table.

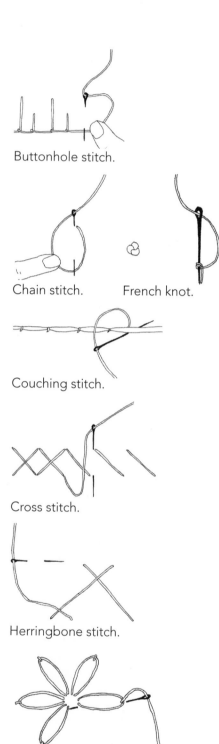

Buttonhole stitch.

Chain stitch.   French knot.

Couching stitch.

Cross stitch.

Herringbone stitch.

Lazy daisy

Supplies

1 yard muslin (or the amount necessary for the size of your project)

1 yard backing (or the amount necessary for the size of your project)

An assortment of cloth that holds special meaning for you

Quilting thread

Cotton embroidery floss in assorted colors

Optional: Photo transfers

Directions

1. For these blocks we are using ½-inch seam allowances around the outside edges. To end up with a 12-inch square, cut a 13-inch square of muslin. Cut as many of these squares as you need. For example, if you want a table runner that finishes at 12 inches by 60 inches, cut 5 blocks of muslin.

2. Select your favorite fabric from your grouping and roughly cut out a 2- to 3-inch square. Don't worry if the angles are not exactly square. In this case, the finished product will actually be more interesting if the patches are oddly sized. Lay this piece at the approximate center of

one of the muslin blocks. You don't have to be exact about this either as the block will end up being asymmetrical anyway.

3. Select a second fabric that contrasts in texture or color with the first. Cut a random-sized piece, making sure that one edge is as long as one of the edges of the first patch. Lay these two fabrics with right sides facing each other, matching up that one similar-length edge. This second fabric will be covering both the first fabric and the muslin block underneath it. Use quilting thread to hand stitch a running stitch ¼ inch from that matching edge. This is one of those circumstances where it's easier and more fun to work by hand, but if you prefer the machine, that will work equally well.

4. Turn the second piece to show its right side. The sewn edge is now hidden, and you now have two fabric pieces sewn to each other and the muslin.

5. Continue in this fashion, adding different random-sized fabric pieces and working your way out from the center until the muslin is completely covered. Trim any excess that goes beyond the muslin edge, ending up with a 13-inch square.

6. Complete all the blocks in this fashion, and piece them into one long row. You have completed the crazy quilt top.

7. Now you can add decorative embroidery stitches over the top of as many of the seams as you like. The more embroidery you do, the better it will look. Start with a simple backstitch and feel free to experiment with a variety of stitches and thread colors.

8. When all the embroidery is completed, cut a backing fabric that is 1 inch bigger along all four edges of the Crazy Quilt top. Lay the patchwork top on top of the backing, wrong sides facing each other.

9. Fold the outside edges of the backing in to meet the outside edge of the top, and then fold the backing in once again to form a binding around the outside edge of the Crazy Quilt top. Hand stitch the binding in place, and add embroidery to the bound edge as you desire.

A Pilgrimage for Brokenness

Terry Taylor

A pilgrimage is a journey to a site that has the potential to connect us with something important in our lives and bring meaning to our experience. It is not a vacation or a trip to "get away from it all," but rather a journey to honor, to witness, to understand. It is the journey of a seeker looking for a connection, an answer, an insight, a resolution....

Pilgrimages require us to leave the familiar to find something spiritually satisfying, something deeper than we currently know. We might come because we are in crisis, or we might come to find the truth of what happened to us in that place. But most of all, we come to seek mending, an inner peace, and empowerment over what keeps us feeling broken.

Phil Cousineau, author of *The Art of Pilgrimage: The Seeker's Guide to Making Travel Sacred*, points out that "pilgrims undertake arduous journeys because they believe that there is something vital missing in their lives. They sense that vitality itself may be lurking on the road or at the heart of a distant sanctuary." And he poignantly adds, "The ritual act of pilgrimage attempts to fill that emptiness."

A pilgrimage is not something to enter into casually. While a pilgrimage to a key place where your story developed can bring new meaning to your life, it can also be painful. Yet, paradoxically, the difficulty of such a journey can be essential to its meaning, and to your mending. The keys are preparation in advance and contemplation after its completion....

Terry Taylor is a workshop leader and frequent commentator for public radio and other media on topics related to spirituality, peace, and justice. He is executive director of Interfaith Paths to Peace, an organization dedicated to fostering interreligious dialogue, and author of *A Spirituality for Brokenness: Discovering Your Deepest Self in Difficult Times* (SkyLight Paths).

Making a Pilgrimage

I'm grateful to Phil Cousineau for his descriptions of pilgrimage and, in particular, his understanding of how a pilgrimage unfolds in distinct stages. As I've reflected on my own experience, I see my pilgrimages encompassing five stages, with an element, reflection, that is integral to each stage:

Stage 1: The Call

Stage 2: The Preparation

Stage 3: The Journey

Stage 4: The Arrival

Stage 5: The Return

Stage 1: The Call

Before you start out on a pilgrimage, an idea usually gets you thinking about making this particular journey to this particular place. You may start having memories of an important event or place from your past, or you may hear from someone you haven't heard from in a long time and start to think about an emotional encounter, or you may find yourself in a situation where you are traveling on a business or family matter in the area of a place where you experienced a childhood trauma. The more you reflect on the idea, the more you feel compelled to go back to this key place where a piece of your life story developed.

For some people, the call is not so obvious.... However your past calls to you, ultimately, you are the only one who can decide when it is time to make a sacred journey to come face-to-face with a piece of your life story.

Stage 2: The Preparation

Preparation may well be the most important step in your pilgrimage process. Without careful, thoughtful, and heartfelt preparation, even a trip to the holiest place on the planet can end up as empty as a tourist "drive-by." Successful preparation includes careful attention to the specific details of your travel plans (including how much time you will need to allow for careful reflection on your experience). In addition, your preparation needs to include time for visualizing the journey before it happens and perhaps journaling on a number of important questions, such as:

Why am I going?

What do I hope to gain from the experience?

What challenges or problems am I walking away from?

What challenges and opportunities am I walking toward?

It is also important to prepare yourself for the emotional impact your sacred journey may have on you.... It is important to make your *hajj* when you have the support you need, and when you have the time to process the feelings and memories your trip might bring to the surface. This trip should not be a threat to your well-being, but rather a fruitful spiritual journey to help mend your brokenness. I recommend that you think about a simple ritual or ceremony that you might perform for yourself when you reach your destination. Not only will it be a tool to help you honor the sacred nature of the site you are visiting, but it will also be a way to help you cope with your feelings when you arrive.

Stage 3: The Journey

The journey itself demands constant mindfulness and a commitment to, as Ram Dass would say, "be here now." Such a journey begs you to be aware constantly of how and what you are feeling, and of the need for self-care—not just for the blisters you may develop on your feet, but also for the blisters that may pop up on your emotions and on your soul.

If you have prepared yourself well, you won't need to spend the time of the journey thinking about getting to your destination or fretting about what emotions you may feel when you arrive. You may instead use the time of travel in a relaxing way, seeking comfort, being particularly mindful of what you encounter along the way.

While it isn't exactly possible to reflect on a journey while you are in progress, adopting an attitude of mindfulness as you travel can arm you with a special form of reflection-like experience that enables you to tune your mind and senses to a level of maximum awareness of what is happening around you. This will also help you reflect more fully at a later time.

Stage 4: The Arrival

After all the preparation and travel, you finally arrive at your destination. You've made it! But this stage of coming to the crux of your journey can be a double-edged experience. You might have a sense of joy at having achieved a goal after overcoming obstacles. You might "meet your demons," so to speak, or you might make a new kind of peace with your past. Your *hajj* might be the powerful spiritual experience you were looking for—or not. Either way, you might be left with a kind of postpartum depression that the journey is over. You might be asking, "Is that all there is?" This is a point where performing a ritual or ceremony can be very helpful in coping with powerful emotions and thoughts.

Give the experience the time and attention it deserves. Don't rush through your arrival. Before or after your ritual, you may want to embrace silence. If you are traveling with a friend or partner, you might want to spend time talking about the ideas and feelings you are experiencing. Even if you are traveling by yourself, you might want to use both spoken words and silence. Let your heart be your guide.

Stage 5: The Return

No pilgrimage is complete until you return home and begin to process what you have experienced. When you return, you will need to look at what you have brought back with you, by way of both physical treasure and emotional baggage. In this fifth stage, the element of reflection is perhaps the most crucial. Everything I know about travel and about struggle tells me that no pilgrimage is complete until the pilgrim has undertaken a period of deep reflection: savoring the moments of joy; wincing at the painful times; thinking about the meaning of the people and places encountered; recounting the events witnessed or in which you participated. I strongly urge you to take time, such as a Sabbath experience, to reflect on the meaning and implications of the journey you have undertaken....

Hajj Alternative: A Virtual Pilgrimage

One option would be to take a "virtual" pilgrimage in which you imagine and write in great detail what such a journey would be like. The techniques of creative visualization can help you take a virtual pilgrimage by letting your imagination carry you back to your destination. In the same way that the immersion experience technique can help you go deeper into being in a story with *Lectio Divina*, you can invoke all of your senses in imagining your *hajj* in as much detail as you like. Find a comfortable place, close your eyes, and imagine what you might see. What does the air feel like at your destination? Is it cold? Warm? Hot? Is there wind or rain or snow? Do you feel pain? What emotions are you experiencing? Fear? Anger? Sadness? Happiness? Are you aware of aromas or odors? Does the experience leave any taste in your mouth? Bitter, sweet, salty? What sounds do you hear? Birds singing? Traffic whizzing by? People talking?

You may find journaling helpful, either as a means of making the trip itself, or as a way of reflecting on what you have imagined. You might also want to pore over old photos.

If you do decide to make a virtual pilgrimage, don't feel that you must make the journey in just one sitting. You can make the trip over a period of days, weeks, or even months.

Hajj Alternative: A Pilgrimage in Retrospect

Another *hajj* option is to consider a pilgrimage you've already taken. Let me explain. You may have already made a trip that has all of the elements of a *hajj*, but you just didn't realize it at the time. Only later, upon deeper reflection, can you come to see that a particular experience was a sacred journey of the greatest depth, a once-in-a-lifetime pilgrimage.

Look back over your life to see if there has been a journey that, in retrospect, has the elements of a *hajj*: a visit to a site that is sacred to you because of what happened there and how it has shaped your life. If you have made such a trip, write down the story of your experience in as much detail as you can conjure. Break your pilgrimage into its stages and see what you can learn from reflecting back on them. Be deeply aware of each phase of the journey because each may hold its own significance. Ask yourself what you learned from that trip. Explore how that trip helped or hindered your mending process....

It is important to be aware that the pilgrimage you plan may ultimately not hold the meaning you were seeking. Or it may take you to a destination that surprises you. Be open also to unexpected opportunities to make sacred journeys that present themselves from time to time. Take advantage of them, if you can. Sometimes you may consciously choose to make a pilgrimage, but at other times a pilgrimage may choose you. Wherever your pilgrimage takes you—whether it is a literal trip or a virtual journey—you can return with new eyes that help you continue to find the meaning in your experience of brokenness.

Partingway Blessing for a Pet

Lynn L. Caruso

The Navajo believe that all creation is given life through *nilch'i* (holy wind). We are all interconnected with this common breath, and we cannot help but notice when that wind shifts. *Nilch'i* enters a being at conception and is breathed in at all times. At death, this holy wind leaves the body.

During times of loss it seems that all is still—that the breath of joy is unmoving within us. But as we leave this place today, let us be aware of the presence of the wind—in the shifting leaves, in the bending grass, in the wings that play among the clouds. Let us always remember that with one common breath, we were all created, and in the end we shall all return in one holy inhale. Look to the gentle winds this day, and as you move forward, be ever mindful of your companion's presence.

Partingway Blessing

Leader: As we reflect on the passing of this companion let us share
    communally in this responsive blessing:

Leader: Upon the Earth with gentle caregivers
All: With gentle caregivers this companion was blessed.

Leader: Upon the Earth with wanderings through green spaces
All: Through green spaces this companion was blessed.

Leader: Upon the Earth with long naps in a patch of sun
All: In a patch of sun this companion was blessed.

Leader: Beneath the Earth with the warmth of our love
All: With our love this companion is blessed.

Lynn L. Caruso is an inspiring educator, writer, and parent/child advocate and editor of the first-of-its-kind *Blessing the Animals: Prayers and Ceremonies to Celebrate God's Creatures, Wild and Tame* (SkyLight Paths).

Leader: Beneath the Earth with the turning of all things done, into
   seeds
All: Into seeds our companion is blessed.

Leader: Upon the Earth with the sprout of loss blooming into rose
All: Into rose our companion is blessed.

—Lynn L. Caruso,
inspired by a Navajo Blessingway

Prayer

In the beginning, all creatures were hidden treasures—longing
to be known, and brought into being. God then exhaled a sigh
of compassion, and with that great sigh, the world was created.

—Sufi parable

Loving God,
Before _____ came to share our home, you knew him [her],
   knew that he [she] longed to be brought into this loving family.

Compassionate God,
With your breath you created the world in one sacred exhale. And
   in that breath, _____ first came into being.

Eternal God,
We return this treasured companion to you. We place him [her]
   in your loving arms, where he [she] was known even before
   the call of his [her] first bark [adapt appropriately]. With your
   breath that created all in one compassionate exhale, draw this
   companion home to you in one loving inhale.

Amen.

Walking a Labyrinth for Healing and Connection

Rev. Dr. Carole Ann Camp

Walking is one of the various practices in use today for seekers of the transcendent experience. By walking a labyrinth, one can travel long distances in a small space. The labyrinth walk overflows with metaphor and meaning. The labyrinth represents a journey, a pilgrimage, a conscious taking of time to seek God.... Making the choice and taking that first step into the labyrinth is to risk discovering the mystery at the very center of our being. The good thing about labyrinths is that you cannot make a mistake. There are no wrong turns. You cannot get lost. Symbolically, what could be better than knowing that by staying on the path, by following all the turns, you will eventually find the center—the Holy of Holies?...

The Preparation: Before You Start

Although it is possible to run in and quickly walk around the labyrinth, by doing so you run the risk of missing the power that the labyrinth has for you.... Take off and put aside, in a conscious and ritual way, those things that may prevent you from the full experience. Some acts of preparing are like prayers of letting go and putting aside. The act can be as simple as taking off your shoes, or putting your purse, laptop, or backpack aside. The act could be taking off as many layers of clothing as climate and society allow or putting on and wearing some special ritual clothing.

Choose your favorite scripture or spiritual source for prayers and mantras that you can use in your labyrinth experience.... During your preparation time, read your passage aloud several times. Close your eyes and allow a

---

Rev. Dr. Carole Ann Camp, founder of an ecumenical spiritual community called Seekers and Sojourners and a retired United Church of Christ pastor, has walked labyrinths on three continents. She is coauthor with Rev. Dr. Donna Schaper of *Labyrinths from the Outside In: Walking to Spiritual Insight—A Beginner's Guide* (SkyLight Paths).

word or phrase to come into your mind. Use that word or phrase as your mantra for the inward journey.

Take some time with your preparation. Your time of putting aside, letting go, and getting ready is very important. The more you are able to let go of and to put aside, the more your labyrinth walk will be able to lift you to the joys of ecstasy.... When you have finished the physical preparations and before you start your walk, you may want to say or sing a prayer of invocation.... An invocation can be as simple as saying, "Come, Holy Spirit." You may prefer a familiar prayer from your religious tradition. Invocations can also be in the form of a hymn, a song, or a dance.

The Inward Journey: Walking the Labyrinth In

Once you have prepared and are ready to begin the inward journey, remember that to enter the labyrinth is to open yourself to profound and life-changing possibilities. The path inward to the center is the path that leads to the very heart of God—a path that leads to the very center of the self and to the very center of the universe. To put oneself on the path is to make the choice that you are now ready for the insights and the wisdom that your deity, the center, the Holy of Holies, has in store for you. This is not a frightening experience, but it is one that is filled with awe. As your feet touch the path, become aware of the path. Even if the path is some paint on a piece of canvas, forget the mechanics of the actual labyrinth that you are walking on and focus on the path—the path that is leading you inward, inward to a kind of transcendence. Allow others who may be walking the path to be there and not be there at the same time. With each step and with each breath, allow your *self* to go deeper and deeper into the center—the center of you, the center of the universe, the center of God. Do not worry about whether you are walking in the right way or doing the ritual in the right way. There is no "right way," there is only your way. Allow yourself to walk as slowly as you can. Focus on *your* path....

Reaching the Center

When you reach the center of the labyrinth, take some time to experience the center before stepping out on the outward journey: sing there, dance there, or have intimate conversations with your friends. The center is also the perfect place to meditate....

The Outward Journey: Walking the Labyrinth Out

When you are ready, begin the journey outward. Remember that the path out is of equal length to the path in. It is important to be as intentional about the outward journey as the inward journey. The genius of the labyrinth lies partly in the fact that the journey inward is the same as the journey outward—into the center *and* out into the world; not either/or, but deliberately and intentionally both/and. As you take this outer journey, you may notice that your body feels lighter and more relaxed. You may experience a feeling of great joy or ecstasy. Do not be surprised if you feel taller and find yourself walking with more intention and integrity. As you take the journey back out into the world, imagine taking a gift to the world from the center of the labyrinth. The gift could be in the form of something you are going to do for the greater good, or an act of creativity like a song, poem, or piece of writing that you will share with the world. It does not have to be a tangible gift. You already are a gift that God has given to the world.... Take some time as you step out of the labyrinth to say a prayer of thanksgiving....

After each walk and journey, take some time to record your experience, either in total or in snippets, words, or pictures. You may find that one journey gives insight and texture to the ones that follow. You may discover that you are directed to explore variations. Be gentle with yourself. Go well.

Falling Apart: A Walk for Times of Difficulty

There are times in our lives when it seems that everything is falling apart. Ritualize the feelings. As you take the inward journey, imagine in your mind's eye each part of your life that is falling apart. Metaphorically catch it and gently lay it on the path of the labyrinth. Allow it (or them) to fall. Instead of madly trying to keep it all together, just let the parts fall away. As you gently catch it (or them) and lower it to the path, thank it for falling away in order to give you some time to put yourself back together the way you want to be. During your meditation time, decide which things you are going to put back together and which things you are going to leave on the labyrinth path. On your outward journey, gently pick up those parts that you have decided to take with you and tuck them neatly into your imaginary backpack. Do not worry about those parts of you that you have left behind. They are safe in the labyrinth if you ever want to come back and retrieve them.

Commemorating Separations

Joinings and partings are the fabric of life. Imagine a macramé work of art. Sometimes the threads are knotted together; sometimes they are not. Different strands intimately knot and reknot with the same strands. Some never knot together, whereas others knot together once or twice, with each going its separate way never to meet again; so it is with life. Some people are life friends; others bless us only for an instant. Walk the labyrinth with the one from whom you are about to be separated. As you walk, reflect on how the labyrinth path brings you close together at times and takes you far apart at other times. notice that sometimes you will meet face-to-face and at other times go in the same direction. Sometimes it feels as if you will never find each other again, and then you are united in the center. When you reach the center, share with each other stories of your time together. Tell each other what gift the other has been to you and your life. Allow yourselves time to laugh and cry. After the outward journey, give thanks that this person has been part of your life and your journey....

Walking to Grieve the Death of a Loved One

When someone dies, we wonder how God could do such a thing. We forget that death is part of life. We are angry with God. The feelings of anger toward God are especially strong when the person who died is a son or a daughter, a parent, or a partner. It is okay to be angry. It is okay to be angry with God. It is okay to scream and shout and throw a tantrum. Being angry is part of the grieving process—a necessary part that cannot be denied. Many of us have grown up in a society that tells us not to cry. In an attempt to shield us from sorrow and grief, funeral directors cover the earth at the gravesite with plastic grass. Except in Jewish tradition, it is very rare to be allowed to stay at the grave when the coffin is lowered into the ground. Whenever someone we love dies, we have to grieve. Other cultures have something to teach us about dying and about grieving. In some cultures, there are women who have the specific responsibility of mourning. They cry and wail and make moaning sounds. The women lead the others in the grieving process. When you walk the labyrinth after the death of a loved one, use the meditation time to grieve by making moaning sounds, allowing your whole body to cry and wail.... Honor your body's need to have some time to experience the deep sadness resulting from the loss of a loved one. The closer the relationship, the longer the grieving process; do not hurry it. Allow yourself to visit the labyrinth at least monthly for a year with the only intention being to walk through the grief.

Preparation

Place mementos of your loved one who has died in the center of the labyrinth with white candles and flowers.

Inward Journey

Try one of the following, or something similar from your own religious tradition:

- Repeat the mantra "The Lord God will wipe away the tears from every cheek" (Isaiah 25:8, author's paraphrase).
- Repeat the mantra "God, I am coming to you" (John 17:11).
- Reflect on "Show me the way in which I should walk" (Psalm 143:8 NASB) or "Make me to know your ways, O God" (Psalm 25:4).
- Reflect on "God is my refuge and strength, a very present help in trouble" (Psalm 46:1).
- Allow yourself to remember your life and the life of your loved one and how they blessed each other. Allow the tears to flow.

Meditation

Allow yourself to weep by holding the mementos of your loved one. Say good-bye.

Outward Journey

Walk in silence or sing a song or hymn that is your favorite or the favorite of your loved one.

Heal

Reaching Out for Comfort and Strength

> I yearn to be different from the center out, to re-create myself somehow, over and over again, from the raw materials of my soul. I ask only to be who I was created to be, each time closer and wiser and better and nearer to the Source of all things.
>
> —Karyn D. Kedar

The "valley of the shadow" is a devastating place. But the intense darkness of the valley doesn't have to last forever. Though what you have lost can likely never be regained, there is healing in this valley.

This section contains active practices for when you feel motivated to do "grief work." It also contains prayers and meditations for when you need to simply let healing come to you.

There is no way to rush this time in darkness and sorrow. Have patience with yourself as you heal. Don't try to skim over grief, but allow yourself to be sad, despite the many tasks, relationships, and emotions that may try to push you to be "okay" before you really are. Above all, even when the valley is at its darkest, hold on to the hope that healing will come.

WIN A $100 GIFT CERTIFICATE!

Fill in this card and
mail it to us—
or fill it in online at

**skylightpaths.com/
feedback.html**

—to be eligible for a
$100 gift certificate for
SkyLight Paths books.

SKYLIGHT PATHS PUBLISHING
SUNSET FARM OFFICES RTE 4
PO BOX 237
WOODSTOCK VT   05091-0237

Place
Stamp
Here

Fill in this card and return it to us to be eligible for our quarterly drawing for a $100 gift certificate for SkyLight Paths books.

We hope that you will enjoy this book and find it useful in enriching your life.

Book title: _____

Your comments: _____

How you learned of this book: _____

If purchased: Bookseller _____ City _____ State _____

Please send me a free SKYLIGHT PATHS Publishing catalog. I am interested in: (check all that apply)

1. ☐ Spirituality
2. ☐ Mysticism/Kabbalah
3. ☐ Philosophy/Theology
4. ☐ Spiritual Texts
5. ☐ Religious Traditions (Which ones?) _____
6. ☐ Children's Books
7. ☐ Prayer/Worship
8. ☐ Meditation
9. ☐ Interfaith Resources

Name (PRINT) _____

Street _____

City _____ State _____ Zip _____

E-MAIL (FOR SPECIAL OFFERS ONLY) _____

Please send a SKYLIGHT PATHS Publishing catalog to my friend:

Name (PRINT) _____

Street _____

City _____ State _____ Zip _____

SKYLIGHT PATHS® Publishing Tel: (802) 457-4000 • Fax: (802) 457-4004

Available at better booksellers. Visit us online at www.skylightpaths.com

Tending Your Grief-Seeds

Diane M. Millis, PhD

Where will you plant your grief-seeds? We need ground
to scrape and hoe, not the sky of unspecified desire.
—Jellaladin Rumi

Loss rose from her garden,
spoke gently between plantings,

conversed softly of death
and dianthus, of despair and dahlias.

Guided by grief, heart in dust,
mind in memory, tears fell, sank,

into the loam of soul. Each turn
of hoe, every scrape into ground,

became honorable labor, honorable
in its intention to transform.

Digging, unearthing, seeing,
she beheld her father, followed

his image as he tended to tea rose
and tulip, dianthus and dahlia;

she watched his eyes brighten
as he handled, cupped, the stuff of life.

Diane M. Millis, PhD, is an inspirational speaker, workshop and retreat leader, organizational consultant, and spiritual director. She is author of *Conversation—The Sacred Art: Practicing Presence in an Age of Distraction* and *Deepening Engagement: Essential Wisdom for Listening and Leading with Purpose, Meaning and Joy* (both SkyLight Paths) and is founder of the Journey Conversations Project.

Buried in darkness, stirrings
pushed where seedlings emerged,

where buds reached for the sky, grew
with the specified desire to live!

Blossoms rose from her garden;
they swirled in crinolines of green,

delighted in bonnets of petalled-softness,
as if to say, *Dance with us, laugh,
we're your grief-seeds—transformed!*[1]

—Jeannie E. Roberts

My maternal grandmother was renowned for her gardening. When someone took her picture, she loved to be photographed in her flower garden. Earlier in her life, she had tended many vegetables during the years she and my grandfather lived on their farm in central Minnesota. It was on that farm that their second child and only son, Donald, died in my grandmother's arms from whooping cough. He was four at the time. It was on that farm that my mother, Rosemary, was born the following year. While she was a child, my mother doesn't recall her parents ever speaking about her brother's death. What she does remember is that after she was diagnosed with polio at age five, her parents sold their farm and bought a house in the nearest city, St. Cloud. There, my grandmother's flowers blossomed.

Each of us experiences grief over the course of our lives. It may be the seeds from the loss of loved ones, the loss of our health, the loss of a job, the loss of our home, the loss of our youth, or the loss of a dream for our life. Whatever our particular medley of seeds, psychologists speak about the importance of honoring our grief rather than denying or striving to overcome it. How we do that is unique to each of us, although the terrain we travel may be similar.[2]

I never had the chance to ask my grandmother about how she tended the seeds of her grief because she died when I was nine. Ironically, her death was the first loss I experienced in my life. All I can recount is the blossoms I witnessed. Like her flowers, she was deeply rooted. I know she was a woman of prayer. Although she never spoke about her way of praying, I could feel the energy of her prayer emanate from her bedroom. It was my favorite spot in her home. I used to love sleeping in there and the time I could spend there alone, gazing at the twinkling candles above her prie-dieu kneeler. I have since learned from other family members that the loss of her son never embittered her; rather, her capacity to love became all the more tender. I too can recall the tenderness in her eyes and the hint of sadness at their center. Grief is like that—although the anguish may lessen over time, an ache still lingers.

Whether or not we are gardeners, each of us holds seeds of grief in the palms of our hands. Some of us may keep our hands tightly clenched, preferring to pretend those seeds are not there. Some of us just want to get rid of them—to throw them out into the sky or the nearest receptacle. Yet the process of honoring our grief invites us to examine the seeds from both the losses in our lives (deaths, illnesses, jobs, and dreams) and the endings (of relationships, of work, of various life stages).

Anthropologist Angeles Arrien offers us a process for working with our grief-seeds, which she calls honorable closure. Honorable closure is based on a ritual practiced among indigenous people to mark endings, to acknowledge the impact of our experiences, and to glean wisdom from them.[3] It consists of four questions:

- What am I grateful for from the experience?
- How was I positively impacted?
- How was I stretched or challenged?
- Is there anything I need to say or do to feel complete?

Throughout her lifetime, my mother has displayed a picture of the brother she never met in the living room. I love that picture and make a point to gaze at it whenever I visit her. I can't imagine anything more painful than having my child die in my arms. I don't know how I would have survived it. I am grateful that my grandparents had the courage to love another child after such an immense loss. The impact of their love shaped my mother in indelible ways. Every time we are with our mother, she never ceases to remind us (my two younger sisters and me, and now our children) that we are the biggest blessings in her life. My grandparents' steadfast

For reflection: Out of your grief, what have you created or what do you hope to create?

commitment to keep reaching out in love in the midst of their loss challenges me to do the same. I can only hope that my life is worthy of their example.

Grieving with Water

Cait Johnson

Author's note: This activity is based on cross-cultural water-burial traditions that have been practiced unchanged since before the beginnings of recorded time. It may seem simple, but it contains a surprising depth and capacity to move and transform.

Just a few days after the World Trade Center disaster, still in shock, fear, and grief, a friend and I went down to a gentle shore of the Hudson River, north of New York City. We found a piece of birchbark on the ground and took turns writing a prayer on its smooth inner surface. We put a dried rosebud on the bark, placed this bundle on the river, and watched it slowly float downstream toward the place where so many mourned. We sang as we watched it disappear, our voices rough and unsteady. But when we finally turned away to go home, we felt more deeply at peace.

Placing Your Grief in Water's Arms

Water gives us a way to honor our mourning over the loss of something dear to us. When we place our grief in Water's arms, she will hold it for us.

Write something that you are mourning on a piece of bark (preferably found on the ground, not removed from a tree) and place it on the surface of a river or stream where the current can carry it away. You may want to pray or sing as you watch it travel out of sight. If feelings come up, let them flow. People have offered their dead to water in just this way for millennia, knowing that she is large enough to hold it all. Now take a deep breath, and turn back toward the rest of your life.

Cait Johnson, author of *Earth, Water, Fire and Air: Essential Ways of Connecting to Spirit* (SkyLight Paths), teaches workshops on connecting to Spirit, seasonal elemental approaches to self-healing, poetry writing, and conscious eating.

The Well of Sadness

Molly Srode

Without choice, like a bucket
I am lowered into the well of sadness.
Falling with uncontrolled speed,
I careen
into the black abyss
and plunge into the icy waters.
Numbed by the cold,
I am unaware of being filled
until I feel a gentle pull.
My spirit begins to rise.
Illusion gives way to reality.
The light and warmth of the sun touch me
as the bucket is passed around
for all to drink.

Molly Srode, a retired hospital chaplain and former Catholic nun, is author of *Creating a Spiritual Retirement: A Guide to the Unseen Possibilities in Our Lives* and coauthor of *Keeping Spiritual Balance as We Grow Older: More than 65 Creative Ways to Use Purpose, Prayer, and the Power of Spirit to Build a Meaningful Retirement* (both SkyLight Paths).

Valley Journeys

Dr. Nancy Copeland-Payton

Even though I walk through the darkest valley,
I fear no evil;
for you are with me ...

—Psalm 23:4

With each passing of one we love, a journey through the valley of the shadow of death looms ahead. We've walked here before in our everyday losses and dyings. We're familiar with the lonely emotions of all who traverse the valley floor—shock, bewilderment and disbelief, lament and hopelessness, anger and fear. This journey through grief will take us ... as long as it takes us. There are no shortcuts through the valley, no timetables for the passage. At times, this "valley" seems more like a narrow canyon with formidable walls above which ravens circle in silence. We must navigate through dark shadows as we walk every twist and turn of the chilling canyon floor. Sometimes the path seems to double back as we tread through the same emotions again and again in varying degrees of intensity.

Mourning the death of his wife, Joy, in *A Grief Observed*, British lay theologian C. S. Lewis states:

> Grief is like a long valley, a winding valley where any bend may reveal a totally new landscape ... [but] not every bend does. Sometimes the surprise is the opposite one; you are presented with exactly the same sort of country you thought you had left behind miles ago. That is when you wonder whether the valley isn't a circular trench. But it isn't.[1]

Dr. Nancy Copeland-Payton, a pastor, hospital chaplain, and physician who practiced medicine for twenty years, leads retreats at church centers, monasteries, and with church groups to help people explore their experiences of loss. She is author of *The Losses of Our Lives: The Sacred Gifts of Renewal in Everyday Loss* (SkyLight Paths).

From deep within the valley of death's shadow, we may hear a coyote howling once again in the dark of night. And on more than one occasion, we might find ourselves wistfully calling out our longing for what we've lost into the wind. Woven into our grieving is the deeper mourning and primal yearning for our sacred home—some of my African friends speak of death as a home-coming. As we feel our way alone through the valley of mourning, our longing for God and divine presence is acute. It seems we are very far from home.

The only way to embrace the rest of our lives is to journey completely through this valley of grief. The choice is ours. We can cling to our loved one and bury our future with him or her. Or we can unclench our hands and let this person go. Mourning is the lengthy process of accepting the finality of physical loss of our loved one, so that we can continue our journey in the land of the living. Eventually, we will come out on the far side of our grief. Towering canyon walls shorten into rounded hills that flatten further still. And the valley floor widens out into a light-filled land of acceptance. We are forever changed by our valley sojourn....

Here again is the difficult learning that something in us must die for new birth to happen. After naming and fully acknowledging what we've lost, after crying our tears of mourning for as long as it takes, we must let go of the gift we've lost to accept the gift of the next moment. The alternative is to entomb our losses and roll the burial stone firmly against the entrance, memorializing the loss of one we loved in a stone-cold tomb and closing ourselves off in their dark burial place to hang onto fading memories. This is a way of death. This is a path of burying our present life alongside our loved one in the grave.

There is a different path we can walk. After we gaze unflinchingly into the terrible depths of our loss, we name everything that's been torn from our hands and journey the valley of death's shadow to become a radically changed person. We can let the stone be rolled away from the tomb of our loss to expose our anguish to the wind of God, hovering over the deep, waiting to breathe new life into being and to create once again. This way does not bury our pain and our loss, but beckons us to accept it. The one we loved is rewoven afresh into our daily life, awakening as a life-giving presence within our self to accompany us every step of our journey.

Prayer for Trust and Healing

Peter Bankson and Deborah Sokolove

O Holy Fount of every blessing,
    your passion for diversity is clear.
    You make each leaf, each cat, each bird,
    each one of us, unique.
    We marvel at the breadth of your imagination,
    and we strive in vain to love creation
    with the grace you pour out without ceasing.
Although we find life easier
    if we can guess where you are taking us,
    we know the future is beyond our divination.
We know the love
    you poured into the world through Christ
    can overcome the pain and suffering we see around us.
We pray for trust to bring our pain and grief to you,
    believing that your love is present
    even in the uttermost places of despair.
Hear now, O Holy Healer,
    our prayers for those in need,
    and for ourselves, for we are broken, too,
    in ways we may not understand.

Peter Bankson has been a popular preacher, regular presider at worship, and spiritual guide for Seekers Church since the mid-1980s. **Deborah Sokolove** is director of the Henry Luce III Center for the Arts and Religion at Wesley Theological Seminary, where she also serves as professor of art and worship. They are coauthors of *Calling on God: Inclusive Christian Prayers for Three Years of Sundays* (SkyLight Paths).

Recognizing and Honoring Grief after Divorce

Rev. Carolyne Call

One of the consistent surprises of working with those going through divorce is how seldom they recognize what they are experiencing as grief. There is a great deal of anger, there may be feelings of betrayal and rejection, and there may be fear, anxiety, and a deep ambivalence about the future. All these may be manifestations of grief. Perhaps it is hardest to see grief when you are in the throes of anger and rage. You want the suffering and the pain to be over and you want this person out of your life.

However, while wanting a clean break is understandable, making it happen can be a bit more challenging. Divorce means the rending of a profound emotional bond that is forged through the attachment process. *Attachment* is the technical term used for human bonding, and attachment patterns and experiences begin when you are an infant. From the design of your brain to the role of hormones in your body, you are built for attachment and bonding. In marriage you come to experience the deepest expression of human bonding (outside of parenting) as you mesh your life with that of another human being. So when that enmeshment tears, you suffer the pain of grief as your individual self begins life without the one with whom you shared that life (however imperfectly). Put simply, the deeper the attachment, the greater the grief at the loss.

Besides the loss of a relationship and the attachment that defined it, you also grieve for the loss of dreams, hopes, plans, assumptions, and beliefs. In reflecting on her own divorce, Mallory called it the "death of a thousand dreams." Part of the deep investment in marriage is the belief that you can plan your life around your union. You will have children, you will have dogs,

Rev. Carolyne Call, an associate conference minister in the United Church of Christ, is author of *Spiritually Healthy Divorce: Navigating Disruption with Insight and Hope* (SkyLight Paths). She serves as a spiritual adviser for those in the process of divorce while also conducting workshops and retreats on spiritual, psychological, and moral development.

you will have a house and a yard, you will travel, you will retire together, and you will build something of significance.

However these dreams manifested themselves in your marriage, you will grieve for them in your divorce. There comes a time when new dreams grow out of the seemingly barren soil of divorce. But until that time comes, I encourage you to allow room for grief in your life and respect it.

Honoring grief can be more difficult than it appears. The process is even more challenging when those close to you do not understand why you are mourning, especially if you were treated badly at the hands of your spouse. But grief is natural and it is normal. Even though you may want to say to yourself, "Oh, get over it! I'm better off without him!" you need to recognize that your emotional system will require time for that to actually happen.

As you grieve the loss of your marriage, you should avoid the quick fix of new relationships and being redefined by a new person. Even if you move out of a marriage into another relationship, you might consider taking at least some time to be on your own. Aloneness is the ability to be comfortable with your own company. Admittedly, this can be challenging, especially when being with another intimate partner can soothe your pain and bring you a sense of comfort that is difficult to find alone. Reaching out to others and to God can bring you to new understanding of who you are, but it cannot be done out of desperation.

Finally, it may be helpful to recognize the spiral nature of grief. It rarely progresses in a straight line, and this can be frustrating and confusing to us. Time passes and you may feel upbeat and focused, and then suddenly you'll be reduced to tears or to guilt or to anger by someone's offhand comment or an object that sparks unbidden memories. Grief moves in spirals. You revisit places you have already been (such as anger toward your spouse), but now you have new perspectives and new insights. Even with the new insights, the emotional triggers can still pack a powerful punch.

Ten years after my own divorce, if I come upon a note written by my former husband tucked in the pages of a book, I may be struck by overwhelming sadness. While I recover quickly and move forward, the emotional reality of divorce has a very long shadow. Respect it. And be patient with yourself when you come upon emotional anniversaries (such as your former wedding anniversary). Respecting time goes hand in hand with recognizing grief and its power.

The Gift of Tears

Christine Valters Paintner, PhD, Obl. OSB

> It was said of [Abba Arsenius] that he had a hollow in his chest channeled out by the tears which fell from his eyes all his life while he sat at his manual work. When Abba Poemen learned that he was dead, he said weeping, "Truly you are blessed, Abba Arsenius, for you wept for yourself and this world! He who does not weep for himself here below will weep eternally hereafter; so it is impossible not to weep, either voluntarily or when compelled through suffering."
>
> —*The Sayings of the Desert Fathers*

Penthos are tears of compunction, a puncturing of the hard shell of the heart, which pierces to our core, reminding us of who we most deeply are. This "gift of tears," as they are sometimes referred to, reveals to us the misguided perfectionism, games, and manipulations we struggle to achieve, as well as the stories we tell ourselves.... Tears of compunction fall when we are awakened to realities that had been, until now, hidden beneath our conscious awareness. Often they are stirred when we deepen our contemplative practice and begin to get in touch with all the ways we have turned away from God and from ourselves. We discover something authentic and meaningful, and grief is unleashed over having ignored it for so long. Compunction comes both through God's grace and our own open-heartedness. Benedict writes in his Rule: "We must know that God regards our purity of heart and tears of compunction, not our many words."[1]

Christine Valters Paintner, PhD, Obl. OSB, a Benedictine oblate, is the online abbess of www.abbeyofhearts.com and frequently leads retreats and teaches on the wisdom of Benedictine, Celtic, and desert ways of praying. She is author of *Desert Fathers and Mothers: Early Christian Wisdom Sayings—Annotated & Explained* (SkyLight Paths), among other books.

You have likely had the experience where you were sitting in silence, and suddenly a great sadness rose up in you, and you weren't certain where it came from. Prayer works through the many layers of our defenses so that we keep discovering what feels like new levels of grief and sorrow at how far away we have allowed ourselves to wander from the heart.

John Chryssavgis writes: "Tears and weeping indicate a significant frontier in the way of the desert. They bespeak a promise. In fact, they are the only way into the heart."[2] This frontier is the boundary between our old way of seeing and believing and the wide new expansiveness into which contemplative prayer calls us. Compunction awakens us to all the ways we have been false to our own deepest self and to the profound longing that is kindled when we pay attention to the heart....

Compunction is an interior stance of grace-filled and humble self-knowledge, recognizing that you are always on the journey and have never arrived. It is the combination of two words from the Greek: *penthos* and *katanyxis*, meaning "a sudden shock, an emotion which plants deep in the soul a feeling, an attitude, or a resolution."[3]

In the ancient monastic tradition, the connection between these two was understood as a moment in a monk's life when something happened that caused the monk to become deeply aware that he had made a choice to move away from God. Compunction leads to sorrow and a gift of tears. These tears begin as an experience of reconciliation, and then move toward joy and the experience of being received back into the arms of God no matter how far the monk has strayed.

These tears come through a recognition of our own limitations. They are tears of profound honesty with ourselves about the ways we have sabotaged ourselves or hurt the ones we love. Tears of compunction are like a great cleansing river running through the heart of the desert, releasing our sorrow and grief, so that we might return to God free of encumbrance....

Tears are agents of resurrection, ushering us into new life—life lived awake and fully present. St. Ephrem writes: "Give God weeping, and increase the tears in your eyes, through your tears and his goodness the soul which has been dead will be restored."[4]

Reclaiming Riches from the Past When You Retire

Marjory Zoet Bankson

Winter arrives with no warning. Increasing darkness tightens its grip on our consciousness no matter how many lights we turn on. The temperature drops, and a freezing rain strips the trees bare. Extra layers of clothing muffle movement, and a fire beckons us inside. Winter is the season for introspection, for remembering and restoration.

In the life cycle of a new call ... we must attend to needs and wants that our professional lives have pushed underground, out of our consciousness. If this period of life is to bear fruit, we must let winter do its work on the seeds of a new beginning.

During this period, we may also feel as if we are wandering around in the desert because we do not have a clear direction. It is a churning period between ending and a new beginning, between a consuming career and a new start. Old ways cling, and we obsessively replay interactions that we might have done differently. New efforts fizzle. We may feel uncreative and out of sorts. We may feel as if we are wasting time, spinning our wheels, going nowhere. Outwardly, there is little to show for our efforts. We might as well be hibernating. Stagnation seems to have settled in for the duration. It is the interior season for the soul, urging us to slow down and turn inward to reclaim energy from the past. Unused gifts may surface. Gestation is just beginning.

When I first retired from Faith At Work, other people expected me to plunge into my basement pottery studio because for a long time I had talked about wanting to do this when I had more time. But once I had more time,

Marjory Zoet Bankson, an artist and spiritual guide, is author of *The Soulwork of Clay: A Hands-On Approach to Spirituality* and *Creative Aging: Rethinking Retirement and Non-Retirement in a Changing World* (both SkyLight Paths) and former president of Faith At Work (now called Lumunos).

I didn't do it. Instead, I found myself sorting through drawers, cleaning the basement, and washing windows—preparing the space for something new. I bought cozy casual clothes and put my suits away, joined a dream group, began to exercise again. It seemed important to reclaim my body and make space for whatever was going to emerge. What I didn't realize was that the work ahead of me was to reclaim my true self, especially the less honored parts I had buried or set aside.

Parker J. Palmer, author of *A Hidden Wholeness*, describes how easily we develop a public face that is divided from the true self (or soul) we are born with. We develop the *public face* to protect our vulnerabilities. It is shaped by our interactions with others, by what gets rewarded and reinforced by success or failure. The *true self* is mute and increasingly hidden, even from ourselves. Feelings of shyness and inadequacy are simply not allowed to surface because they contradict the public persona that we show to others. When we are split this way, we literally do not know our true selves....

Signs of True Self

The phase of reclamation often begins with some signs that our true self has something to say to us. Depression and listlessness may be suggesting that we need to tend our inner life more carefully. If we can't shake some incident or interpretation of events that seems frozen, perhaps there is a secret asking for airtime. If we are especially critical or excessively concerned about time, perhaps our ego is trying to stay in control of something our soul is wanting. These are outward signs of inward distress, the signs of a divided self. They are signs that it's time to reclaim what we may have been ignoring, or even forgotten....

Creative aging is a process, not a race or a benchmark of enlightenment. In fact, in this part of the neutral zone we will probably feel lost, lonely, and small. If we can give ourselves permission to *not* know the next step, to stay in the womb of remembrance and let the natural process of gestation occur slowly, we are more likely to birth a whole and healthy inner core. Learning to pay attention and trust our inner wisdom for guidance about the next step underscores the words of Psalm 139: "I praise you, for I am fearfully and wonderfully made" (Psalm 139:14)....

Reclamation doesn't happen overnight. It is a process of drawing energy from the past, discovering forgotten loves, and exploring deeply buried veins of precious resources that have been ignored or repressed. Digging up gifts from the past requires space and time for musing, for following intuitions and feelings to uncover yearnings that have stayed mute in the background. In the midst of a busy career, we seldom have or take the time for this kind of exploration....

Although it is important not to romanticize pain or loss, a new call can sometimes arise out of suffering—our own or our response to someone else's pain. Reclaiming the parts of ourselves that we have denied or set aside to be "successful" in the eyes of the world can indeed open our hearts to the reality of pain and suffering. When we allow that to happen, we become more fully human, more integrated as our true selves, capable of deep connection with the needs of others.

Dreaming as a Means of Spiritual Healing

Lori Joan Swick, PhD

Spirit is perfect. We can't lose it, though we can lose contact with it; we can even forget that, beyond the skin, we *are* spirit. Soul is a different matter. It's our vital essence, and it is in a body to have adventures and to grow. Spirit does not evolve, but soul surely does. Also, you can't expect soul to stay in one place. When we suffer trauma or bitter disappointment or violent shock, soul may leave the body to escape. This produces the phenomenon that psychologists call dissociation and shamans call soul loss.

—Robert Moss, *Dreaming the Soul Back Home*

For shamanic dream teacher Robert Moss, spirit is a sacred field of Ultimate Reality that permeates everything and everyone, while soul is a spiritual reality related to the body and mind of each individual person.... The soul is not confined by the embodiment of the dreamer. Moss reminds us that in Greek, the word for "soul" is *psyche*, which also means "butterfly." The soul flits in and out of the body, and when we lose our connection with it or with parts of it, we lose energy, memory, identity, personal gifts and skills, and the abilities to feel deeply and to choose and act from the heart. In all, we become lost to our life's purpose.[1] We can learn, however, to reclaim through our dreams the parts of our souls that have wandered away from us.

Lori Joan Swick, PhD, is a popular speaker and retreat leader specializing in women's spirituality and religious, mystical, and mythological topics. She is an adjunct professor of religion, mythology, and philosophy at St. Edward's University in Austin, Texas, and author of *Dreaming—The Sacred Art: Incubating, Navigating and Interpreting Sacred Dreams for Spiritual and Personal Growth* (SkyLight Paths).

Moss recognizes that what he sees as "soul loss" is regarded within the discipline of modern psychology as a state of physical or mental denial, which results from the depression we enter when we suffer loss, oppression, or physical or psychological trauma. As Freud and especially Jung claimed, because within dreams we can more easily access the areas of our consciousness where these repressed feelings are stored, by analyzing these dreams we can reclaim lost parts of ourselves and effect psychological and sometimes physical healing.

Sacred Dreamself Mapping

I have adapted this method of dream healing from a practice of dream body mapping designed by Daniel Deslauriers that I learned in a seminar I took during my doctoral studies. The practice is deeply meditational. In the seminar, Deslauriers had recorded audio directions to guide the dreamer throughout the process, which was very effective. Because I cannot replicate that experience here, I suggest you familiarize yourself with steps one through three before you begin, and then try to work through the entire process from memory to avoid having to disrupt the meditative quality of your work. Wait to read the fourth and fifth steps until after you have created your dreamself map. If you do this, you will avoid unconsciously drawing based on the interpretive steps, and your map will more accurately convey the condition of your dreamself.

1. **Draw a contour outline of your physical body.** Make this drawing life-size if possible. If you can, enlist the help of a friend to draw around the outline of your actual body. A smaller replica will suffice, but because mapping can require a lot of space and detail, make it as large as you feasibly can, and leave some blank space around the contour. Have coloring or drawing materials handy. I suggest using soft colored pencils or pastels, because they come in a wide range of colors, can be used without preparation, mixing, or blending, and can convey hard lines or soft, blurred edges—all of which may be extremely helpful in conveying the details of dream imagery. Select a dream that you felt contained a sacred healing message and read your journal entry about it. If you have not written about it in your journal, spend some time free writing about it.

2. **Meditatively visualize yourself within your sacred dream.** Reenter the mystical realm of dream consciousness through meditative breathing.... Sit in a comfortable position with your spine fully extended, or lie in the

posture in which you usually sleep. Take a deep, comfortable breath and feel it filling your whole self. Hold the breath momentarily before exhaling slowly. Repeat breathing in this manner as you meditatively reenter your dream. As you breathe, be mindful of how your breath feels as each part of your being fills and deflates. Note any areas where your energy seems especially dynamic or blocked. Keep breathing until you can physically, mentally, emotionally, and spiritually feel how you felt within the dream. Your feelings may have changed or evolved within the dream. That is fine. Concentrate on your feelings of self as they flow throughout the dream.

3. **Map your dreamself.** When you have recaptured the feeling of yourself as you were within the dream, spontaneously draw these feelings onto the map of your body contour.... Let the colors choose you, and allow yourself to create your dream image as you remember how your dream body felt. If it changed throughout your dream, draw the later senses of your dreamself right over any earlier ones.

4. **Use your dreamself map to understand the dream's sacred healing message.** When you look over your dreamself map after your meditation, you will probably be astounded to see how different parts of your body are holding your concerns and worries as well as your joys and triumphs. Thousands of messages about the state of your physical, psychological, and spiritual health may manifest themselves in thousands of different ways. Follow your instincts in interpreting your map, just as you would in interpreting your sacred dreams. Within your analysis, however, I suggest you ask yourself these questions:

   - What parts of yourself seem tight or congested, and what parts seem open and free to function normally?

   - Where does your energy reside, and from where does it seem to radiate? Does it extend beyond the confines of your embodiment?

   - Where is your soul in your map? Is in intact, scattered, or missing altogether?

   - Where is the sacred presence in this map?

   - How does your map relate to other symbols in the dream once they are amplified?

Write your answers to these questions and all your other thoughts and discoveries about your sacred dreamself map in your sacred dream journal.

5. **Honor your dreamself by attending to its needs.** If your sacred dreamself mapping indicates there might be a physical or psychological problem, seek the proper medical or psychiatric care. If it indicates you are too stressed or overworked, find a way to relax. If tension or dynamism seems localized on or near one of the body's natural chakra energy centers, check to see if any of the symptoms, fears, or strengths above seem to apply. Aided with this knowledge, you might find that regular meditation on scenes from dreams that were located within certain energy centers can work wonders. If the dream imagery was troubled, meditate on the same setting while creating a calmer, more satisfying dream sequence. Use this imagery as an intention with which to cultivate future healing dreams. Above all, trust your instincts in interpreting your dreamself image, and trust that your sacred dreams are perennially trying to heal you.

Your Unfolding Forces—
In Times of Disappointment

William Cleary

Holy Creator Spirit,
the memory of disappointments,
of "what might have been,"
brings back sorrow and bewilderment.
We are vulnerable—as you understand so well.
We are easily frayed and wounded,
and often afraid to hope for healing.
In fact, illness threatens us constantly
and saps our energies of creativity and accomplishment.
Yet, around us are your sacraments of hope
great and small:
the night sky full of creative fire, the migrating geese,
the promise-rich crocus of early spring,
the serenity of sleeping infants.
You are here, Holy Mystery, singing in the wind,
comforting us with human laughter,
coloring our life from your rainbow of possibilities
in an evolving world.
Your way is best:
it fills us with hope beyond every sadness.
May it be so.

William Cleary was a Jesuit priest for over twenty years, a filmmaker, and a composer. He is author of many books on spirituality, including *Prayers to an Evolutionary God* (SkyLight Paths). His musical *Chun Hyang Song* was performed at the Seoul Olympics.

No Holding Back

Jan Phillips

My relationship with my back changed dramatically one day when I was hit by a car, which then landed on top of me and pinned me under its burning exhaust system. I ended up with third-degree burns on my back and hip that required skin transplant surgery.

On the night before this surgery, I engaged in a ritual of thanksgiving for my body that had so narrowly escaped death and now was about to undergo yet another trauma, the harvesting of skin from one side of my back to be grafted onto the other.... "Thank you, back," I began, shifting my attention up to the most injured part of me as I called to mind all the ways my back had served me in my life. "Thank you for supporting me, for carrying me and my belongings everywhere I've moved in this world. Thank you for helping me carry others who've been too weak to carry themselves. Thank you for carrying me into the majesty of the Himalayas, into the hunger and haunting mysteries of Calcutta, into the numinous quietude of temples and monasteries and cathedrals around the world. Thank you for carrying me into the lives of people who have taught me everything I know about love and kindness and not giving up no matter what. Thank you for bearing the weight of my cameras, my guitars, my tape recorders, so I could bring music to others and bring back home the music and images of people from other places."

My litany went on, but it stayed on the surface, focusing on the back in its most literal, physical sense. It wasn't until after my surgery that I began to get a sense of the *metaphysical* aspects that were crucial to my healing....

It's been nearly two years since my accident, but I noticed recently that I was still holding remnants of that trauma in my back. It came to my attention

Jan Phillips is an award-winning photographer, writer, and national workshop leader. She is cofounder of *Syracuse Cultural Workers*, a publisher of artwork that inspires justice, diversity, and global consciousness, and is author of *Divining the Body: Reclaim the Holiness of Your Physical Self* (SkyLight Paths).

when I began this chapter and found myself frozen in front of the computer. I was afraid to go there, afraid of the images it conjured up. I had spent so much energy trying to get past it that I had never processed my way *through* it. I never expressed my terrible sadness at what my back had gone through. I never released the grief of being nearly killed, of having so much of my flesh burned away, of the awful shock it was to my back and spine, of being hit from behind by such an incredible force. I told myself how lucky I was to still be alive and tried to carry on like nothing had happened. But something huge had happened, and it called for my attention and tender love. Energy was locked up somewhere, and I had to find a way to let it go.

I made an appointment with a bioenergetics therapist who was referred by a trusted friend. When I went for the session, I explained to the therapist what had happened and asked for her help in releasing the pain. I showed her my scars, then lay down on the floor in the position I was in under the car. She asked if it would help if she touched my back, and I said yes, that would be fine. Then she asked, "What would you like to say to your back?" I started to talk to my back and my spine, to all my cells and vertebrae, to my new skin and old, crying out in sorrow for the pain and loss. "I'm so sorry this ever happened to you, so sorry for the burning, and for that terrible moment you were struck so fiercely and by surprise." As I returned in my consciousness to the moment of the accident, I thought of the massive impact of the initial hit, the hurtling through space, the crashing of my body on the ground, then the weight of the car landing on top of me, and the burning of my skin under the muffler. I relived every moment, crying my way through as I spoke with deep love to my poor little body.

When the therapist asked, "Are there any sounds associated with these feelings?" I began to moan, then whimper, then wail, and as I let out these sounds I felt an energy coming to life at the base of my spine. It felt dark and massive, but it climbed up my spine and settled in my heart, causing a fear that my heart would explode. "Breathe into your heart," she said, as I grasped at my chest and held on tight. "Breathe, breathe, breathe," she repeated, and as I breathed, the energy moved again, settling now in the middle of my fore-head. I grabbed my forehead, felt its pulsing, and tried to breathe and help it along. Within a few moments, the energy traveled upward and suddenly left through the top of my head. And I felt light and calm in its place. The old had left and made room for the new.

Whether our traumas and upsets are physical or emotional, mild or severe, they have a power that needs to be dealt with. If something happens that disturbs our balance, violates our spirits, causes us horror or heartbreak or anger, it impacts our energy in a major way and can obstruct its flow if we don't tend to it consciously, physically, and energetically. Talk therapy is good, but if we keep talking about the same old things without relief, we might be better served by going within, listening to what the body has to say about the matter. In my session with the bioenergetics therapist, I spoke to my back in my language, and she spoke right back to me in hers—a language of sensation that I could feel in every fiber of my being....

Uncovering the truths buried within our bodies grounds us to the earth, focuses our attention, hones our survival skills, and lessens our fear. When we're grounded, survival is not a concern. We know the universe is *for* us, that people enter and leave our lives for the lessons they offer. We know that everything we need comes to us if we don't stop the flow out of fear or greed. When we're grounded, we know that we have more than enough and that generosity of spirit is what sustains the flow.

Healing Light Visualization

Lie down on your bed and begin to breathe deeply from your belly. Focus your attention on your back. Visualize your spinal column as a tunnel through which energy travels, communicating important information throughout your body. This tunnel may be clogged with emotional debris and energetic blockages, but you can clear it out with the power of your imagination and the flow of your breath. Beginning with your first chakra, imagine a healing vortex of light spinning away and clearing out this tunnel that is your spine. Visualize this radiant light working its way slowly up your spine, swirling around every vertebra, and opening every chakra and meridian it comes in contact with. Your spine has twenty-six vertebrae. See if you can hold your attention on one at a time as you continue to breathe and let your energy rise from vertebra to vertebra.

Finding Healing and New Perspectives Through Prayer

Monica Furlong

Prayer, to pray, are words that are so much part of our language that we rarely examine the idea and ask what it means. The obvious meaning, the one that a child would probably give if asked to define the word *prayer*, is "talking to God" or "asking God for something." Many of us, whether we believe in God or not, find ourselves blindly asking for help when our need is great enough—it is an aspect of our helplessness in the face of illness, death, bereavement, and other painful aspects of being human. The idea of talking to God opens up a vista. It beckons us out of a purely human perspective, and invites us to try to see the world, and ourselves within it, from a different angle. "It draws God who is great into a heart which is small" said Mechthild of Magdeburg.[1] It is almost like the experience of the early astronauts, looking at earth from distant space instead of from a position on the earth itself. They found that first external vision astonishing, a source of wonder, and perhaps they experienced an impulse to reassess the human place within a much vaster context.

Mystics of all cultures have been similarly affected by a sense of wonder and vastness as they contemplated the presence of God. It is part of the human condition that we get stuck in our own local perspective.... Geographically, nationally, intellectually, and emotionally, our natural tendency seems to be provincial, chauvinistic, lacking in imagination about, and sympathy for, what we do not directly know, though we can and should struggle against this blindness. But our personal experience, our joys, our loves, our worries, our labors, and our sorrows fill our consciousness until our personal concerns can block out all else. The great religions of the world, however,

---

Monica Furlong was a British author, journalist, and activist; editor of *Women Pray: Voices Through the Ages, from Many Faiths, Cultures and Traditions*; and author of *Zen Effects: The Life of Alan Watts* (both SkyLight Paths).

have always reminded us that we need release from that cramped perspective. We need stories, festivals, Sabbaths, ceremonies, meditations to jolt us out of our pathetic narrowmindedness, our obsession with the internal village street. They remind us that we are bigger than our egos, that we belong to a larger enterprise altogether....

Prayer, then, which may take the form of meditation as well as the simpler forms of asking, or thanksgiving, or praying for others, is about a shift of consciousness, or at least an attempt at a shift of consciousness, to a new perspective. If we are less preoccupied with ourselves, we are less likely to see others as competitive egos or deadly rivals. Many religions suggest that in some sense we *are* one another. The Anglican poet John Donne famously said that we are not islands—"No man is an island"—but all human beings are "part of the main." Rabbi Shmelke of Nikolsberg said that to strike another human being is like striking ourselves—it is bound to cause us suffering.

Prayer *for* other human beings involves us in their well-being, their health and happiness, and religion has often encouraged its adherents to carry their prayer forward into practical concern—to feed the hungry and house the homeless. Late in the twentieth century and on into the twenty-first, many have started praying also for the earth and its creatures, as the threat to *its* health and survival has become ever plainer. Tribal peoples have usually had an acute awareness of the welfare of the natural world, since their survival depended very directly on the animals and plants that they hunted and gathered. In more "sophisticated" and industrialized cultures, where for generations townspeople have had little to do with the growing or gathering of food, this knowledge is returning only slowly.... If people need to be cherished, healed, and sustained, then so does the natural world, Westerners are painfully learning. Having lost the old awe and wonder in the face of nature, modern civilizations have plundered the earth, destroying habitats, poisoning waters, and hunting or fishing creatures to extinction. The only way back from this desperate situation is a new perspective, a collective turning away from the ego and its greed that all religions have taught.

So prayer is about a new perspective on the world about us, or perhaps the recovery of an earlier perspective. It is about a rediscovery of awe and wonder, of love and joy, of a transforming of grief and pain and loss, of a turning to one another and to the world in which we find ourselves.

This Season of Life

Nancy L. Bieber

While each stage or season of our lives brings changes, sometimes we don't recognize the freedoms and limitations different seasons offer. In this exercise you will look at the present and discover how it has both limited and freed you.

Limitations and Freedoms

1. Specify the season of life you are in right now. While there are broad life stages that are widely recognized (early adulthood, parenting preschoolers, retirement, etc.), you might need to be creative in describing the unique season you are in now. It could be the "newcomer in town" or the "leader who is no longer leading" phase of your life.
2. Reflect on the limitations that are built into this stage of your life. These may be in areas of responsibility, relationship (family or others), economic security, health, or energy levels.
3. Reflect on the freedoms you have in this stage of your life. Sometimes freedoms are more challenging to identify than limitations, particularly if the new freedom involves diminishment (such as the loss of a spouse). You still have the freedom to choose how you live with the loss.
4. Sometimes the same reality both limits and opens your life. Retirement or job loss can severely limit your spending but open you to a different way of living.... What aspects of this season both limit and free you?
5. As you reflect on what you have written, use it to remember your desire to live this season guided by God's wisdom and light. What would it be like to live the limitations gracefully? What would your life look like if you really embraced the freedoms offered by this season?

Nancy L. Bieber is a Quaker spiritual director, retreat leader, psychologist, and teacher and author of *Decision Making and Spiritual Discernment: The Sacred Art of Finding Your Way* (SkyLight Paths). She teaches at Lancaster Theological Seminary and is a core leader with Oasis Ministries for Spiritual Development.

Rewriting Disturbing Messages

Jim Sharon, EdD, and Ruth Sharon, MS

I magine that you are born holding a paper sign that reads, *I am lovable and capable*. Then, starting as a young child, each time you hear a negative remark or judgment about yourself, a piece of your sign gets ripped away.... As an adult you still carry the rips and tears of your childhood, and they still hurt. The emotional weight of these negative influences may be lowering your self-esteem.

In your journal, list some particularly painful or upsetting messages from your parents, teachers, peers, and others that you have internalized and considered as true. For example, your aunt would regularly bump into you and call you clumsy. For years, you thought that you indeed were clumsy or a klutz. Perhaps you have come to realize that you are actually graceful and balanced. She was the one who had trouble with spatial relations!

Complete these sentences with several of your strong childhood memories or impressions:

- I was told I was ...
- I believed I was ...
- I now regard myself as ...

How much does each of these messages still affect you? What do you tell yourself that further undermines your self-esteem? For each of the items that you list,

Jim Sharon, EdD, and **Ruth Sharon, MS**, are dedicated to helping people improve their well-being by seeing their lives as individuals and couples through the lens of their soul. Jim has worked as a licensed psychologist; Ruth has been a professional counselor—both serving in private practice and leading seminars and retreats for over four decades. They are coauthors of *Secrets of a Soulful Marriage: Creating and Sustaining a Loving, Sacred Relationship* (SkyLight Paths).

counter your hurt with a few statements that dispute the validity of any negative messages that you received. For example:

- "I was told I had no athletic ability, but I run five miles a day, five days a week. I'd certainly consider that an athletic achievement."

- "I was told that I would never amount to anything, but two generations of kids have graduated from my classroom. I have many boxes of letters from former students thanking me for being such a positive influence in their lives."

What Would Happen If We Laughed?

Rev. Susan Sparks

For thousands of years, arks have been an archetype of protection and safety. The book of Genesis tells the story of six-hundred-year-old Noah building a wooden boat and saving creation from God's great flood.... An ark in a different form, laughter can act as a lifeboat for those in crisis: a place of protection, a means of moving to and through grief, a vessel that can carry us above the pain, a second chance....

Moshe Cohen, founder of the American branch of Clowns Without Borders, tells a story of doing therapeutic work with children in Kosovo, a country that had been destroyed during ethnic conflict. Cohen invited these kids to pretend to be wolves howling at the moon.

"All of a sudden, I saw all these adult faces popping over the wall to see what was happening. Everyone started laughing."

Suffering is not who we *are*; it is what we are *experiencing*. Laughter is what can protect us from being defined by our pain. It holds our spirits safe while we sail treacherous waters. It's our own personal version of a gopher-wood hull, reassuring us that no matter what comes at us, even if it defeats us, it will never define us.

Tears of Laughter

It was my first funeral as newly ordained clergy. The service was being held an hour and a half from my church on the far end of Staten Island. It was pouring rain. Three strikes! The funeral was for Mary, the ninety-five-year-old

---

Rev. Susan Sparks, the only female comedian in the country with a pulpit, is senior pastor of the historic Madison Avenue Baptist Church in New York City (the first woman pastor in its 160-year history). She is author of *Laugh Your Way to Grace: Reclaiming the Spiritual Power of Humor* (SkyLight Paths).

matriarch of a large family in my congregation. A beautiful woman full of life and passion, Mary always took pride in her appearance.

When I arrived at the funeral home, I was escorted by Mary's daughter, Nancy, over to the casket to say a prayer. As we bowed our heads, I placed one hand on Nancy's shoulder, and with the other I reached into the casket. When I touched Mary's arm, I froze. It was hard with sharp edges—almost square.

"What is this?" I blurted out, pulling my hand out of the casket. (Probably not the most pastoral of responses.)

Nancy opened her eyes, looked down at Mary, and then broke out laughing. "Oh, I forgot," she said pulling out a box from within Mary's sleeve. "We slipped in a bottle of Miss Clairol hair color for Mama's journey. She always worried that they might not have her exact formula on the other side."

We laughed until we cried, and then cried until we started laughing again. That was our prayer.

Tears of laughter and tears of mourning are virtually the same. The unfortunate difference is that we learn to share our tears of joy and hide our tears of sorrow. To do so makes us feel strong, as if we are somehow beyond the pain and grieving.

Unfortunately, sometimes we get stuck in this place of no tears, a place where we don't even remember how to grieve. Humor can help break this block. Like Noah's ark, humor can transport us from one point to another: from laughter to tears, and tears back to laughter....

Humor as a Second Chance

In early 2005, I took a trip to Death Valley. Clearly, this is not everyone's first choice of vacation spots. But at this particular time and at this particular place, it was mine. A miracle was happening in the California desert. The previous winter had brought the area a few more inches of rain than normal, and in February, its otherwise bleak sand dunes and rocks were covered with tiny wildflowers. Desert gold, blazing star, poppies, verbenas, and evening primrose blanketed the landscape. I immediately bought a ticket and flew there to see this phenomenon: a place of hope and renewal, life from no life; a second chance.

As I walked through those desert blooms, I was reminded of Noah and how he must have felt when the rain stopped and the mountain tops appeared and the dove he sent to search for land returned with an olive branch. Finally ... at last ... life.

In every crisis and every place of pain, there comes a second chance, a place where we can reclaim our spirit and our power. And like the flowers in Death Valley, that point is usually marked by some tiny sign of life breaking through: a smile, a laugh, a small signal of resurrection. When we find something to smile about in a place of pain, the balance of power shifts and we reclaim control. We take life back.

The Wellspring of Life

Nancy Barrett Chickerneo, PhD

> Above all else, guard your heart, for it is
> the wellspring of life.
>
> —Proverbs 4:23 (NIV)

Think of your wellspring as a metaphor for the condition of your spirit. How clear or cloudy is it? How many layers of muck has life on this broken planet built up? How blocked are your streams of energy and creativity? No matter what the state of your wellspring is, the condition is not hopeless. Listen carefully: *If you can remember the clear, fresh wellspring you started with, you can restore it.* The path to clearing your wellspring is almost literally a "path"—any path that will take you outdoors.

In nature you have access to a part of yourself that you may have forgotten or that may have gotten lost in the stream of life. And in nature you have more access to your *memories* of being in nature. That's a valuable gift because as you are able to reaccess your childlike sensate experiences, you will be able to connect with those core qualities that make up the real you.

In the book of Job is an ancient truth that I believe we each knew as children, before we got caught up in the rush to live: "Ask the animals, and they will teach you. Ask the birds of the sky, and they will tell you" (12:7 NLT). Children are incredibly present to the moment and to their senses. They see, hear, touch, taste, and smell their environment with immediacy. By being fully immersed in nature, in your senses, you can get back to this wonder of your lively, whole self.

Nancy Barrett Chickerneo, PhD, is director of SPA Sisters: Spirit, Place, and Authentic Self, a nonprofit organization whose mission is to awaken women to their true selves through interaction with nature, creative expression, and connection with other women. A licensed clinical professional counselor, Chickerneo is also author of *Woman Spirit Awakening in Nature: Growing into the Fullness of Who You Are* (SkyLight Paths).

In SPA Sisters,[1] we help women restore their blocked wellsprings by starting with the question, "Who was I before my wellspring became blocked?" We ask each woman to recall an early memory of being outdoors, a memory that tells them something about their original senses and natural connection with the earth, something that tells them who they were before their wellspring became unclear. And, as you might guess, we ask them to go outside, to allow nature to awaken these memories.

Over and over again, I have heard women return to describe how being conscious and aware of nature helped them reaccess their childhood memories in a sensate, present-oriented way. They describe vivid scenes of exploration, surprise, delight, contentment—a natural way of being at one with the earth. And, most important, they recognize at some deep level that what was true about their child self is still true for them today. For many, this is the start of a rich spiritual journey of reclaiming their authentic self.

Finding Your Child Self in Nature

For this experience, gather what you need to be comfortable outdoors. If it's winter, bundle up with a favorite hat, scarf, and mittens; if it's summer, your outdoor venture may call for less clothing and more sunscreen. Whatever the weather is, give some thought to what would make you as comfortable as possible in the elements. Then collect your journal, crayons, pencil, and whatever else you would like to take along.

Ready? Find a place outdoors where you can be quiet and attentive to the nature around you, as well as to your thoughts. Settle yourself someplace where you can relax and become aware of your breathing. Then ease into this meditative exercise: I put myself into a contemplative mood. I look slowly, carefully, taking in what I see, one thing at a time. I listen with sensitive ears to what I hear, becoming more conscious of the many layers of sound as time passes. I take in deep breaths of air, focusing on each distinct smell I am able to sense. I become aware of how my body feels, of what is touching me.

As you pay thoughtful attention, look and listen for something in nature that attracts you. Where does your attention rest? What seems to call to you?

When you find yourself drawn to something, think about how you are connected to it. What does it say about where you are in your life right now? Take some time to enjoy and experience the moment.

Then allow yourself to become centered and think of an early recollection in nature, some experience that you had as a child that involved being outdoors, interacting with the natural world. When a memory surfaces, consider these two questions:

- What does this recollection tell me about who I was before my wellspring became unclear?
- What is the contrast between my childhood memory and where I am right now in my life?

Many women find it helpful to write a description of their memories in their journals, with as much detail as they can remember. This is an excellent way to capture the alive sense of how you experienced the world as a child. Don't try to polish your writing; keep your words as close to your natural childlike state as possible.

Then take some time to reflect on how you feel about this memory. Use meditation (just being in the moment, aware of your senses), art, journal writing, poetry, movement—however you feel moved to respond.

When you are ready to return to your everyday life, take a moment to give thanks for the inner beauty you were born with.

Change for the Sake of Transformation

Karyn D. Kedar

I wonder what it feels like when a snake sheds its skin. Does it hurt, like ripping a bandage from your skin? Does it feel light and clean, like the first haircut of the summer? Is there a sense of sadness and loss, or does the snake feel oddly free of old and familiar constraints?

What does it feel like when that snake forms a new skin? Does it prickle and sting? Does it itch like the healing of a wound? Is there a sense of awe at the newness of it all, or fear that what is new will not be as comfortable as what is old?

What does it feel like during those moments in between? Is that ever-so-thin layer between death and rebirth raw, tender, or numb?

These are, I believe, the sensations experienced during a shift of consciousness. It is not a simple thing to shed the beliefs, assumptions, and perceptions that we hold as tightly as skin to the soul. Yet we must shed them if we are to change in a fundamental way. It is not simple, because our very identity is based on those assumptions. It is not simple, because our beliefs have served us for a lifetime. It is not simple, because to shed a skin, to rip away our self-image, our sense of truth, is terrifying. It is not simple, because we are invested in the way things are. It simply is not simple. We feel like a snake who first sheds its skin, then is skinless, then forms a new one.

Ralph Waldo Emerson writes in his essay "Self-Reliance," "A foolish consistency is the hobgoblin of little minds.... With consistency a great soul has simply nothing to do. He may as well concern himself with his shadow on the wall. Speak what you think now in hard words and to-morrow speak

---

Karyn D. Kedar is senior rabbi at Congregation B'nai Jehoshua Beth Elohim in the Chicago area and the inspiring author of *Our Dance with God: Finding Prayer, Perspective and Meaning in the Stories of Our Lives* and *God Whispers: Stories of the Soul, Lessons of the Heart* (both Jewish Lights).

what to-morrow thinks in hard words again, though it contradict every thing you said to-day."[1]

Consistency, complacency, and compliance with old ideas nullify any sense that change is essential. They lull us into a sense of stagnation, and we then believe that if it has always been this way, it will always be this way.

The spiritual path is never straight. Rather, we travel it like the sailor who, in order to move forward, tacks from one point to another. At times we find ourselves zigzagging, thinking that we must always move forward, precisely and concisely. We fail to recognize that the crooked path is indeed a path, though it could make you dizzy. As we travel this path, we perpetually change our vantage point. We see things, including ourselves, from a different angle, for the points of reference are forever shifting. Moving along on our spiritual journey, we are asked to examine all that is previously thought to be true.

We cannot change without experiencing change. We cannot grow without growing. We cannot rise to the next level of understanding without leaving the level that has been our perch for so long. So why do we resist change all the time when it is a basic fact of life?

To change we must simply live, but to experience transformation we must undergo a sort of collapse, or a stripping of what we thought to be true....

I have been called to shed a skin many times—to change a perspective, an internal barrier that may once have protected me but now serves as a block to growth. I have been called to peel away a persona that simply does not fit the evolving truth of who I am. I have been called not once or even twice, but many times to reconsider what I believe to be true, to strip away assumptions, to form a new skin, born of the raw materials of the old one, but somehow different. I have been called to get out of my way and allow newness and grandeur to emerge. All this and more is the nature of change that becomes transformative. It is the difference between what changes as a matter of course, like the flow in a stream, which knows only perpetual motion, and a moment of redemptive transformation.

I yearn to be different from the center out, to re-create myself somehow, over and over again, from the raw materials of my soul. I ask only to be who I was created to be, each time closer and wiser and better and nearer to the Source of all things.

Creator of the universe, push me, pull me, strip me of what is no longer of service. And as You do, use me, as I unfold like a miracle before my very eyes.

Reorient

Finding Yourself in an Upside-Down World

Sure, it's safer to keep both feet on the ground, but it's even safer to crawl. Pushing past fear is the only way to stand tall or fly.

—Edith R. Brotman

Rather than despise himself as dust and ash, Job finds comfort in being dust and ash, knowing that dust and ash are the very stuff of divine creation and creativity. Job isn't made small by God's revelation of the enormity and wildness of the universe, he is made large through the realization that he too is this enormity and wildness.

—Rami Shapiro

Your world will never be the same again. No matter what you've lost, the grief has likely changed you for good. And somehow in the midst of sorrow, you must begin to remap the world, to reorient to a landscape that has changed dramatically—whether through the loss of a loved one or job or physical ability or identity.

Through your loss, you may have begun to question your understanding of yourself, how the world works, or the existence or power of any kind of Divine Spirit. There are no answers here, but there are wise companions and assurances that, though coming to terms with your new reality will be difficult, it is also very possible—and worthwhile.

The contributors to this section acknowledge that pain and fear will inevitably accompany you as you peer out into this new world. They gently coax you to take a few steps outside anyway, to consider what has changed, to begin assembling an idea of the new terrain of your life.

Hope in Spite of Uncertainty

Marica Ford

In an insightful column expressing outrage at Americans' lack of outrage over the news that the government has been tracking our phone calls, *Washington Post* writer Eugene Robinson offered up this wonderful visual analysis of what ails us as a nation:

> If a psychiatrist were to put the nation on the couch, the shrink's notes would read something like this: "Patient feels vulnerable to attack; cannot remember having experienced similar feeling before. Patient accustomed to being in control; now feels buffeted by outside forces beyond grasp. Patient believes livelihood and prosperity being usurped by others (repeatedly mentions China). Patient seeks scapegoats for personal failings (immigrants, Muslims, civil libertarians). Patient is by far most powerful nation in world, yet feels powerless. Patient is full of unfocused anger."[1]

We do live in a time of uncertainty, don't we? On September 10, 2001, we were the most powerful nation in the world, and we knew it. A day later, we faced the reality that we could be taken down. Despite the rhetoric from politicians and leaders who have trumpeted America's greatness ever since 9/11, many of us are not so sure anymore about our greatness. If we're so great, how could one terrorist group cause so much devastation to our country and so much damage to our collective psyche? If we're so great, how come so many manufacturers have fled to other countries, and how come many that remain can't produce a quality product? If we're so great, why can't we get the rest of the world to like us?

As we lie on the couch waiting for the psychiatrist, who we're convinced is busy with far more important patients, we wonder: "Am I paranoid, or are

Marcia Ford is author of *The Sacred Art of Forgiveness: Forgiving Ourselves and Others through God's Grace* and *Finding Hope: Cultivating God's Gift of a Hopeful Spirit* (both SkyLight Paths), among many other books.

these threats, these perceptions, these fears valid?" After more intolerable waiting, we answer our own question: "Probably both." And then we ask another question: "So who needs a shrink?" We already have the answer.

We're back to square one, but at least we've been able to admit that the very real threats to our safety and security have created a cultural paranoia. The question now is: "What are we going to do about it?"

I like this thought from mind-body expert and best-selling author Dr. Bernie Siegel: "In the face of uncertainty, there's nothing wrong with hope."[2] When it comes to the real threats, the best we can do is remain vigilant and support the government's efforts—the reasonable ones, that is—to keep us safe. (Better security at airports, train and bus stations, and shipping ports is a reasonable effort, even if it inconveniences me. Probing into my phone records to discover that I called my gynecologist on June 8 at 2:26 p.m. is not reasonable.)

When it comes to our paranoia, there's plenty we can do. Here are some things I've learned about nonclinical, garden-variety paranoia (which several mental-health experts have dubbed "paranoia lite")—not that I've ever had firsthand experience with it or anything:

Paranoid people ignore color wheels. Everything's black or white— that's it. Learning to see the gray, and all those other colors, helps immensely in avoiding or overcoming paranoia. One of the best moves I've ever made was toward a "gray" perspective with regard to political parties. It keeps my anger in check, and it helps me to make wiser choices in the voting booth. Graying our perspectives also enables us to maintain a fair and reasonable attitude toward ethnic groups, regional factions, political parties, and religious persuasions.

Paranoid people make lousy Buddhists. That's because they can't get the hang of living in the moment. Learning from the past and preparing for the future are critical skills to have, but trying to live in either dimension will only make you crazy. Enjoy this moment—*this* one, right now. And then enjoy the next moment when it comes. It's awfully hard to remain fearful and threatened for very long when you live in the moment.

Paranoid people make great egomaniacs. After all, the world is out to get them, so why shouldn't they be obsessed with their very own selves? In all the volunteer work I've done, I can honestly say that I've never met a committed volunteer with a heart to serve others who gave any hint of being fearful or paranoid. When we begin to live outside our own heads and start to live in service to others, it's amazing how quickly our perspective on life changes for the better.

Paranoid people are the death of the party. They have no sense of humor. None. Everything is deadly serious. By lightening up and allowing ourselves a little amusement—even about deadly serious matters—we become increasingly aware of just how comical our rigid, intense perspective is....

Paranoid people live in tight spaces. Small world, narrow focus, limited viewpoint. What kind of life is that? Broadening our perspective on life makes room for the best antidote of all to paranoia—hope.

I say we abolish paranoia lite altogether. Let's train our minds to stop thinking and worrying about things that may not ever happen. See the gray, live in the moment, serve others, lighten up, expand our world. Not a bad prescription for living with uncertainty

Keeping Perspective

In the days following 9/11, many of us developed coping strategies, even though at the time we were oblivious to the fact that that's what we were doing. In the intervening years, I've come to appreciate some of the measures I took to keep things in perspective, which was especially critical in 2001 when my daughters were both teenagers. These are just a few practical guidelines for living with uncertainty:

- Learn all you can about the situation without becoming morbidly obsessive. Like many people, I watched television nonstop right after the attacks (I happened to be watching a morning news show when they occurred, so I was inundated with those horrific images from the moment they first aired). But within a few days, I turned the television off, took a break from the horror of it all, and

For reflection: Several years ago a scholarly book about the current challenges facing the Jesuit order was released. The content of the book is not as relevant here as is its title: *Passionate Uncertainty.* Think about that phrase.

began reading up on terrorism and Islam from reliable sources. If your uncertainty is related to a health issue or finances or any other area of your life, learn all you can about the problem and the solutions—again, from reliable sources. Sometimes what we learn can be frightening, but that knowledge can also empower us if we allow it to.

- Return to your normal routine as soon as possible. "As soon as possible" is a relative concept, of course. In the aftermath of a minor fire in our home, we were displaced for almost two months—two months filled with uncertainty about things such as what our insurance would and wouldn't cover, which is never as clear-cut as it should be; what needed to be done to the house, and when and how it would get done; how much danger we had been exposed to by inhaling toxins right after the fire. Six months later, we're still not back to normal. We've returned to our usual routines, even though that delays restoring our house to its former condition.

- Talk things out, but avoid unhealthy disagreements and attitudes. No matter how legitimate your anxiety over the war in Iraq may be, digging your heels in and engaging in pointless debates with those who disagree with you will only increase your anxiety level. Be patient and gracious with those who try to fix you and your situation; some people don't under-stand that when you're expressing your feelings, all you want is a listening ear, not a prescription. If you tell a friend that you've just been diagnosed with diabetes, and he launches into a detailed description of the perfect diet and treatment plan that he just knows will work for you, take a deep breath, remind yourself that he means well, take another deep breath, and ask God for a triple dose of patience.

- I know you don't want to hear this, because I never like to hear it either, but it really is important to eat right and stay active in times of high anxiety. Living and working from a makeshift office in a hotel room with nothing more than a refrigerator and microwave wrought havoc on my dietary health, but I ran around handling so many fire-related chores that I managed to compensate for the intake of restaurant and fast food (which made me gag after a while). The "running around" was fairly stressful and hardly qualifies as exercise, but you take what you can get sometimes. Anyway, the right food and the right level of activity really do help decrease our anxiety.

Cherish Each Day

Translated and Annotated by Rami Shapiro

Just as none can know
the way of the wind,
nor predict the life
of one as yet unborn,
so you cannot fathom the way of reality.

Nevertheless, plant seed in the morning,
and do not let your hands be idle in the evening.
There is no way to know
which of your efforts
—this one or that one—
will succeed,
and perhaps both may turn out for the good!

Light is sweet,
and it is good that the eyes see the sun,

so cherish each day
no matter how many you have;
and yet know that days of darkness, too, will be many.
For all that arises is fated to fall.

Let the young rejoice in their youth
and follow their heart's desires,
pursuing all that the eye sees;
but know that every choice has its consequence,
and reality will call you to account.

Rami Shapiro, a renowned teacher of spirituality across faith traditions and a noted theologian, is the award-winning author of *The Sacred Art of Lovingkindness: Preparing to Practice* and *Ecclesiastes: Annotated & Explained* (both SkyLight Paths), among many other books.

> Banish worry from your heart,
> and do not mortify your flesh,
> for the brightness of youth
> and the darkness of age
> are both empty and impermanent.
>
> —Ecclesiastes 11:5–10

Just as there is no perfect moment, there is no perfect knowing, no certainty. To remain inactive until you are certain of the result is to do nothing at all. So accept uncertainty, and do what you can when you can....

The ceaseless emptying of life and the uncertainty it generates is no cause for despair. There is morning—enjoy it! There is evening—enjoy that as well. While there may be nothing new under the sun, still each moment is fresh. Only the curious live without fear, taking pleasure in each day's unfolding.

Yet do not cling to light or freshness, for dark days—days of suffering, loss, and depression—too will be many. There is no escaping the rising and falling of things, the coming and going of moments. Enjoy what there is while it is, and let it pass when the time to pass comes due.

Wisdom should not make you old before your time. Knowing that everything is in the process of emptying—that nothing is permanent, certain, and secure—should not leave you paralyzed. On the contrary, live always in sync with the moment.... Do not despair over past choices or the consequences they set in motion. There is nothing you can do to avoid the moments to come. So don't worry about the next moment, and seek only to engage this moment wisely and well.

Accepting the Life That Awaits You

Rev. Jane E. Vennard

Think back to when you were a teenager or young adult and your life stretched before you. Most likely you had ideas of where you were heading and held pictures in your heart of what your life would be like. Maybe you imagined a life of adventure or marriage and a family. You might have had a certain job or career in mind—the military, medicine, teaching, or construction. You may have made plans to make your dreams come true, such as more education or ways to find the perfect mate. You probably began to follow these plans in pursuit of your dreams. Are you now living the life you planned?

When I ask this question of adults in the second half of life, the answer is almost always no. Some are deeply disappointed that their lives didn't turn out as planned, and others rejoice in the life they are living. As one woman said with glee, "I couldn't have imagined this life, let alone planned it. It is pure gift!"

Rejoicing in the life you have does not mean that there has not been pain and loss. Death, divorce, illness, job loss, bankruptcy, and accidents often interrupt our plans and cause our dreams to die. However, pleasant surprises can also cause a change in plans if we are willing to entertain them—such as an invitation to travel, a proposal of marriage, or a job offer outside your chosen career. How do the losses and surprises that are common in all our lives lead some to deep disappointment and others to lives more fully lived?

The answer is not to stop planning. There is nothing inherently wrong with setting goals and making lists of how to proceed. The problem comes when we become attached to our plans and get upset, angry, or depressed when the plans don't work out. I like to plan as much as the next person, maybe more.

Rev. Jane E. Vennard, a popular teacher on prayer and spiritual practice, is ordained in the United Church of Christ to a ministry of teaching and spiritual direction. She is author of *Fully Awake and Truly Alive: Spiritual Practices to Nurture Your Soul* and *Teaching—The Sacred Art: The Joy of Opening Minds and Hearts* (both SkyLight Paths).

I love planning trips—airline schedules, what to take, where to eat. As I finish reading one book, I plan what to read next. I enjoy planning celebrations for my family and friends, and I am an inveterate list maker. I have been learning to hold these plans lightly and have discovered that the easier I am with the small disappointments, the more prepared I will be for the next inevitable major interruption. So I practice letting go in ordinary situations.

When the book I had planned to read is not available, can I let go and find another or go without a book for a while? When the family celebration must be cancelled due to illness, can I simply be sad and let it go? When the route I planned to travel is closed by construction, can I let go of my irritation and find another way? Might I even discover that these changes in plans hold new possibilities? Life becomes full and exciting when we learn the rhythm of planning and letting go.

For reflection: How do you respond when your plans are stymied? If you pay attention, I imagine you will have a chance to answer that question today!

Even when people's lives are tragically interrupted and plans are turned upside down, it seems that the ability to move on is grounded in a willingness to let go of what was and embrace what is and what will be. In the most difficult situations, such as the birth of a special-needs child, the sudden early death of a spouse, or the collapse of a business, some people are able to let go—not without profound grief and disappointment, but with grace and trust in what will follow.

A friend told me of her nephew who at the age of forty-five is retiring from the navy. "How exciting," I responded. "The whole second half of life before him!" "He's not seeing it that way," she said. "From his college days of ROTC, his commission, and further education, he's had his heart set on regular promotions so that some day he would retire as an admiral. He was passed over the last time, and in the military at his age it is either 'up or out.'" Everything in this man's life has gone according to plan. And now he is faced with a major loss. He will not have the life he imagined. Will he sink into despair and depression, or find the courage to see this as an opportunity to take his life in a new direction? I wonder if the key to which way he will go will be his ability to trust—trust in a reality that is unfolding toward healing and wholeness.

If we look back over our lives to those moments in time when our careful plans were mangled by circumstances, we may see the new possibilities that have grown from them. When a friend of mine was fired from her prestigious job, she felt her life was over. Her self-esteem plummeted, she wondered how she would support herself, and her natural hopefulness turned to despair. She sought help, knowing she could not travel this journey alone. She began to recognize the need for patience and the uselessness of urgent striving. She remembered the times in her life and the lives of family and friends when the greatest loss contained a gift. Time passed (not as quickly as she would have liked), new opportunities presented themselves, and with new confidence her hope was restored. Five years later she feels she is now living the life that was waiting for her.

Trust and surrender seem to be at the heart of the spiritual practice of letting go. The paradox is that we cannot experience trust or surrender unless we are willing to let go in the small everyday experiences and in the larger, more life-shattering events. As much as we would like to practice trust first and plan for periods of surrender, the process does not work in that linear fashion. We must learn by letting go....

For reflection: When faced with the need to let go of your life plan, how have you responded? What have you learned?

Beginning to Let Go

Although the trapeze artist lets go of everything at once, that is not the way in most of our ordinary lives. In fact, it is probably wise to proceed gradually, letting go of our grip gently, softly. Where do you need to begin? Letting go of your stuff? Fasting from habits and behaviors to create empty space in which the spirit can move?

At the heart of this practice, as in every other practice, is the willingness to pay attention to your inner and outer worlds. If you do not pay attention, you will continue to hold on to what you have always held close....

Spend some time looking back and then forward. Courage is necessary to look at these issues, to accept what you see, and then to transform old patterns of holding on to a new willingness to let go.

To remind yourself of the power of letting go, practice tightening your fists and gently opening your fingers wide, closing and opening, closing and opening. Do this anywhere and anytime. The wisdom of your body will guide you to the next step in the practice of letting go, freeing you for a life not yet imagined.

Discovering God in the Midst of Evil

Tom Stella

The experience of life's trials and tragedies brings some people to believe in God as a Supreme Being, for it is in these situations that we can feel the need for a relationship with an entity we imagine to be more powerful than ourselves. That was the case for a woman I encountered in the hospital not long ago. Sheila was in her midforties and was in constant and intense pain as she faced serious back surgery. She told me about her concern for her son, a drug addict who could not hold a job; her daughter, who had a penchant for abusive relationships; and her alcoholic ex-husband, who had left her years ago but continued to disrupt her life with his angry outbursts and constant pleas for financial assistance. I was amazed at how upbeat Sheila was, despite her circumstances, and when I asked how she managed to maintain such a positive attitude, she replied that her situation had brought her to her knees. She said that she used to be angry at God for not sparing her the hardships she experienced, so she had turned away from God and religion years ago. But now, out of a sense of desperation, Sheila had begun praying to God and felt that doing so was helping her to cope. The saying "There are no atheists in foxholes" can apply to everyday life as well as to war.

There are many people who do not feel the comfort of God's presence in their darkness, as Sheila did. For some, God is a source of punishment. But rather than blaming God for the events that bring them suffering, they blame themselves. They think that if they had been better people, the tragedy they experienced would not have occurred. It is not uncommon to hear someone say, in the midst of difficult times, that they think God is punishing them for wrongs they had done or are now doing.

Tom Stella is a hospice chaplain, retreat facilitator, former Catholic priest, and a cofounder and director of Soul Link, a nonprofit organization whose mission is to bring spiritual seekers together. He is also author of *Finding God Beyond Religion: A Guide for Skeptics, Agnostics & Unorthodox Believers Inside & Outside the Church* (SkyLight Paths).

But people often turn away from God when their lives take a "wrong turn," for their understanding of God as loving, fair, and in charge is undermined by the evils they experience. I see this phenomenon as tragic and unnecessary, an evil in its own right. I see it as the fault of churches whose failure to educate their members beyond the images and stories that were appropriate in their childhoods has left these people without a theology that could serve them as adults. Such stories portray God as one who protects from harm those who are good and punishes all who are not. A better image, a story closer to the truth, would present God as an incarnate presence who, like a faithful and loving spouse, parent, or partner, accompanies us in life for better or for worse, in sickness and in health, through death and beyond....

I have seen the pain in the eyes of parents as they stand by helpless at the bedside of their hospitalized child. They may feel responsible that their son or daughter is ill, for prevention and protection are deeply embedded instincts in every good parent. But the reality is that by their loving, compassionate, and helpless-to-help presence, parents give witness to the abiding truth that God is one with us through thick and thin.

Theodicy is the defense of God's goodness and omnipotence in the face of evil. An apology of sorts, theodicy attempts to prove what has come into question, to make a case for God's benevolence despite evidence to the contrary. But when we realize that the problem of evil is a problem with our concept of God, theodicy becomes irrelevant. What is needed instead is a theology that allows God to exist *in the midst of evil.* Episcopal priest and theologian Robert Farrar Capon addresses this point:

> If God seems to be in no hurry to make the problem of evil go away, maybe we shouldn't be either. Maybe our compulsion to wash God's hands for him is a service he doesn't appreciate. Maybe—all theodicies and nearly all theologians to the contrary—*evil is where we meet God....* Maybe—just maybe—if we ever solved the problem, we'd have talked ourselves out of a lover.[1]

In dealing with the problem of evil Capon is not interested in its origin or in the fact that evil calls God's presumed goodness and power into question. Rather, his concern—and mine—is that we not allow the reality of evil to blind us to the loving Presence present in and with us in our suffering.

Why? Perennial Wisdom on a Perennial Question

Rami Shapiro

Job and the Question *Why?*

In the book of Job, the protagonist, Job himself, demands to know why he suffers, why his children died, why his business and his health have failed. His friends come to comfort him, but after a week of wise silence, sharing only their presence and his grief, they fall into the trap of answering the question *Why?* While each of Job's friends puts his own spin on the answer, their answers are basically the same: Job suffers because there is a flaw in Job's character. Job is being punished, and unless and until Job admits his sins, God will continue to punish him. If Job would only repent, God would then forgive Job his failings and restore his fortune, family, and health.

To his credit, Job will have none of it. He is innocent, and his suffering is undeserved. He demands that God explain the *why* of life's tragedies. Job's plight is universal, and his demand of God no less so. We all want to know why things are the way they are, and we all imagine that only God can answer this for us.

What Job doesn't know, but the reader does, is this: Job is simply collateral damage in a wager God made with Satan. During one of the periodic meetings between God and the angelic host, Satan reports on the doings of humanity on earth, and God brags about Job and Job's love for God. Sensing a need that can be exploited, Satan suggests to God that Job's love for God is contingent on God blessing Job with health, wealth, and a great family. To test this devilish notion, God empowers Satan to take away all Job has that God might at last know whether Job loves God or merely loves what God does for him.

Rami Shapiro, a renowned teacher of spirituality across faith traditions and a noted theologian, is the award-winning author of *The Sacred Art of Lovingkindness: Preparing to Practice* and *Perennial Wisdom for the Spiritually Independent: Sacred Teachings—Annotated & Explained* (both SkyLight Paths), among many other books.

While Job and his friends argue about sin and its connection to punishment, the reader of the book of Job knows that this is irrelevant to the truth: Job is being tortured (and his servants and children murdered) just to see whether Job will, as his wife urges him to do, curse God and die (Job 2:9). Job refuses both to confess to sins he didn't commit and to curse a God he doesn't blame, and he clings mightily to the hope that God will appear and make known to Job just why it is that he and by extension all the innocent suffer.

When God appears, however, the fact of God's satanic wager is dropped in favor of something far more profound. Rather than simply admit that Job suffers as a result of God's self-doubt regarding Job's love for God, God reveals to Job the fundamental wildness of reality that renders mute all questions of why things are the way they are.

God doesn't fall into the trap of answering Job's question. Rather, God shows Job the absurdity of even asking such a question. The liberation that Job seeks, the book of Job seems to be saying, isn't found in answering the question *Why?* but in dropping it altogether.

God, as I read the book of Job, seems to be saying to Job: "Look, the universe is wild and chaotic and wonderful and terrifying all at the same time. You can't pick and choose what happens to you, and in time all of it will happen to you: good and bad, blessing and curse, joy and sorrow. That's the way it is. Your task isn't to erase or avoid suffering, but to embrace it and make the most of it. The key to living well in the madness of reality is radical acceptance, not control and avoidance."

I think Job gets this and, in so doing, comes to a realization that is profoundly comforting. Unfortunately, most English translations of Job seem to miss this and end the book of Job with Job despising himself as nothing but dust and ash, as if God's aim was to reduce Job to a meaningless blip on the cosmic screen of life, when in fact the Hebrew suggests something so much greater.

Rather than despise himself as dust and ash, Job finds comfort in being dust and ash (Job 30:19), knowing that dust and ash are the very stuff of divine creation and creativity. Job isn't made small by God's revelation of the enormity and wildness of the universe, he is made large through the realization that he too is this enormity and wildness.

Job's comfort at the end is in his mortality. The physical body is acknowledged as dust, the personal drama as delusion. It is as if the world we perceive through our senses, that whole gorgeous and terrible pageant, are the breath-thin surface of a bubble, and everything else, inside and outside, is pure radiance. Both suffering and joy come then like a brief reflection, and death like a pin.[1]

What *is* is what matters, not why it is. Once you know who you are, where you came from, where you are going, and how you are to live, the question of why is beside the point. Yet the question never seems to go away....

Suffering and Perennial Wisdom

For some people it always comes back to punishment and eternal damnation, but perennial wisdom doesn't posit such a God. Rather, it teaches that God is all, and being all means including everything and its opposite. To imagine that God could create a world without suffering is to imagine God could create a world with fronts and no backs, with ups and no downs, with ins and no outs. It can't be done because joy and suffering, no less than fronts and backs, go together. But this has nothing to do with God rewarding some and punishing others.

Everything goes with everything else. To have anything is to have everything. Hence the world cannot be other than it is, because there is nothing other for it to be.

Please don't confuse this view with that of the eighteenth-century German philosopher Gottfried Leibniz, who argued that this world is the best of all possible worlds. According to Leibniz, there are multiple options to any given situation, and God chooses the option that is most beneficial at the moment. So this world isn't the best world, but the best of all options available.

The perennial wisdom view isn't that this world is the best option God has, but that this world is the only option God has. Just as it is the nature of a sun to shine, so it is the nature of God to manifest the universe. This is what it is to be a sun; a sun that fails to shine isn't a sun but a collapsed star or black hole. This is what it is to be God; a God who fails to manifest in all as all isn't God.

This answer rarely satisfies. But from the perspective of perennial wisdom there is no other answer. God is not outside the world fashioning it to our benefit; God is the world manifesting the dynamic polarity of God in the seeming opposites that define human experience. Where most people imagine a God who could erase evil but chooses not to, the nondualist understands God as that greater unity embracing and transcending good and evil. Where those who imagine a good God have to explain why God allows for evil, the nondualist realizes Isaiah's God who creates light and dark, good and evil (Isaiah 45:7), and cannot do otherwise. In short, the world is the way it is because God is the way God is....

> Nothing can happen to a man or woman
> which is not according to the nature of a human being,
> nor to an ox which is not according to the nature of an ox,
> nor to a vine which is not according to the nature of a vine,
> nor to a stone which is not proper to a stone.
> If then there happens to each thing
> both what is usual and natural,
> why should you complain?
> For the common nature brings nothing
> which may not be borne by you.[2]
>
> —Marcus Aurelius

Nothing can happen that is not aligned with the nature of those involved in the happening. But, again, this does not mean that what happens should happen, ought to happen, or in some way furthers a plan that only a god knows.

When we say, "God works in mysterious ways," we are merely saying that we don't know why things happen as they do. When we say we don't know why things happen as they do, we are merely saying that things could happen other than they do. But can they? If they could, why don't they?

Things happen the way they happen because at the moment of their happening no other happening is possible. Take something as seemingly random as playing the lottery. You buy a ticket and wait for the numbers to be generated. Could those numbers be any number? Only before they are generated. But before they were generated there was no number at all. So in what way could it be different if it doesn't yet exist? When it does exist, it exists as it is and cannot be other than it is. You can call this randomness or chance, but the label adds nothing to the reality.

The simple fact is this: things happen. They happen because of causes over which you have little if any control. If there is any answer to the question *Why?* it is simply this: Because it cannot be other than it is.

Losing Security, Beliefs, Identity

Dr. Nancy Copeland-Payton

Losing the Illusion of Security

Parents and teachers train us to protect ourselves, to be prudent, and to build safeguards into our lives. But many religious traditions—and life itself—teach us just the opposite: We need to be open and vulnerable, to trust in something other than ourselves. No matter how much planning we do, we are not in control.

A window is forced open and our house is burglarized. Our friend is mugged in the city, a little girl disappears while walking to school, another inner-city shooting is on the newspaper's front page. Around the globe, gunshots ring out, land mines explode, and bombs are dropped in acts of piracy, terrorism, and war.

Hackers steal our identity, a virus crashes our hard drive, unwanted phone calls and text messages invade our privacy. National and global economies ebb and flow and crash as we watch our life savings hemorrhage. At work, we are downsized and told to clean out our office.

Volcanoes spew ash skyward and bubble up molten lava. Green skies warn of tornados that rip through towns, while hurricanes, tsunamis, and floods drench everyday lives. Fires roar through buildings and forests, earthquakes shake homes into rubble, and drought silently steals life as babies and children cry from hunger.

Life is obscenely exposed as a ridge walk where terrain plummets dizzily downward on either side. All our moats, barrier walls, and safeguards can be

Dr. Nancy Copeland-Payton, a pastor, hospital chaplain, and physician who practiced medicine for twenty years, leads retreats at church centers, monasteries, and with church groups to help people explore their experiences of loss. She is author of *The Losses of Our Lives: The Sacred Gifts of Renewal in Everyday Loss* (SkyLight Paths).

breached. We are not invulnerable. Eruptions of both creation and human-kind can harm, even kill us, and those we dearly love.

Our illusion of control is shattered. Reality's undertow pulls us under the surface of the delusion of human-made security. If we can neither control life's explosions nor guarantee safety from them, how do we live day to day? If our fantasy of a protected life rests on quicksand, upon what beliefs and understandings can we ground our lives?

We wrestle with pivotal questions. Easy answers and simple platitudes do not work in the maelstroms of real life. As we confront the loss of our notions of control and physical security, our deepest beliefs are challenged.

Losing Beliefs and Identity

Early in life, firm beliefs ground us. Certain principles and values form us and guide us through myriad decisions and actions. Clear ideals provide meaning and purpose and give us identity. Rock-solid faith in the tradition in which we worship tethers us tightly. Our fervent beliefs anchor us in a world of shifting sand and flowing water.

But a day may unexpectedly dawn when the moorings of our convictions slip. We go from confident walking propelled by our beliefs to blind groping in the dark or even to paralyzed immobility. It can happen gradually over time. Life experiences repeatedly crash against our certainty and undermine our beliefs until they collapse.

Or it can happen all of a sudden, like a hand on the light switch. One moment we live guided by the brilliant incandescence of moral values, ideals, or faith. Then—click. What we believed and hoped is extinguished, replaced by an impenetrable blackness that appears even darker to our unaccustomed eyes.

Ideals may shatter when we devote part of our lives to an endeavor that crumples and fails. Our sense of purpose and meaning may be destroyed when we wholeheartedly believe in a community, tradition, or country revealed to be far less noble than we had thought. Surface-deep faith is ripped open when our loved one skids off into eternity on a lonely stretch of slick road, when we hear a dreaded diagnosis in our doctor's office, or when the phone rings at home and a hospital chaplain asks us to come to the emergency department immediately.

Beliefs and ideals are intangible, yet they form the spine of our lives. They grant us significance and identity, sustenance and vision beyond our own narrow horizons. When convictions are dashed against rock-hard life and disintegrate into pieces, we are left bereft of knowing who we are and why we get up each day.

Yet journeys guided by beliefs also traverse through fall and winter seasons. We walk the ever-present terrain of loss and death in our ideals, values, and faith. And we can emerge changed people in a landscape of new gift and mature growth....

Losing Faith

Throughout my faith journey—and probably yours, too—there have been many questions and many losses. There have been multiple times to let go to receive new gifts. Life continually challenges past answers that we either formulate or are taught, that we cling to until one of life's tsunamis breaks them into pieces and sweeps them away. Pain and suffering confront faith and contest easy answers. We let go of well-worked formulas and clichés that fall apart in the face of real life, that address neither the complexity of life nor the depth of suffering. Letting go, we learn to humbly wait for the God who is, the God without a name who is only known as "I am," who refuses to be contained inside human-made boxes. The continuing loss of easy faith, faith filled with certainty and woefully inadequate conceptions of God, is the price of encounter with the God of mystery.

Losing God in the Dark

Thomas sits across from me in this sacred, spiritual direction space in time.

> This is different. There is no life crisis that wipes out my platitudes of faith. This is more like a slow-motion sunset, where the sky's light slowly turns dark blue, then purple, then indigo, then pink. I look up and I'm startled by the darkening sky of my faith world. When did this happen? When did it become night? How long have I not been able to see?
>
> I've navigated my share of life crises. As a priest, I've accompanied countless others through their difficult places. But now, inexplicably, without any discernible cause, my faith is like the sun that has reached the western end of its arc in the sky ... and set.
>
> I am alone, in the dark. The God I used to "know" has disappeared. The ways I used to name God no longer work. Prayer is dust-dry, lifeless. I wonder why I even try. Scripture words, once so vital and

nourishing, no longer speak. I'm bereft, living under a pall of disturbing silence with no image, no sense of God. Church is a struggle. Whatever does it all mean? The way I used to believe is no longer valid—doctrine doesn't mean anything. There are no answers.

This slow slide into darkness is deeply disorienting. Sitting alone in the silence of this spiritual night, our hands cannot grasp or clutch anything. Our mind cannot create human-made constructs in which to house God. The comfort of our "knowing" all about God or soaking up the sweet consolations of prayer does not exist here. With hands pried open of self-assuredness, we approach the mystery of God. Thankfully, we cannot see in our usual way in the dark. Years later, Thomas looks back and writes:

> There's a secret that you won't hear from most spiritual writers, in sermons, or at retreats. There will come a time when the God you thought you knew, who is proclaimed without end to be faithful, loving, and present, will leave. Really leave, not just take a brief vacation or play a quick game of hide-and-seek, but get on a bus and leave for good in a cloud of diesel exhaust. This is the stuff they don't tell you about in Sunday school....
>
> This is a heart-wrenching letting go of knowing God in a way I can name, describe, and control. These last years have been a slow, creeping blindness that inexorably leads into darkness. In the darkness there are no answers to who God is, only the reality that God is.

Thomas grows accustomed to this place of not knowing, of not having answers. With the loss of a God he can contain, perhaps even control, comes a dramatic shift in his relationship with God. He learns to live in the dark, leaving behind his expectations as he humbly shows up for prayer. As he is defined by his relationship with God, when his understanding of God changes, his self-identity in relation to God must also change. Sometimes, he's overtaken by a fearful desire to grab something concrete about God that he can keep in his back pocket to bring out whenever he needs.

> In this place of openness to God as God is, sometimes I panic. I realize I'm floating in the middle of the ocean at night. The ocean is God, and I'm floating in it. But then comes the fear that I'm sinking and will drown. I begin to thrash about and want to grasp at answers again. But

there aren't easy answers. There is just the ocean that is God, and when
I finally let go, the possibility of floating in it.

This is the ultimate letting go, losing all our favored ways to describe, contain, control, and experience God, and in the end, letting go of God.... St. John of the Cross describes the losses of this dark night as leading to sweet gift. But the gift we receive is not a return of confident knowing or past experiencing of God. Rather, as our hands are gradually opened to let go of our certainty about God and of our effort to "attain" God, we're given the gift of receiving God and awakening to an encounter with mystery. This is not the god who fits inside human constructs, about which we can speak with assured knowing. This is the ineffable God who is.

Losses in Life—
When Saddened by Failure

William Cleary

Holy Fire at the Heart of Mystery,
there are losses in life that break our hearts—
especially if we send out our affections profusely.
Losses come, failure happens,
energy dissipates and is lost,
our efforts all in vain at times.
Be near, Holy Wisdom,
and strengthen our hearts if you can,
but above all enable us to befriend
the perplexing world we have
along with all its imperfection, illusion,
and disappointment.
Persuade our hearts to accept the world as it is
and to work for our planet home's survival.
It is the life you have given us for now,
and in your promising presence
we can walk its paths responsibly and courageously.
Be with us.
Amen.

William Cleary was a Jesuit priest for over twenty years, a filmmaker, and a composer. He is author of many books on spirituality, including *Prayers to an Evolutionary God* (SkyLight Paths). His musical *Chun Hyang Song* was performed at the Seoul Olympics.

Cultivating the Strength to See Good

Dannel I. Schwartz

Emotional pain is as debilitating as physical pain. It drags us into a place without apparent escape. It is easy to be consumed by it and to wallow in the loneliness and rage that it creates. When we're in pain, we tend to see everything through its filter. Faced with catastrophe, sickness, and death, even the strongest among us can become weak. Misshapen by a moment's tragedy, we can fall victim to a disaster that lasts a lifetime.

It doesn't have to be that way. A Yiddish proverb states, "To a worm in horseradish, the whole world is horseradish." In other words, to those in pain, the whole world is filled with painful things. But if we find options to a life mired in the anger and self-pity, we can find that elusive inner joy.... To mystics, with all wisdom comes the realization that we have the power to control our reactions to the things life brings us. This is essential to stopping the pain in our lives.

Once we acquire this understanding, we can begin the process described by mystics to conquer that pain. The first step is achieving a sense of what mystics call strength, or *Gevurah*, which is the ability to take control of ourselves mentally and focus on the positive possibilities of our lives. When you feel frustration, anger, self-pity or fear, *Gevurah* helps you realize that those negative emotions are counterproductive and will not help make things right. They do not bring back a loved one or stop the spread of a disease. Instead, anxiety and panic can be overcome by forcing ourselves to be positive and hopeful.

Ancient mystics knew that controlling ourselves in moments of anger or agony is among the hardest things we can do, hence the name *Gevurah*. It

Dannel I. Schwartz, spiritual leader of Temple Shir Shalom in West Bloomfield, Michigan, is author of *Finding Joy: A Practical Spiritual Guide to Happiness* (Jewish Lights) and many articles on religion and spirituality.

requires strength. Once we can stifle the tendency to strike out at others or to retreat into self-pity during the worst times of our lives, we become the master of our grief. With the energy created by focusing on the positive pieces of our world, we can confront and gain control of our pain, rather than let it control us.

Transforming Sorrow to Joy

The second and complementary step to *Gevurah* is called grace, or *Chesed*: The ability and willingness to be kind and to do good things even when faced with the worst situations in life.

What is *Chesed*? Instead of wallowing in her sorrow, a woman who lost her child to a drunk-driving accident started an organization called Mothers Against Drunk Driving. MADD is now a major influence in shaping legislation and public awareness of the dangers of drinking and driving. That is *Chesed*. A woman in Detroit whose young son was killed in the crossfire of a gang shooting could have lashed out at the unfairness of urban life and fled with her family to safer environs. Instead, she started Save Our Sons and Daughters, a group dedicated to eradicating violence among the young. That is *Chesed*, a good, graceful thing coming from one's deepest grief.

Can *Chesed* be achieved in a more personal and private way? A man who had a reputation in business for being hardheaded and tough developed a life-threatening illness. Instead of cursing the doctors or being angry at those who were healthy, he trimmed his working hours and began volunteering for various charitable organizations. His new charm and humor delighted people. Something else happened. His family called it a miracle; his doctors couldn't explain it any better. He recovered his health. This is *Chesed*.

To the person whose losses are immeasurable, kindness may seem an inappropriate response. But because it creates a sudden, yet subtle feeling of well-being, mystics understand that it is precisely the best response to sorrow.

Mystics believed that when *Chesed* and *Gevurah* are both within the shattered heart, something more satisfying than joy develops. This harmony, or *Tiferet*, is felt when we are at one with ourselves and our world. Once we experience it, there's no escaping its lure. Once we know the pleasure of *Tiferet*, we understand that even through loss and disease we can make our lives satisfying and more loving. That supernatural sensation of harmony is so powerful, so mystical, that we want to experience it, again and again....

Perfectionist thinking is the most difficult hurdle to overcome in our efforts to achieve harmony in the face of disease or tragedy. In a perfect world, good people should never have a problem. Storybook lives should continue until the end of time. The frogs we kiss should all become princes or princesses. Intellectually, we know that this view of the world is flawed. Most of the time when we kiss a frog, it stays a frog. We understand this intellectually, but in our hearts we believe otherwise.

We all must realize that things happen in life to make us feel bad, but that they have no relationship to how we live our lives. A very wise man once said that expecting the world to treat us fairly because we are nice people is like expecting the bull not to gore us just because we're vegetarians.

We enter dangerous ground when we convince ourselves that we are victims. This feeling begins a chain of negative thinking that culminates in believing that feeling bad is the right thing to feel. We assume that our lives should mirror the perfect images in our imaginations, that we should be just like the rich and famous we see in our media. We make everything worse for ourselves by believing that we are not as good as we should be. It is not unusual for very rational people to say that they should be above disease or death, that their fine lives qualify them for preferential treatment. This belief is implied whenever people wonder, "Why did God do this to me?" or "Why is this happening to me? What did I do wrong?" These are the laments of the victim trapped in perfectionist thinking, the refrain of people who feel wronged by fate or those certain that there are others whose lives, indeed, are perfect.

To a man without substantial assets, perhaps money can make him immune to life's caprice. Or, more likely, as F. Scott Fitzgerald said, "Money doesn't make you better. It just helps you live better."

An unmarried person might assume that marital bliss will guard them against misery. Certainly, people don't feel this way because they know so many happily married couples. In truth, the happiest married people are those who were happy before marriage.

The Jewish mystics had a simple belief: Not only does perfection not exist, but pain and pleasure are both part of life. When we experience pain, the whole world seems painful. When we are happy, the world is a bed of roses; when sad, a handful of thorns. To the mystic, it is a combination of both. What is real is what we focus on. The thorns will always be on the rose's stem. Indeed, slicing the thorns off the stem shortens the life of the flower.

Jewish mystics believe, though, that we must focus our attention on the flower. Our job is not to make the world perfect or to expect perfection, because the Messiah will do this. While we wait for the Messiah, we are obligated to fix what is wrong in this life. By lessening our own pain, the world becomes a better place.

Strength and Grace: Exercises for the Soul

Monday	Write down these words: "I will not be a victim." Do not let anyone make you feel that you do not control how you act and react. Keep the paper with those words where you can see it during the day.
Tuesday	Silently repeat the words, "Be strong." Whenever you feel emotional pain, do not let it control you. You are no longer a victim.
Wednesday	Repeat the words, "I am strong enough to be kind." Write a letter or make a call to someone you care about, and tell that person how much he or she means to you.
Thursday	Repeat again, "I am strong enough to be kind." Write a letter or make a call to someone you think you may have hurt. Tell that person you are sorry, and try to win a friend.
Friday	Turn every no into a yes. Instead of criticizing what is wrong, find something that is right in everybody and in everything that you encounter.
Saturday	Write down what makes you angry. For the rest of the day, each time you face a triggering event, don't let your anger overwhelm you.
Sunday	Be kind to others for the entire day. In the evening, go to a private place and figuratively pat yourself on the back.

Opening Our Hearts to Change

Nancy L. Bieber

When we begin a discernment process and brace ourselves to make decisions, we are entering a time of change. Some things will drop away, others will rise up, and life will take unforeseen turns. Even when we carefully and thoughtfully conclude *not* to change a situation, such as turning down a job offer that would uproot our children from their schools and their friends, the process of considering it changes us internally.

We can be thoroughly unhappy with a situation and still be afraid to change it. A *familiar* unhappy situation often feels much safer than the unknown.... Sometimes we're afraid that choosing to change will alter our sense of who we are. Letting go of a sense of identity can be scary. Who am I if I'm not defined by my child's needs, by my job, or by anger at my parents? Who am I if I'm not the wallflower, the class clown, the dedicated student? Who am I if I'm not the ever-helpful friend? If we put aside those "truths" we believe about ourselves, we don't know what we'll be left with.

The old self-understanding feels safer than the unknown. All change brings loss, and we might grieve the loss of old self-limiting stories even as we begin to recognize that they have limited us. It can be hard at first to appreciate the new freedom of growing into who we can become.

Sometimes our lives feel just right and we'd like to keep things just as they are. Even so, change will still come to us. We might well be afraid of its arrival. When the last child leaves home, when a spouse dies, when the business closes, unwanted change comes. Our decision then will be how to live with what has changed. We will need the divine Guide to learn to live amid the grief....

Nancy L. Bieber is a Quaker spiritual director, retreat leader, psychologist, and teacher and author of *Decision Making and Spiritual Discernment: The Sacred Art of Finding Your Way* (SkyLight Paths). She teaches at Lancaster Theological Seminary and is a core leader with Oasis Ministries for Spiritual Development.

In the end, we have to allow change, even courageously welcome it, because we know it is the only way to satisfy our innate longing to grow. The resistance to change and the longing to grow into a better life are so balanced that sometimes it seems impossible that either side could give way. The tipping point comes when the Guide teaches us to trust just a bit more than we fear.

Releasing Fear

Fear and resistance are held not just within the mind but within the whole body, so this practice engages the whole physical self in releasing them.

1. Sit comfortably, with your eyes closed or unfocused. Notice your breathing—not changing it, simply observing it. Notice the way you've chosen to sit. Does it stress or tighten any part of your body? Adjust your position to be comfortable.

2. Be aware of how you have been carrying tension within you. Perhaps it comes from a fear that we've named in this chapter. Perhaps it is another fear or resistance that keeps you from moving forward in your life. Acknowledge your desire to release it, not to carry it anymore.

3. Take a deep breath and release your breath slowly. You may wish to repeat words of release, a mantra such as "Let go, let go" or "I am releasing ..." Taking another deep breath or so, let your body begin to relax. Perhaps your palms gently unfold and open, signaling your willingness to release fear and be open to the Spirit. Now allow relaxation to flow down your body, as you release tension in each part of your body. Notice what it feels like to release this tension.

4. Continue to repeat the mantra, noticing your quiet breathing and relaxed body. Remain quiet, allowing the breathing and the mantra to settle your spirit. Stay with this practice longer than you think you need to.

Finding Your Focal Point Through Scrapbooking

Cory Richardson-Lauve

If I asked you to name the focal point of your life, you might think "my children" or "my husband" or "my aging mother" or "my dog, Rufus." But what I really want to know is *what*, not *who*. What is the focus of your energy? When you are being a mother, is it all about nurturing? Or teaching? Or learning? Or feeling connected emotionally? All of these, perhaps, but if you look closely, you will find one thread that connects the important elements in your life. Why do you have the friends you have? Why do you nurture the relationships in your life? Why do you go or not go to a place of worship? Why do you have your particular hobbies and interests?

The focal point of my life is learning. For a while, I thought it was teaching, but after a few years I became restless. I was teaching better than ever, but I had stopped learning. It was time for me to learn something new. I longed to be challenged in new ways. This pattern runs throughout my life. Although I spend a lot of time teaching, it is, for me, a conduit to my focal point—learning.

To find our focal point means to search for purpose and meaning, and to live with that intention. In fact, I would go so far as to say this is our mission in life: to find our focal point, our essence. The rest—whether that is what swirls in our closets or refrigerators or in our minds—is secondary....

In scrapbooking, each page has the potential to return you to your focal point.... You may be looking through a narrow lens at your past, but your mind broadens those images into the fullness of life. The past becomes alive again, and you become aware: aware of yourself as a creator, aware of what

---

Cory Richardson-Lauve, an award-winning scrapbooker, designer, teacher, and artist, is author of *The Scrapbooking Journey: A Hands-On Guide to Spiritual Discovery* (SkyLight Paths).

matters to you, aware of profound connections, aware of the deeper meaning of your life....

This is the way of scrapbooking. When you scrapbook, and when you look at scrapbooks of your past, you find that you are living in a moment that connects you to a larger sense of time, a clearer glimpse of what is important. Even if it seems that your focus is merely on photographs, paper, and words, in the big-picture sense, you are connecting with your memories, with your own creativity, and, most important, with the Source of all that is—past, present, and future.

A Focusing Experience on the Scrapbook Page

1. Start by writing your responses to these questions:

   What motivates you?

   What sustains you?

   What would an observer of your life say matters the most to you?
   Try to respond in terms of a concept or an idea, not a person. Make a list of your responses. If people's names come to mind, write them down, then probe deeper.

   What is it about these relationships that keeps you focused on them?

   What do you do in these relationships that you enjoy or find satisfying?

   How do you find your truest self in the context of these relationships?
   Use verbs as much as possible in your responses. Words such as learn, pray, nurture, create, teach, lead, care, enjoy, defend, make peace, play, unite, communicate, love, protect, laugh, survive, and connect will help you identify your focus more clearly.

2. Look at your responses. Circle the word that best describes the focal point at this time in your life. There are probably several options, but narrow it down to one word to focus on for this scrapbook journal page.

3. Stop and think about your word for a few minutes. Take a few minutes to respond to each question.

   What are the ways you live out this word?

   How does it show up in your life?

   What relationships help you with it?

   How do other people experience this aspect of you?

4. Now choose one or more photographs or pictures that convey this word. (The photographs can be of other people, as long as they illustrate your word.)

   As you select your image, consider the meaning of the photo or picture. Don't just pick the most engaging picture. For example, if you are creating a page about a birthday party, and you have ten pictures from the event, ask yourself some questions. What was meaningful to you about the party? Was it the joy in the face of the guest of honor? The number of candles on the cake? The strength of the community who attended the party? The beauty of the homemade cake? The variety of gifts that were received? Pick one of these themes that spoke to you during the party and choose your pictures accordingly.

   Likewise, for this exercise, consider pictures that illustrate the verb you have chosen as your focal point. Don't just use a self-portrait; try to find pictures of you living out this verb. Take some new photographs if you need to!

5. Consider other elements you might want to add to your page: a title, a drawing, a quotation, some words from your journaling. Such supportive details can create balance and movement....

6. Consider which mediums you want to use to create your page: paint, paper, stitching, stamps, markers, stickers, digital technology. As you become more experienced as a scrapbooker, you will find that certain supplies and techniques speak to you—both in general and on specific pages. There are many supplies available. Be open, but be selective. You don't need them all....

7. Okay, now you're ready to get to the heart of this exercise: how will you emphasize your focal point? Here are some helpful techniques for creating a strong focus on the page:

   - Use contrast. Place a light focal point on a dark background. Or place a light border around a dark focal point. Lighter tones will draw the eye to that element. Use repetition. Repeating an image or a word will highlight its importance.

   - Use size. Enlarge the focal point. Or create a larger border around it to distinguish it from the others.

   - Use line. Draw attention to your focal point with horizontal or vertical lines that lead the eye toward it. You can use lines of text (such as titles), arrows, linear doodles, stripes, lines of the edges of other elements, or lines within photographs....

- Use shape. A circle will stand out among right angles. A square will stand out among natural, flowing shapes....

- Use a frame. Even a two-sided frame will help delineate the focal point.

- Use color. Color is a powerful way to direct the eye.

8. Once you have some ideas in your mind, you may want to draw a quick sketch of your page. It is not necessary to plan all the details, just to start with an intentional idea. You can add other embellishments or supporting images as you work. Creating is a process, and you might be surprised by what appears on the journey. Be open to ideas as they come. Even when you start with a rough plan, your page will evolve as you work.

9. As you work, keep returning to your main idea: the focal point. Make sure that you are emphasizing this idea throughout your design.

10. Continue working until you feel your page communicates your thoughts and feelings and visually pleases you.

11. Then take some time to reflect on your page.

Which elements did you spend the most time creating?

What does the page tell you?

What is most meaningful to you about the page?

Are you satisfied with your focal point?

12. Show your page to friends or family members. Look at their eyes.

Where do they look first?

What draws their attention?

Is it what you had intended?

What does their response tell you?

13. Give yourself some reflection time.

> Are you happy that this is the focal point of your life?
>
> If yes, how can you emphasize this focal point throughout your life?
>
> If no, what do you want to change?

Going Deeper: Options to Explore Your Focal Point Further

- Create a scrapbook page with a song or poem as a focal point. Pick words that are meaningful to you. Try to get the entire page to emphasize your message....

- Create a scrapbook page showing what the focal point of your life was when you were a child (ten years old or so). Use photographs of you or other images that resonate.

- Create a scrapbook page depicting what you want to be caring about ten years from now.

- Draw a sketch for a scrapbook page that illustrates the focal points in your life. Size the photos according to your emotional and spiritual investment in each subject. Now, sketch another layout about those focal points. This time, size the photos according to the amount of time you spend on them. Are the sketches similar? Vastly different? Which page do you want to create?

- Scrapbook a page about a recent day in your life. What was the focal point of that day? What resonated with you? How you can illustrate these gifts with photos and words?

> Either you look at the universe as a very poor creation out of which no one can make anything, or you look at your own life and your own part in the universe as infinitely rich, full of inexhaustible interest, opening out into the infinite further possibilities for study and contemplation and interest and praise. Beyond all and in all is God.
>
> —Thomas Merton

The Yoga of Courage

Edith R. Brotman, PhD, RYT-500

> Fear is the cheapest room in the house. I would
> like to see you living in better conditions.
>
> —Hafiz

Think of someone acting courageously—a person running into a burning building to save a child, a corporate whistle-blower exposing tainted food products, a political activist standing up to tyranny and corruption. In each case, bravery pushes the person beyond the place of safety, certainty, and comfort. Great acts of courage may be less dramatic, as when people make midlife career changes, travel overseas alone, or leave abusive relationships.

With these examples in mind, we can understand courage as a state of expansion. Courage expands what is possible, broadening the conception we and others hold about what can be accomplished in a given circumstance. When we are acting courageously, we step out of our comfort zone, freeing ourself from the limits imposed on us by our own self and by society.

By contrast, a life lived in fear is a smaller life. Fear is contraction, an involution of us into ourself. Living with fear imperils our spiritual journey in two regards. First, it keeps us from doing what needs to be done, seeing what needs to be seen, and learning what needs to be learned. Fear is an attachment to the status quo, no matter how awful, because it is a known entity. It's clinging to the side of the pool, to the same hopeless job or relationship, to the same patterns and habits of being. In addition, fear is the desire to drop and run, to abandon the current state of things.

In yoga, fear can either keep you from lifting your feet off the floor in Headstand or Crow Pose or make you roll up your mat and run out the door. When I am teaching a challenging pose in yoga class, I often remind my students that

Edith R. Brotman, PhD, RYT-500, an experienced educator and highly trained yoga teacher, is founder of Kavvanah/Mussar Yoga. She is author of *Mussar Yoga: Blending an Ancient Jewish Spiritual Practice with Yoga to Transform Body and Soul* (Jewish Lights).

falling is part of the process of growing. Where would we be if, as children, we weren't willing to risk a few head bonks while learning to walk or do a cartwheel (over and over)? Sure, it's safer to keep both feet on the ground, but it's even safer to crawl. Pushing past fear is the only way to stand tall or fly.

A friend of mine once asked a wise teacher how to find the courage to make big changes in her life, to confront her fears of rejection and find another man to fall in love with and marry. The teacher asked her to think about the cost—all that is being lost—by not changing. Fear of getting hurt emotionally or physically often robs us of more joy than an actual injury. In other words, the pain of loneliness can hurt more than a broken heart. A broken foot heals faster than the regret of never learning how to ski, ride a bike, or rock climb. A quotation attributed to James Neil Hollingsworth, a beatnik writer and musician, says, "Courage is not the absence of fear, but rather the judgment that something else is more important than fear."

The other impediment fear brings to our spiritual journey is its tendency to eclipse the Divine Presence and feed the illusion of separateness. Consider what Mahatma Gandhi said about the enemy (of goodness and light). Fear of others divides us and feeds our worst impulses. When we are afraid, we are defensive and prone to fall into the traps of discrimination and prejudice. Fear justifies and embellishes our suspicions and distrust of the motives of others. When we presume that someone is a threat to our well-being, we cut ourselves off from recognizing the divine spark in that person. The more fear, the less light and the darker the perspective....

Courage Versus Recklessness

Sometimes fear is legitimate and a good thing. You should probably not walk down a deserted street in the middle of the night in a crime-ridden neighborhood or go skydiving if you are prone to heart attacks. Being reckless or courting trouble are not acts of courage. Courage involves a certain element of wisdom and awareness. It involves discernment.

Likewise, courage doesn't necessarily mean taking action. Sometimes the most courageous act is not acting at all. Our usual temptation in a time of fear or uncertainty is to force certainty in an attempt to control the outcome. The image that comes to mind is soldiers at a checkpoint confronting a person who seems suspicious. Fear prompts an aggressive approach; courage might call for alert restraint.

Courage may be about surrendering expectations and allowing for uncertainty—a cancer patient trying an experimental treatment, for example. One brave friend of mine got onstage in front of a large group of his peers and began to sing a melody he had never sung before. He mispronounced some words and there were a few snickers in the crowd, but before he was finished, he had everyone on their feet dancing.

Evaluating risks versus rewards is a valuable exercise, but—and this qualification merits attention—take care not to exaggerate the risks (or the rewards). If you love riding a bike but read in the local paper that someone was hit by a car while riding, don't let fear of an accident keep you off your bicycle, but do be sure to wear a helmet and reflective gear. If you presume that people from different religions, ethnic groups, and nationalities cannot be trusted, then you are letting your smallest and most fearful self win. The middle ground requires an honest evaluation of real risks and rewards with an inclination toward living the most expansive life possible.

Mantras for Courage

"Worry is a misuse of imagination."

"Fear no one."

"Fear is the cheapest room in the house."

"Never let your fear decide your fate."

Courage on the Mat

Triangle Pose—*Utthita Trikonasana*

In this pose, in which we expose our most vulnerable parts—our internal organs and our throat—we feel both our vulnerability and our courage. To choose to be vulnerable is an act of courage. Triangle Pose embodies this contradiction.

1. From Mountain Pose, step your left leg toward the back of the mat, allowing your feet to be about three feet apart. Keep your right foot pointed forward (twelve o'clock) while your left foot is at an angle so that your left heel is at six o'clock and your left toes are at ten o'clock.

2. Rotate your hips and your shoulders to the left so that your torso is fully facing the left side.
3. Extend your arms to shoulder height. Turn your head and gaze over your right fingertips.
4. Keeping both legs straight, hinge at your right hip and send both hips toward your left leg.
5. Reach with your right arm forward as far as you can. (Imagine reaching over a countertop for a pen while holding on to an old-fashioned corded phone.)
6. Then drop your right hand to your shin, a block, or the floor to the outside of your right pinky toe.
7. Reach your left arm high and spread your fingers wide.
8. Refine the pose by stacking your shoulders and aligning them over your rib cage and your right thigh. Drop your tailbone toward your left ankle. Draw your chin off your chest and let all the sides of your neck be long....

Crow Pose—*Bakasana*

This is another pose to play your edge if you're a beginner, an advanced student, or in between.

1. Beginning in Mountain Pose in the middle of your mat, toe-heel your feet wider than hip-width apart. Keep your toes slightly turned out.
2. Bend your knees and drop your hips to come into a squat (heels do not need to be on the floor).
3. From the squat, plant your hands on the mat and either squeeze your knees to the outside of your upper arm bones (beginners) or plant your knees directly on your arm bones just below the armpits.
4. Lean your head and upper body forward until you feel the weight of your torso on your arms.
5. Lift one foot and then the other; bring your big toes together while you lift your chest up. Think "up" as you lift through your belly.

6. Beginners can exit the pose by reversing the order, while intermediate and advanced yogis can shoot their legs back into Low Push-up.

Lion's Breath—*Simhasana*

Lions are typically thought of as brave animals. You might feel the need to summon some courage when you try this pose in class for the first time; it can feel a little ridiculous at first. Lion's Breath can be practiced from almost any yoga asana; frequently it accompanies Goddess Pose (*Utkata Konasana*), Fish Pose (*Matsyasana*), or Yoga Squat (*Malasana*).

1. Beginners can practice this breathing technique from Easy Seated Pose or in a low kneeling position.
2. To begin Lion's Breath, inhale deeply.
3. Then forcefully exhale through a wide-open mouth, while sticking your tongue far out and downward, rolling your eyes upward, and making a loud roaring sound from the back of your throat.

Explorations in Courage for Mat, Journal, and Life

When in the past have you exercised braveness on the mat? What was the outcome?

Thinking about the past, when in your life have you been notably brave? What risks have you taken? What was the outcome?

When was the last time you took a big risk?

Identify where and when fear arises in your yoga practice. How do you typically respond to fear in your practice?

Where in your life—work, relationships, leisure—is fear holding you back?

What would you do if you knew you could not fail?

How will you address courage and fear this week? What parts of your upcoming week present opportunities to work on courage? What specifically can you change in your life to act with more bravery? Do you need courage to ask for help? Do you need courage to make a change in your job or a relationship? Do you need to let go of your fear to embark on your life's dream?

Walk Together

Grieving with Others

> May our lives be filled to overflowing by reaching out to one another.
>
> —Steven Greenebaum

> It helps to have others to accompany me in the wilderness, those who encourage me to take my time and listen within, those who embody God's presence when God seems to be absent.... Soul friends help us listen to our lives when we'd rather not or are unsure how to do so.
>
> —Diane M. Millis

You may feel alone in your grief. As you long for connection, consider that the loss you have experienced has likely caused sorrow to others as well. There is power for healing and love in the vulnerability that you share. Reach out to those around you who are also grieving. Cry with each other; remember with each other; ask for a listening ear and offer one as well.

In this section you'll find prayers and practices for joining together in times of grief and reminders of ways you can help lift the burden of isolation from others who are grieving. Allow yourself to discover the depth of love that can grow between mourners who share sorrows, memories, and hopes.

And when the concentration of grief in your days has become less, when you are no longer in the intensity of new grief and pain, you can bring the compassion you have learned to others who have new losses.

Praying Together to the God of Hope

Annotated by The Rev. Canon C. K. Robertson, PhD

We are all interconnected. Family members and close friends walk with us in the journey of life, and when they leave us, we are understandably bereft. These prayers from the Burial Office put words to the deep feelings of grief that can threaten to overwhelm us. In faith and in hope, we affirm that our tearful good-byes now will one day give way to a joyful reunion. These words are meant to carry us through this in-between time.

O God, whose beloved Son took children into his arms and blessed them: Give us grace to entrust [*Name*] to your neverfailing care and love, and bring us all to your heavenly kingdom; through Jesus Christ our Lord, who lives and reigns with you and the Holy Spirit, one God, now and for ever. Amen.

Most merciful God, whose wisdom is beyond our understanding: Deal graciously with [*Names*] in their grief. Surround them with your love, that they may not be overwhelmed by their loss, but have confidence in your goodness, and strength to meet the days to come; through Jesus Christ our Lord. Amen.

—Collects from the Burial of the Dead Rite II

God of hope, we come to you in shock and grief and confusion of heart. Help us to find peace in the knowledge of your loving mercy to all your children, and give us light to guide us out of our darkness into the assurance of your love. Amen.

—From the Funeral Liturgies of the New Zealand Prayer Book

The Rev. Canon C. K. Robertson, PhD, is canon to the presiding bishop of The Episcopal Church, a noted scholar, and a distinguished visiting professor at the General Theological Seminary in New York City. He is author of *The Book of Common Prayer: A Spiritual Treasure Chest—Selections Annotated & Explained* (SkyLight Paths), among other books.

Anniversaries and Holidays after a Disaster

Imam Yusuf Hasan, BCC, and Rev. George Handzo, BCC

One Family's Story

We have a large family spread out across the country.[1] Some of us have been close to each other all of our lives, and some of us have become closer as we have become older. Since 1984 we've had family reunions every two years. Generally about 150 people attend, often coming on chartered buses from all over the county. In August 2005 we had a major reunion in New Orleans. At that time, over one hundred members of our extended family lived in and around New Orleans, many of them in the ninth ward. I remember very vividly how we enjoyed ourselves at the amusement park and at the picnics and banquets. As always, the reunion was a time when we were happy to be together and renew our relationships.

As Hurricane Katrina approached New Orleans, an aunt who lived in New Orleans died. Many of us from outside the area purchased airline tickets and prepared to travel to New Orleans for her funeral. Needless to say, we were not able to go to New Orleans, and there was no funeral. My aunt's body, which was in a funeral home when the hurricane struck, was eventually recovered, but no funeral was ever held. So, one of the immediate and lasting effects of Katrina for my family was the inability to mourn the loss of a beloved member of the family and even to know that she was properly buried. It was particularly difficult for us not to be able to be there or get close to our family at that

Imam Yusuf Hasan, BCC, was one of the first disaster spiritual care responders in New York after 9/11 and helped create a disaster chaplaincy response organization in New York City, within the American Red Cross. **Rev. George Handzo, BCC**, past president of the Association of American Chaplains, is vice president of pastoral care leadership and practice at the HealthCare Chaplaincy (HCC) in New York City. They are contributors to *Disaster Spiritual Care: Practical Clergy Responses to Community, Regional and National Tragedy* (SkyLight Paths).

particular time. This loss and the inability to properly observe my aunt's death continues to be a part of our family. In this instance, a disaster interrupted our family process and prevented us from observing an occasion that would have been very important to our whole family—even to those who had not planned to attend the funeral. Our anguish over not being able to go to New Orleans and be close to our family as the storm approached was compounded by our grieving the loss of a family member. It was difficult for us to lose an aunt, a mother's sister, and never have a chance to say good-bye with a formal service.

For a long time after the storm, we did not know whether many of our family members were alive or dead. Many of them had never left New Orleans in their lives. It was traumatic to know that they were likely in another state where they knew no one, scattered about, and trying to reach each other in panic. Meanwhile, the rest of the family was collecting money to support them. Often, it was impossible to even get this support to them. Two years after the event, many of our family were still not established back at home. Some were in Texas. Some were in other parts of Louisiana. For our family, Katrina remained very much both a present and a past tragedy, highlighting how long the effects of events like this can persist in the life of a family. It is also forever linked to my aunt's death.

The Role of Family Events

How can we help one another cope with the effects of these tragedies, mishaps, and calamities? How can family events be both a resource and an impediment in this process?

In August 2007 we held our first family reunion since Katrina. The coincidence of this event with the second anniversary of Katrina and the second anniversary of my aunt's death gave it special meaning. The matriarch of our family attended, along with about fifty family members from New Orleans. Of the 160 attendees, thirty-three were under the age of thirteen. Significantly, the children of the aunt who died in New Orleans attended for the first time.

In planning any family anniversary, reunion, or similar event, or in celebrating any significant family occasion in the aftermath of a disaster, several levels of need should be accommodated. You should consider the special needs of those who were directly involved in the disaster as opposed to those who were not. You should consider the needs of different age groups and those with different degrees of relationship, especially those of the same generation. You should hold in tension the need to remember and process the effects of the disaster and the need to move on. Lastly, you should always understand that individuals need to feel free to participate in the event only to the degree that they choose, no matter what others think they should do.

Needs of the Survivors

You need to anticipate that those closest to the disaster will have the most lasting effects and wounds that are deeper and therefore heal more slowly. At any point in time, they will not be as far along the continuum of returning to "normal." As mentioned, many of our family who survived Katrina were still not resettled two years after the storm, or had to relocate entirely. While many of the rest of us have been able to move on with our lives, the aftermath of Katrina is still a daily reality for them. After any kind of major loss or disaster, the first set of anniversaries, holidays, or other such events will bring its own challenges as participants work to integrate the particular loss into their routine. The first Thanksgiving dinner without the person who sat at the head of the table for years confronts the family with the reality of their loss, but also helps the family move on through seeing someone else sitting in the chair. For our family from New Orleans, the August 2007 reunion was their first chance to reunite with family from other parts of the country. For them, this was far from a routine reunion. For the whole family, this was the first reunion without our beloved aunt and sister.

Our goal was to take this dynamic seriously while not allowing it to dominate the event. We went out of our way to welcome those from New Orleans without making them feel self-conscious.... We honored their need to talk about what life was like for them, as well as their need to simply enjoy the fun and find something "normal" in their lives. We wanted it to be safe for them to talk about their hurt and anxieties or to simply get away from that reality if they chose.

Generational Needs

As mentioned, many of the attendees of the reunion were children. Many of them were from New Orleans. In general, children are less able to cope well with loss and exposure to disaster; some of this inability has to do with a lack of skill in verbalizing feelings and asking for help directly. Also, the everyday survival demands a disaster puts on adults often leaves them with little time or other resources to pay attention to their children. However, children do draw consolation from being in familiar groups and from doing the normal tasks of life. Children need opportunities to grieve, but also opportunities to move away from their grief to play. They express many of their feelings through activity rather than words. Family events and celebrations, such as holidays and birthdays, give children the opportunity to be assured that their life is going on. It also gives them a safe environment to process some of the feelings they do not feel free to express otherwise.

In planning our reunion, we were very aware that many of the children had lived for two years under the stress of relocation and crowded conditions with no mental health support available to them. Having the major part of the reunion in a park gave us the perfect opportunity to have an abundance of time for both free play and organized games. Children who recently had not had the opportunity to play in a safe, well-equipped environment could do so. We also had two child psychologists in attendance in case any of the children wanted to talk about their experiences. Finally, at the banquet, each child was called on individually and given a special gift so that he or she would feel special in the midst of the greater family. Even though the event was not about the children specifically, we were able to use the time and opportunity to do some things that hopefully helped their healing.

The other group we paid special attention to was the elderly. We were aware that my mother and her five surviving siblings had not had the opportunity to grieve together for their sister who died in New Orleans and never had a funeral. So, the reunion became an opportunity to do some of the work that would have been done at the funeral. We made sure they had time together for that purpose.

While using religious beliefs and practices to cope with loss is not restricted to the elderly, older people are more likely to want to incorporate religious rituals and practices into these special occasions. They may want to go to a worship service at a local church, synagogue, mosque, or temple, especially if the place itself holds special meaning for them. They may want to read their holy books alone or together. They may want to include prayer as a part of the occasion. Even if the day itself is marked by partying, laughter, and jokes, some people might want to maintain a somber tone—at least for themselves. They might want to remember God more during those particular times.

Remembering—The Role of Ritual

It is safe to say that every special event in a family has rituals attached to it. These may be formal and religious in nature, or they may be patterns of behavior that we think of as traditions and that describe the way we normally do things around a certain occasion. For example, Thanksgiving may always be celebrated at a certain family member's house. The meal may always include certain dishes prepared according to a certain recipe. Certain people may always be in charge of certain parts of the meal. It may be expected that part of the day is devoted to telephoning members of the family who are elsewhere. As children grow up and marry, the tradition is amended according to which side of the family the couple will generally spend Thanksgiving with. As members of the family die or are no longer able to fulfill their normal roles, decisions have to be made about who will take their place. Making these decisions, by whatever process, affirms the permanence of the family. It communicates, at least implicitly, that the family will go on despite losses and other changes and will continue to be a support to individuals within it.

Rituals are extremely important to our lives in numerous ways. They function as formularized interactions that affirm our relationship to each other and to powers beyond ourselves. They are patterns of behavior that we share in common. Especially in the context of disaster, they affirm and confirm that life goes on. They represent the normal and the expected. They can also represent, as in the case of a wedding or a funeral, processes for incorporating new members into the family or saying good-bye to other members. They often have ways to incorporate changes in the family experience built into them. Conversely, if rituals or traditions are interrupted, it often signals that life is unreliable, maybe even random.

After disaster has affected a family or some members of it, it is extremely important to continue treasured rituals and, to the extent possible, to observe special occasions in the usual way. At our recent reunion, in addition to the many rituals normative to the reunion itself, such as the banquet, we celebrated two birthdays. We also remembered in prayer our aunt who died and two members of the family from New Orleans who remain missing. Through these simple rituals we gave place to the grieving that Katrina had both caused and prevented us from expressing. We also reaffirmed that while Katrina could change our family, it did not destroy it. We would continue to celebrate our life together.

Interfaith Prayers for Grieving and Healing

Rev. Steven Greenebaum

The Overwhelming Call of We

Editor's note: Words in plain type may be spoken by a leader or leaders. The rest of the group may respond with the words in italics.

Sometimes ... the world seems to come at me from all sides.
Sometimes ... I hurt, I hunger, I thirst, and I am filled with wanting.
Sometimes ... I forget that I am, I truly am, and I have a place in this Universe.
Sometimes ... I forget my value, and see only my faults.
At these times, I can tend to turn inward and see only myself.
At these times, I may see only my hurt, my thirst, my wants.
At these times I can forget you, my brother; and you, my sister.
At these times, my humanity ebbs.
Let me never forget that I am called not only to love and to compassion, but also to community.
And there is no community, if there is only me.
O, Hope of the Universe, we are all children of the universe.
Let us refuse to divide into camps of gender, "race," or spiritual path.
But let us come together.
May our lives be made richer and more whole by reaching out to one another, in times of joy and in times of terror.

Rev. Steven Greenebaum, an Interfaith minister and founder of Living Interfaith Church in Lynnwood, Washington, is author of *Practical Interfaith: How to Find Our Common Humanity as We Celebrate Diversity* (SkyLight Paths). He speaks and leads workshops on Interfaith and compassion as the core of our diverse spiritual traditions throughout the United States and Canada.

May our lives be filled to overflowing by reaching out to one
   another.
Let us answer with unswerving faith, the overwhelming call of we....

Bring Us Together

Bring us together.
We walk this one world
In different worlds.
Bring us together.

Help us see each other.
We tend to see what we expect,
Even when what we expect has fled.
Help us see each other.
If I need to stand upon your
shoulders
To see across the field,
Let me not forget that you've a right
To stand on mine as well.

Let us "be" together.
Each ourselves
And yet as one united,
Let us "be" ... together.

Interfaith Prayer for Peace

May peace find a welcoming home in my heart.
May peace envelop me and flow through me in all that I embrace
   and all that I do.
May I be a beacon of peace.
And may I always remember that only a diversity of beacons can
   bring sufficient light to our paths to show us the way.

Receptivity, Presence, and Hospitality with Family

Rev. Nanette Sawyer

There is receptivity in the simple awareness of being present, together, here and now. This kind of deep presence is so precious that the mere fact of it occurring can create between you and your loved ones a feeling of mystery and joy. This is the essence of reverence—it is love, honor, respect, and tenderness. Once reverence arises in you, generosity flows out naturally. We want to express our care for those we love.

The gift of full attention is a powerful one that will make hospitality grow in you and flourish in your family. My very best memory of my grandfather is from one time when he looked me in the eyes with full attention. I must have been about four or five years old because I was little enough for him to pick me up by the waist and set me on the edge of the dining room table. There he played a game with me. He said, "I bet I can make you blink just by looking at you." I was very certain that I could resist his will and hold my eyes open forever. And so the contest began, me sitting on the dining room table, legs dangling over the edge, him standing in front of me. As the urge to blink grew bigger and bigger in me, I opened my eyes wider and wider and began to tilt my head slightly forward as though the angle of my head would help my eyes stay open. Eventually, of course, I blinked.

"Aha!" he teased. "You blinked! I knew I could make you do it!" With a big smile and a joking haughty attitude I told him that he didn't make me blink; I only blinked because I wanted to. He laughed and picked me up again by the waist and stood me back on the floor. "Now you'll blink all the time," he

---

Rev. Nanette Sawyer, teacher and spiritual counselor, is author of *Hospitality—The Sacred Art: Discovering the Hidden Spiritual Power of Invitation and Welcome* (SkyLight Paths) and a founding pastor of Grace Commons, an innovative Christian community in Chicago that holds hospitality as a core value.

said. And it was true; I did. And for the longest time I believed that I had never blinked before my grandfather made me do it.

In that exchange with him, I knew that I was loved. He invited, welcomed, and nurtured me in an attentive, loving, and generous way. That was the gift he gave me, a form of hospitality expressed through giving me his deep presence and full attention. This is something that you can do with your family in innumerable ways. If you would like to begin developing this, here are just a few ideas to help you practice hospitality toward your family:

Try instituting regular signs of affection to be shared with family members. I have a friend whose husband brings her a red rose every single Friday night. This is one of the things they do to welcome in the Jewish Sabbath. Even if they've had a fight, he brings her a rose. There will always be time to continue the fight after the Sabbath is over, but the rose comes as a sign of commitment to love. This, too, is a form of hospitality: to remain receptive, reverent, and generous to a loved one, even when it requires consistency that feels bigger than us, even when we feel angry or hurt or particularly vulnerable. Vulnerability creates intimacy if we treat each other with respect and tenderness.

Practice talking to your family members in intentional ways. It's surprising how little we really do this. Find out what's important to them, what they spend time mulling over as they are about to drift off to sleep at night. Ask questions. Act interested. You might be amazed at how this simple added effort can make a big difference.

Be generous in sharing yourself, naming your needs and desires honestly. Be clear and direct to the best of your ability, saying what is true for you instead of expecting your loved ones to know intuitively what is important to you.

Set aside consistent, quality time to be together, not just to do together. This might be time for dinner, trips to the park, going to the movies, or just sitting around on the porch or in the living room. Are there games your family might like to play? We're so used to being busy all the time that this might be more difficult to do than it sounds. If you can enlist the commitment of at least one other family member, you may have better luck actually pulling it off. Even if no one else joins you at first, your having fun might begin to attract greater attention and participation.

Try the once-a-month gift-giving experiment, especially if you're struggling with a particular relationship. You can tell the recipient of your gifts what you plan to do, or you can just start doing it and see how long it takes the person to ask you what you're doing! As you go through the process, be intentional about becoming aware of your feelings and making decisions about how to respond to them. Remain aware, also, of the preferences, feelings, and desires of the person you are giving gifts to. Be sure to give presents that he or she is likely to enjoy, rather than gifts that you *wish* the person would enjoy. If you don't know what the person might enjoy, that is part of the marvelous adventure! Now you have to be an undercover detective and find out. Ask questions about what she enjoys, what she wishes for, or what she used to do but now misses. Conversation can go a long way toward identifying potential gifts.

Receptivity and reverence go hand-in-hand for this practice, since giving another person what he would enjoy requires becoming aware of what he might like, as well as honoring his desires and his personality with respect. This is what makes the action generous: grounding it in awareness and acceptance of the other person. It will be interesting to see how this kind of persistent focus on expressing your care for a person changes you and changes your relationship.

Speaking Love and Healing

Jay Marshall, PhD

Just as knowing God's love for us is our greatest resource for healing inner wounds and fears, our love for others is the greatest contribution we make toward healing and transforming a world in desperate search for wholeness. We can enter the world projecting an ambiance of love that can subtly but powerfully alter the way we see and interact with others....

- Messages of love affirm, empower, and strengthen, serving as a healing balm to the weary soul. Put the resource of your words to work for loving purposes:
- Let your speech flow from the deepest reservoir of love that resides within you by virtue of the Light Within. Let it be filtered by the Inner Witness, who in a moment recognizes your true motives and can offer an accountability checkpoint.
- Monitor the motivation of your speaking.
  - Are you about to speak in order promote or draw attention to yourself?
  - Are the words hurtful, even if true?
  - Can they be restated in ways that allow love to wrap the message's content?
- Commit to bring forth only those responses that desire what is best for the other and offer words in ways that convey that desire....

As the people in your most immediate circles are touched by this love, their attitudes and activities toward you will transform. In this new ambiance created by the intersection of the Divine Light with your own light, your life's

Jay Marshall, PhD, a gifted teacher noted for his ability to express spiritual insights with compassion and grace, is dean of Earlham School of Religion, a Quaker minister, and author of *Thanking & Blessing—The Sacred Art: Spiritual Vitality Through Gratefulness* (SkyLight Paths).

encounters will become a series of thankful and blessed exchanges—not perfect, but never bereft, because the mood is bathed in the greater reservoir of blessed love that keeps you securely within the care of the Divine. Such blessing begets love, which lays the foundation for a differently ordered world.

Listening to Your Life

Diane M. Millis, PhD

Surely the Lord is in this place—and I did not know it.
—Genesis 28:16

Each of us will inevitably encounter times in life that don't go according to *the plan*. Whether it's the breakup of a relationship or leaving our homeland, a diagnosis we've received or a loved one's illness we must endure, a period of long-term unemployment or the need to make a transition from a job that no longer fits us, we find ourselves in a wilderness, that is, a destination not of our own choosing.

Time in the wilderness is an archetypal theme found in the stories of various faith traditions. As we read the stories of the Hebrew people, Jesus, Muhammad, and the Buddha, we learn how wilderness times provide a catalyst for spiritual awakening. Such times invite us to increase our awareness of, and receptivity to, all that surrounds us, and perhaps, more important, all that resides within us. Although some of us may plan excursions into the wilderness, most of us are busy enough just trying to keep up with the demands of everyday life. It isn't until we find ourselves in what the poet John O'Donohue refers to as a "Genesis Foyer"—a key threshold or an unplanned wilderness experience in our lives—that we begin to pay attention within. O'Donohue offers the following counsel for when we find ourselves at such a threshold: "Take your time; Feel all the varieties of presence that accrue there; Listen inward with complete attention until you hear the inner voice calling you forward."[1] I find O'Donohue's eloquent words inspiring. Yet, let me confess. I don't like to take my time. I don't want to feel all the

---

Diane M. Millis, PhD, is an inspirational speaker, workshop and retreat leader, organizational consultant, and spiritual director. She is author of *Conversation—The Sacred Art: Practicing Presence in an Age of Distraction* and *Deepening Engagement: Essential Wisdom for Listening and Leading with Purpose, Meaning and Joy* (both SkyLight Paths) and is founder and director of the Journey Conversations Project.

varieties of presences accruing in an experience, especially if they are painful. Even though I've gotten better at listening intently to the inner voice, I'm not always certain whether the voice I hear is the voice of God's Spirit beckoning me or my own very real need to just get on with it.

So, when all else fails, I have found that it really helps to have others to accompany me in the wilderness, those who encourage me to take my time and listen within, those who embody God's presence when God seems to be absent. In my faith tradition, Christianity, we refer to those who accompany us as spiritual companions, or *anamchara*, soul friends. Soul friends help us listen to our lives when we'd rather not or are unsure how to do so. Through their attentive presence, they invite us to pay attention to the sacred Mystery at work in our lives....

Each time we listen to our life, we have the opportunity to discover, notice, and name more fully how God is at work. When we tell our stories in conversation with others, we create the occasion both to listen to our lives and to draw upon our life experiences as a source of truth. It is through listening to and sharing the stories of our life that we begin to make new maps for our journey.

Reflecting on Our Story

The capability to make meaning of our lives, and to tell our own distinctive story, begins to take shape in late adolescence and young adulthood. For those of us who are new to sharing the story of our journey, we may find it helpful to reflect upon the arc of our lived history as if we were preparing to write a book. We can begin by considering how we might respond to each of the following questions:

If my life's journey were a book, I would title it ...

The reasons I give my life this title are ...

The chapters in the book of my life are ...

The chapter I am in right now is ...

I am currently discerning and trying to figure out ...

As I imagine the next chapter on my journey, I hope ...

The first time we respond to these questions, or invite others to do so, we may find that our responses are fairly brief. We might only be able to respond to each question in a sentence or in a few words. However, the more we commit to listening to our life and composing our story through journaling or conversation with others, we find that our short responses begin to lengthen....

Perhaps the most significant aspect of listening to others' stories and sharing our own is the realization that our stories are not set in stone. In listening to and composing our lives, we abandon the notion of the past as having a meaning and work to extract alternative meanings that may prove more life-giving. God's action in our lives is always open to new interpretation.

Through their genuine curiosity, commitment, and alertness to our verbal and nonverbal communication, really good conversation partners help us notice aspects of our stories that have particular energy for us. They ask us meaningful questions that invite us to step back from the action and to reflect on our wishes, motivations, values, and beliefs.[2] They encourage us to not settle for thin narratives, to continue to listen for the enigmatic expression of the Spirit whose meaning isn't readily apparent and continues to be revealed over time. In considering others' questions and observations, we can't help but examine our stories in new ways.

Letting Our Life Speak Through Storytelling

We need to create more occasions for listening to our lives and letting our lives speak, for people typically don't tell their story in much detail unless they are asked to do so and an occasion for doing so is created....

In 2003 Dave Isay set up a recording booth in New York's Grand Central Terminal where forty-minute interviews were conducted between family members and friends. Isay believes that each of us has a valuable story to tell. His StoryCorps Project is based upon a few ideas: "That our stories—the stories of everyday people—are as interesting and important as the celebrity stories we're bombarded with by the media every minute of the day. That if we take the time to listen, we'll find wisdom, wonder, and poetry in the lives and stories of the people all around us. That we all want to know our lives have mattered and we won't ever be forgotten. That listening is an act of love."[3]

Listening is an act of love. As we listen to another's story, our role is not to interpret the meaning of how God is at work in another's life. Rather, we strive to listen for the sacred currents *beneath* the stream of the person's life. As listeners, our intent is not to challenge a narrative but to invite the teller to dig deeper, to unpack it, to thicken it, to offer the possibility of considering it from a different perspective.[4]

Our stories—the ones we tell and those we are told—shape us. Each of us is a story catcher, or more accurately, a story sponge, absorbing stories from many different sources (our family, culture, faith traditions, and the media, among others). It's not what's happened in our past that defines us, but the stories we attach to the past. For example, there are many adults like me whose parents divorced when they were children. Some of us may tell a story about being the victim of such an event, for example, how their parents' divorce debilitated them and kept them from ever experiencing true intimacy with others. Others may tell a more redemptive story recounting how their resilience increased as a result of the disintegration of their family.

Perhaps the most important response that we as conversation partners can offer one another is the encouragement to practice what narrative therapists refer to as "relentless optimism," the recognition that "God is constantly at work in our personal and collective stories to realize God's dream for us. Although we may not pay attention to this ongoing work, it's there nonetheless—God's persistent, compassionate presence ... is always at work to offer an alternative narrative."[5]

Gathering with one another to practice relentless optimism and help each other notice and name the particularities of our lived experience nurtures our awareness of how *God was in this place even when we did not know it.*

Steppingstones on the Journey

Begin by journaling your responses to one or more of the guiding reflection questions. Bring one or more of the following questions into a future conversation and invite others to respond:

- At this time in my journey, I am ...
- As I take the next step on my journey, I hope ...
- As I take the next step on my journey, I seek ...
- As I take the next step on my journey, I wonder ...
- As I take the next step on my journey, I fear ...
- What I have learned from earlier steps I have taken on my journey is ...
- As I take this next step, I want to remember ...

A Touch on Her Head

Rev. Martha Spong

I could hear the mother while I was still around the corner from the entrance to the neonatal intensive care unit. Her keening accompanied me in the required ritual of thorough hand washing before I passed through the door. As it closed behind me, I could see instantly where I needed to go, to the huddle of stricken people in the corner: a middle-aged woman and a man of about twenty, neither trying to soothe or hold the new mother whose wail expressed their shared lament.

That night, I had been rushing to get dinner ready before a trustees meeting at 7. Just before 6, the phone rang. I stretched the cord to its limit, searching for a pencil to take notes. The volunteer chaplain on duty that night wanted help with a call from the NICU. A young woman had given birth to a baby at twenty-one weeks' gestation, not even old enough to inhabit the borderlands where doctors consider treatment, four weeks shy of the "very premature" date when they certainly will. The baby was alive, but not for long.

She told me all these things hurriedly. "I don't think I can do it," she said. "Will you go?"

"Of course," I said, scribbling what little information she could give me on a scrap of paper. We didn't know each other well. She called me only because my name came first on the backup list. She didn't know that I had lost a baby in the same hospital.

I told my children to eat without me and kissed the top of my nine-year-old daughter's head, the one born after. "Oh Mom," she said, and shrugged me off, tossing her long hair. On the short drive to the hospital, I called a trustee from my cell to say I might be late to the meeting. A short fifteen

Rev. Martha Spong is a United Church of Christ pastor and is director of RevGal-BlogPals (revgalblogpals.org), a social media ministry making community for clergywomen across lines of denomination, generation, nation, and orientation since 2005. Spong is editor of *There's a Woman in the Pulpit: Christian Clergywomen Share Their Hard Days, Holy Moments and the Healing Power of Humor* (SkyLight Paths).

minutes from the time I got the call, a nurse brought me sterilized water in a sealed container, which she opened carefully. She stood beside me while I spoke to the mother.

"I'm the chaplain. I've come to baptize your baby."

The mother was nineteen. I knew people would promise her there would be another baby someday, knew people would try to retell her story for her and make it "right," but where we stood there was no future, no hope, only a smaller-than-small baby girl with closed eyes and purple skin.

"We know that Jesus loved children," I said, "because when the disciples tried to keep them away, he said, 'Let the children come to me.' Baptism reminds us that we all belong to God; we are all God's beloved children. It is a sign of God's love and a promise that we will never be separated from God's love."

I'm not sure anyone heard what I was saying. I turned to the nurse and took the water, then poured some in my hand. I baptized the baby, Anne, in the name of the Father and of the Son and of the Holy Spirit. I touched her precious head. Anne's mother trembled beside me while the father and grandmother stood, seeming helpless to scale the walls of her grief.

Her sobbing rose again as I offered a closing prayer. At the nurse's prompting, I stepped away to fill out the hospital's baptismal certificate, a slim piece of evidence that God knew about a parent's love and loss, a paper promise that the dear, brief life would not go unmarked.

Anne died a few minutes later.

The baby I lost years before had only a funeral for a blessing, no baptismal touch on his head. We buried his ashes in the church garden and planted a dogwood tree there. I wanted to hear my pastor say his name, Christian, but it never happened. There are many ways people can fail to hold you.

I drove across town to church, just a few minutes late for the meeting. The trustees awaited me, a group of older, crusty, and inherently suspicious men. Each monthly meeting revolved around repetitive points of contention, from their suspicion of the "budget year-to-date" line on the financial reports to complaints about how many times the nursery school children flushed the toilet.

We don't tell each other about these things, the losses that happen outside safe and understandable boundaries. We don't hold each other, even though when we witness a baptism, we promise we will. We promise to love the child and support the parents. That's easy when everything goes smoothly.

"I've just come from the hospital," I told them, "and I can't stand for you to argue tonight." In an unaccustomed display of mercy, they did not. Instead, they listened to the story. They bore witness, and, although they never touched me, they held me that night as we prayed for Anne's mother.

I hope someone held her too.

Being a Healing Presence

Ron Miller

"When you go into a region and walk around in the rural areas, whenever people receive you, eat whatever they provide for you, and heal their sick" (Gospel of Thomas 14b). One notices the open-endedness in this injunction. The disciples are just "walking around" in a rural area. They encounter some people who receive them; presumably, others don't. They are offered food to eat, and at a time when dietary laws were one of the primary norms for judging who was religious and who was not, Jesus is telling them to eat whatever is provided. The one clear command is to be a healing presence.

This saying stands in such sharp contrast to the average proselytizing scenario we have all experienced. There is a knock at the door and when we open the door we find one or two smiling people who are eager to help us. They never ask about the way in which we experience the divine mystery. They have the answer, the right answer, *our* right answer. They know how we should find God better than we ourselves could possibly know. Why is that? Because they have the infallible book—the Bible, the Book of Mormon, or whatever. Or they have the infallible leader or the infallible method of salvation—we just need to accept Jesus or Krishna. There's no reciprocity here. We have no "food" to offer them. They are full, full of themselves, full of ego, full of indoctrination, full of other people's answers....

There is a beautiful Jewish story about a young man who is deeply attached to his rabbi. He feeds on his every word and spends every waking moment with him. One day he says to the rabbi, "Rabbi, I love you." The rabbi responds, "Ah, you love me, do you? Then tell me where I hurt." The young man, startled by this response, replies: "Rabbi, I have no idea where

Ron Miller was chair of the religion department at Lake Forest College in Lake Forest, Illinois, where he taught for thirty years. He is author *The Hidden Gospel of Matthew: Annotated & Explained* and *The Gospel of Thomas: A Guidebook for Spiritual Practice* (both SkyLight Paths).

you hurt." "In that case," the rabbi tells him, "you cannot possibly love me." This is as true of healing as of loving; healing, after all, is a form of loving. We can't love or heal another until we take time to learn where they hurt, to feel the world from their side.

What is healing? It is whatever leads to wholeness and, therefore, it naturally involves many of the practices we have been considering. It entails, for example, a capacity to be present to others. This in turn means that we are present to ourselves. Neither of these qualities can be taken for granted in our society. As a matter of fact, they are more often lacking. Most of us operate at a hectic pace of mindlessness where we are present neither to ourselves nor to others. There have been numerous studies in which chosen researchers move around at cocktail parties, smile at those they meet, and mention that they are dying of cancer. No one hears them. People merely smile, utter a cocktail party cliché ("Aren't these canapés delicious?"), and disappear in the crowd.

Healing involves a form of generosity, a giving of our time to another's hurt. When my mother was dying in the hospital, I noticed the mechanical nature of the procedures employed by many of the medical personnel. The hospital chaplain, however, was a skilled minister who brought true compassion to her ministry; she spent real time with my mother and was with her when she died. There was also an African-American custodian who would come in now and then to empty waste bins and tidy up the room. She would walk over to my mother, take her hand, and ask her with total sincerity, "How are you doing today, sweetie?" My mother would always manage a smile for these two women. They were healing presences in her final days on earth. And they are as rare in hospitals as in any other institutional settings in our culture.

Offering Healing

Is there a set form for healing? There need not be. One can, however, use forms that have been part of healing traditions for centuries. We read, for example, in the letter of James 5:14–15 that believers can anoint the sick with oil and pray for them. This is the origin of the Christian sacrament of "extreme unction," which is now called "the sacrament of the sick." During my years of clerical ministry, I found this a very beautiful way to bring healing to the sick. I spent the summer after my ordination in a parish and my mornings were filled with visits to hospitals and nursing homes, administering this sacrament to countless people who needed spiritual comfort and healing.

This is something any Thomas Believer can do with any ailing friend for whom this would be appropriate. Create a pleasing environment. Light candles or incense, if these are agreeable to the person who is sick. Then take a small dish of an oil pleasing to you and your ill friend (I prefer eucalyptus) and anoint the person as you pray or sing a message of healing. Remain together in silence, opening yourselves to the healing environment.

There are also ways of praying for the sick when they are at a distance. See the person you are praying for as clearly as you can in your mind's eye. Then raise your right hand, palm outward, and envisage healing energies being transmitted to that person. If you know the place of the pain or disease, imagine the energies touching the body at that point. Some people see the energies as color, especially blue. Meanwhile, place your left hand on your own heart, and feel those same energies and colors healing you.

You might want to use a healing prayer. I learned a beautiful prayer from a Jewish friend of mine who has a healing ministry. "God is my strength; God is my light; God is my life; God is my healing." This prayer also honors the four great archangels: Gabriel, Uriel, Michael, and Raphael, for the roots of their names relate to those divine qualities. You can repeat this prayer together for several minutes, silently praying between the repetitions.

For reflection:

- Am I a healing presence? Or am I so consumed with my own agenda that I have no room for the needs of others?
- Do I try to hear where others are hurting? Can I read between the lines of what they are saying to me?
- Have I ever tried some kind of ritual for sending healing to others, whether they were nearby or far away?

Coping with Grief as a Caregiver

Marty Richards, MSW, LCSW

Have you ever felt that you needed to "walk on eggshells" around someone who was grieving? Or maybe you've been hesitant to encourage your care partner to share their innermost concerns because you're a bit fearful of your own reaction, or you're not quite sure how to "handle" their strong feelings. Being present or "with" another is a wonderful gift, but it can be difficult to do. Some emotions are very raw and tender. You do need to walk gently with your care partner and realize that what they share about their grief will bring you together in a very sacred space and time.

Over my years of practice, I've seen many different ways that people deal with grief, and I've collected here some of the practices that I have seen help people. Although sadness and grief may be omnipresent in caresharing, there are things you can do to help yourself and your care partner cope.

Name the Sadness

Too often I've seen that the immediate reaction to someone feeling sadness and grief is to offer comfort. A very wise counselor I know cautions, "Don't immediately jump in to dry the tears. Don't give the tissue ... let the person reach for it." In other words, don't shut off a person from sharing what is very important to them. Naming the sadness and the losses is the first step toward coping.

Contrary to what many believe, talking about losses does not make a situation worse. It may well be that both you and your care partner (consciously or unconsciously) are looking for the acknowledgment that someone "gets

---

Marty Richards, MSW, LCSW, is a clinical social worker, an affiliate assistant professor at the University of Washington School of Social Work, and a popular speaker on the topics of chronic illness, Alzheimer's disease, elder care, and spirituality and aging. She is author of *Caresharing: A Reciprocal Approach to Caregiving and Care Receiving in the Complexities of Aging, Illness or Disability* (SkyLight Paths).

it." Naming the sadness will help you recognize and face the grief before it becomes so overwhelming that it makes functioning difficult.

I want to add a special word here to you, as a caregiver. In situations of loss, it is imperative to name the grief and loss that *you* are feeling as well. If you only suffer silently while you take care of your partner, any platitudes you might offer to them will ring hollow. Many caregivers I have known often express a wish that there were someone in their family, circle of friends, congregation, or care network that they could be honest with and share the difficult feelings of grief. While I certainly suggest that you share what is appropriate with your care partner, I also urge you to look for support, either in a friend or counselor, with whom you can share your toughest feelings and questions, "no holds barred."

Give Permission to Grieve

Be sure to give your care partner (and yourself) permission to grieve each loss. This includes giving your partner a chance to clarify why this is an important loss, and what it meant in the past (if an old grief has resurfaced) or in their present reality. Don't feel as if you have to have all the answers. Don't worry so much about saying something "wrong" that you don't say anything at all. Let go of trying to come up with "solutions." There is no "solution" to grief, only resolution over time. Grief resolution will be uniquely defined by you and your loved one, but generally it means that you are able to live out your life in as normal a way as possible, with as much quality of life as possible.

If you're at the point where your care partner is coming to terms with losing their life, they may need your permission to "let go" of all the things and people around them. Your permission to fully grieve their losses may be one of the greatest gifts you can give them, even though it may be a very difficult experience for you. Remember: Though you will be losing the person as you have known them, they are losing everything. As you share this grief with your care partner, it might be especially important for you to have someone—other than your care partner—to support you in your grief, someone with whom you can share your deep sadness so you can be available to help your loved one let go.

Give It Time

When you are dealing with losses, working through grief and transitions always takes time. This is especially true as someone copes with chronic illness, changes in mental ability, or getting used to a body that does not work the way that it used to. If your care partner is aging, it may take even longer to process grief because there may be more losses to face at the very time they have fewer physical, emotional, and spiritual reserves to help them cope.

While, on the one hand, you should be concerned if your care partner is not functioning because of a long, drawn-out grief process, on the other hand, you need to remember that they need to grieve at their own rate. You cannot do the grief work for another, but you can stand by them. This kind of support is invaluable as your care partner navigates their grief journey....

Listen

As obvious as this may sound, taking time to listen is critical. In the daily needs of caresharing, time out for listening often gets shortchanged. Allow time—even to carve out time, if necessary—for personal sharing, time when your care partner can tell their stories and know that you are trying to understand. Your listening will let them know that they do not have to face their struggles with loss, grief, sadness, and pain alone. If you are fearful of not knowing what to say, I have found that people really do just want you to listen; they do not need you to have answers. Sometimes, in sharing something with a supportive person, they can work out their own answers. And sometimes it is best to say nothing except that you care and that you will be with them through this difficult journey.

Listen Beneath the Words

When you are listening to your care partner's words and expressions of grief, it is important to hear not only the words but also the underlying feelings. For example, if you hear a barrage of angry accusations or complaints from the one you are caring for, ask yourself: "What is really happening here? Is this anger about what just happened, or might it be connected in some way with their grief and loss?"

Be especially aware of nonverbal communication. Even though our society tends to be "word-bound," people do not need words to communicate what they are feeling. Don't be quick to try to fill in all the empty spaces. Silence is important. It gives you and your care partner time to respect the depth of their feeling and absorb the many layers and associations of their grief.

If you are in a situation where your care partner is using language that seems strangely out of place for the grief they are expressing, you may need to respond to their "symbolic language." Their words may relate to their experiences over a lifetime or to their work. A pilot, for example, may talk about going on a flight as he tries to verbalize his thoughts about his own impending death. It is important not to mistake such verbalizations for confusion, but to be open to what your care partner is attempting to express. What they are saying may include glimpses of another world, or the way they view this world. A good reference on this subject is Maggie Callanan and Patricia Kelley's book *Final Gifts: Understanding the Special Awareness, Needs, and Communications of the Dying.*

Help Resolve Unfinished Business

At times in the long caring process, your care partner may request that something be done before they can let go and die. This "unfinished business" may involve old conflicts or resentments, guilt, or anger, or it may be something as straightforward as making sure that things are taken care of.... As a caregiver, you may also have some unfinished business with the person who is dying. Try to work out any unresolved issues—such as asking for their forgiveness or offering your forgiveness for an old hurt—so the unfinished business will not get in the way of being open to your care partner. This is also an important part of taking care of yourself in the situation you are in.

Take Care of Yourself

I can't stress enough how important self-care is, especially when you are dealing with issues of loss and grief. You need to be honest with yourself, and others, about how you are feeling. Remember, as a caregiver your nonverbal expressions are coming through even when you are valiantly holding your emotions in check. Your care receiver will likely perceive the nonverbal expression of your grief negatively, and you may end up adding to their stress rather than helping to ease it.

The reality is that you need to care for your physical, mental, and spiritual needs in order to care for another. The old sayings that you cannot get "water out of a dry well" or "blood from a stone" ring true. If you are feeling emotionally exhausted and physically depleted, you will be of no help to your care partner. Taking care of yourself is not selfish; it is imperative. I would even say that the standards for self-care apply doubly because of the extra stress of grief in caresharing: Get enough sleep, exercise, eat healthfully, and socialize with friends. Be gentle with yourself as you walk with grief—hopefully, with others by your side. Try to carve out time for spiritual comfort and nurture as you deal with the loss and grief issues in the dance of caresharing.

Although loss and grief are almost always present in caring, they can be shared, and you and your care partner can grow emotionally and spiritually as you navigate the grief process together. If either of you tries to hide feelings, perhaps to "protect" the other, you will miss out on a very special intimacy. Walking alongside someone who is going through difficult losses, transitions, and grief is treading on sacred ground.

Leaving a Legacy of Love

Rabbi Jack Riemer and Dr. Nathaniel Stampfer

Editor's note: Ethical wills are precious spiritual documents, windows into the souls of those who write them, and are often a treasured part of a family's history. These "legacy letters" sum up what you have learned in life and what you want most for, and from, your loved ones.

The following section contains suggestions for writing an ethical will. The presentation here is neither lengthy nor exhaustive. It doesn't need to be. Our observation has been that writing a *tzava'ah* (will, instruction) is something that most often comes quite easily, possibly because the impulse to write it is deeply human as well as sanctified by tradition. In our practical experience, a small number of strategies prove sufficient for stimulating remembrances and feelings and for outlining useful writing procedures.

Writing an Ethical Will

There is no *one* way in which to write an ethical will. Feel free to write yours in whatever style or tone you want to. But as every writer knows, the hardest thing is to get started. And so we offer these suggestions and guidelines based on our experiences and on the wills in this collection. These are only a number of topic headings under which you can structure what you wish to say; you may choose other topic headings, as you wish....

Step I: How to Decide on Topics: Some Suggestions

Getting started can be challenging. Here are some introductory sentences to help you enter this rewarding effort.

Rabbi Jack Riemer, a well-known author and speaker, is rabbi emeritus of Congregation Beth Tikvah (now Shaarei Kodesh) in Boca Raton, Florida. **Dr. Nathaniel Stampfer** served Spertus Institute for many years as dean, vice president for academic affairs, and professor of Jewish education. They are coeditors of *Ethical Wills and How to Prepare Them: A Guide to Sharing Your Values from Generation to Generation* (Jewish Lights).

These were the formative events of my life ...

This is the world from which I came ...

These are some of the important lessons that I have learned in my life ...

These are the people who influenced me the most ...

These are some of the favorite possessions that I want you to have and these are the stories that explain what makes these things so precious to me ...

These are causes for which members of our family have felt a sense of responsibility, and I hope you will too ...

Some of the scriptural passages that have meant the most to me ...

These are the mistakes that I regret having made the most in my life that I hope you will not repeat ...

This is my definition of true success ...

This is how I feel as I look back over my life ...

I would like to ask your forgiveness for ... and I forgive you for ...

I want you to know how much I love you and how grateful I am to you for ...

Step II: How to Organize and Write What You Want to Say

Having selected and completed some of the topics suggested above, and/ or written down a number of your own, write each of these at the top of a separate sheet of paper. Treat each statement as a topic sentence and expand it into a paragraph or develop it into a section of any number of related paragraphs. Many or all of your topics may warrant such development. Some topics may require more than one page. In that case, attach same-topic pages to each other.

Arrange the pages in sequence, that is, in the order in which you wish the parts to be in the final form. Rearrange the parts until you arrive at the sequence you desire. Read all the parts through for coherence, making needed changes or corrections. If you have used quotations, now is a good time to check their accuracy.

Rewrite or type the entire manuscript. It is recommended that this be considered a *draft* of the final document. It is useful to set it aside for a few days or weeks then re-read and edit it from the perspectives presented in the next section....

Step III: How to Personalize and Strengthen the Links

Special Words

Some words are worth a thousand pictures. Are there such words and expressions loaded with special meaning for you and your family? Your use of these in your ethical will are bound to resonate for your loved ones. In re-reading your draft, therefore, consider including some of these to evoke important memories and insights....

Favorite Sayings

Are there favorite sayings often used in the family that should be preserved? One family recalls that their mother used to tell the children at meal time *Est Kinderlach, vet ihr hobn koyach tzum lernen.* (Yiddish for "Eat children, so you can have strength to study well.") It is for them a deeply cherished recollection, which they have in turn transmitted to their children.

Anecdotes

Do you have or wish to find a suitable anecdote to help illustrate a point you have made in the draft of your ethical will? Here is an example:

> A skier, separated from his comrades in a blizzard, became lost and disoriented. He fought valiantly to stay awake and moving, against the bitter wind and the blinding snow. But after several hours, his strength ebbing, feeling his struggles to be in vain, he lay down to comforting sleep but certain death.
>
> But as he moved to lie down, he stumbled over an object in the snow. Glancing at the object that had made him fall, he realized to his surprise that the object was a *man*. He cleared the snow from the face and body, placed his ear to the man's chest, and detected a heartbeat. Quickly, he began massaging the limbs of the other vigorously to restore circulation, and in so doing, he restored his own. When the man returned to consciousness, he helped him to his feet.
>
> Supporting each other, the two walked on ... until they reached safety together.

This story has appeal in the context of an ethical will because it underscores the ethical view that brotherly love demonstrated by kind deeds, charity, encouragement, volunteerism, etc., is as basic as any necessity for maintaining human life and preserving the human image in man....

Step IV: How to Prepare the Ethical Will Document in Other Formats

The great majority of ethical wills are prepared, in written or printed form, on paper. Although some have been audio- or videotaped, the favored mode has been the written. In this form it is durable, easily reproduced, and framed. Keep in mind, too, that even if recorded, your text needs to be written out first.

If written or typed, it is advisable to use acid-free paper. Many documents written on acid-free paper have remained in superb condition for hundreds of years. Such papers are widely available in specialty stores. Also, if the ethical will is to be written by hand, a fountain pen should be used rather than a ballpoint because the ink in ballpoint pens is usually oil based and very often causes the ink to "bleed" through the paper. These precautions will help preserve the valuable document against time and environmental factors....

Step V: How to Convey the Ethical Will

Each individual can decide when it is the right time to present an ethical will to loved ones. Some prefer to present it soon after writing; others prefer to review and revise it over time, even over a period of years. Some leave this spiritual legacy to be given after their death, often as a codicil to the material will; some do both—presenting one while alive and a second loving message as a codicil. Either way, the will should be reviewed and updated over a period of time.

Step VI: Some Other Considerations

If you have written a *living* will, tell your children what is in it and where it can be found.[1] If you have made a decision about donating your organs after death, they should be told about it. In both these matters, you should first discuss the details with rabbinic authorities or the clergyman of your faith.

If you have divided your goods among your survivors, you may want to explain to them the reasoning behind your distribution.

And if there is any more unfinished business between you and them, this is the time to resolve it and make peace.

Into a Larger Existence

Rabindranath Tagore

Peace, my heart,
let the time for the parting be sweet.
Let it not be a death but completeness.
Let love melt into memory and pain into songs.
Let the flight through the sky end
in the folding of the wings over the nest.
Let the last touch of your hands
be gentle like the flower of the night.
Stand still,
O Beautiful End,
for a moment,
and say your last words in silence.
I bow to you and hold up my
lamp to light you on your way.

Rabindranath Tagore is to the Indian subcontinent what Shakespeare is to the English-speaking world. A poet, playwright, painter, and educator, Tagore was also a mystic of great complexity and depth. He was awarded the Nobel Prize for Literature in 1913. His work can be found, among other places, in *Tagore: The Mystic Poets* (SkyLight Paths).

The Dharma of Dying

Gordon Peerman

Should someone ask
where Sokan went,
just say,
"He had some business
in the other world."
        —Death poem of Yamazaki Sokan, died ca. 1540

During the time of Dad's dying, my wife, Kathy, reminded me of John Tarrant's remarkable account of his mother's death in *Bring Me the Rhinoceros*—remarkable in its lyrical and humorous honesty, and remarkable that this Zen teacher had just the word I needed to hear at the right moment, in this instance in the form of a Zen koan:

The great way is not difficult
if you just don't pick and choose.

Jon Kabat-Zinn, founding director of the Stress Reduction Clinic at the University of Massachusetts Medical School, makes an observation in *Full Catastrophe Living* about weaving a parachute. He says that if you are going to jump out of a plane, it is wise to have begun weaving your parachute before you take the plunge. Fortunately, I had begun to weave the parachute of mindfulness practice some time before my father's dying, and like other contemplatives caring for the sick and dying, I found mindfulness practice made all the difference—especially as Dad descended into terminal agitation in his final weeks, when there was no more medical cure at hand. Practice helped me be present to whatever the moment was bringing, whether sweet or sad or maddening or humorous.

Gordon Peerman is an Episcopal priest, psychotherapist, and teacher. He is author of *Blessed Relief: What Christians Can Learn from Buddhists about Suffering* (SkyLight Paths) and is an adjunct faculty member at Vanderbilt Divinity School.

I found myself often moved to tears of gratitude for the great kindness of Willie Jackson, Dad's companion in the final weeks of his life. This giant of compassion was able singlehandedly to move Dad physically from bed to chair and back again when the strength of Dad's legs had deserted him. Even more amazing to me, Willie was able to hold Dad emotionally, easing his suffering with a calming presence when no medicine seemed quite adequate to the moment. Willie and Dad had both been in the navy, and before Dad's terminal phase, they would talk about where the navy had taken each of them. When Dad would drift into a period of rest and quietness, Willie would reach into his backpack and draw out his book of Bible stories to read to himself. Willie told my father he would stay with him to the end, which is just what he did.

As Tarrant's mother was dying, he noticed that whenever he found himself wanting anyone to be different, when he was picking and choosing for things to be other than they were, his mother's hospice room filled with sorrow and pain. But when he wanted no one to be different, when his own heart was spacious toward whatever was happening, the room was large and at peace.

Tarrant's simple observation was a lamp to guide me along the dying way with my father and my family. I, too, found that the way was not difficult if I wasn't picking and choosing. Not picking and choosing whether Dad was doing well or poorly. Not picking and choosing how we as a family were handling things. Not picking and choosing how others were reacting to this time in our family's life. Each moment, pleasant or unpleasant, was as it should be. Of course, there were moments when precisely what I was doing *was* picking and choosing. But noticing, "Ah, here's a moment of picking and choosing," offered me the freedom to choose. I could continue my struggling or I could drop picking and choosing in favor of being present in a more open and spacious fashion.

Along the way, there were decisions to be made about the particulars of Dad's care and the best setting for his care, decisions around the obituary and the memorial service, the burial and the family gatherings. In these decisions, I found a focus and energy to do what needed to be done, but at night I found it hard to slow my mind and body down. I would awaken in the small hours, my mind slipping into the gear of what next needed to be done. When I became aware that this planning energy had taken over, I would purposely shift gears and listen to the night sounds, to the owls calling to each other in the autumn darkness. I would follow the tidal in-and-out of my breathing, letting the breath cradle and rock me back to sleep. To my surprise, I found myself enjoying the quiet and solitude of these nighttime awakenings—as long as I was not picking and choosing that I needed to be sleeping. Not picking and choosing, sleep would come again, all by itself, when it was ready. I couldn't help noting how easily my own breath came and how different it was from my father's labored breathing.

On the morning after my father died, I arose for my morning bike ride. The sun was just coming up, and on this first dawn without my father, I found myself pedaling in and through an unexpected beneficence. The soft pinks and salmon color in the sky, the familiar early bird sounds—these seemed to convey that all was well. A grouping of a dozen deer stood at attention as I rode past them—a quiet salute to my passing biking cortege.

Just a week before, I'd told Dad I'd seen a fox on my morning bike ride, an unusual sight, and he'd managed a slight smile. This morning he would not be there in the flesh to receive my story about what I had seen, so I found myself telling him right there, on the spot. And then, as I pedaled along, I wished my father well in Buddhist fashion, and to my surprise felt him wishing me well: "May you be filled with lovingkindness. May you be calm and peaceful. May you be safe. May you be well."

At the graveside service a few days later, I read the burial office from the Episcopal prayer book, and I offered my own remembrances for a small gathering of family and friends. My father's West Highland terrier, Bonnie, white ears pricked up, was seated next to my mother at the graveside. My son, Alex, read from Psalm 90: "Lord, thou hast been our refuge from one generation to another (Psalm 90:1 Douay-Rheims Bible). After we had committed my father's ashes to the earth and to God, Alex came and took the shovel from my hand, turning the first spade of earth into the grave. As he reached for the shovel, Alex touched me on the arm and whispered, "Good job, Dad."

Words of praise had never come easily from my father, and I had spent much of my life longing for his approval. Hearing these words from my son on the day of my father's burial was mysteriously healing. The timing was perfect, the right word from the right person at a moment with my heart wide open to receive it.

I closed with the traditional Christian blessing: "The Lord bless him and keep him, the Lord make his face to shine upon him and be gracious unto him, the Lord lift up his countenance upon him and give him peace." Then, in the Buddhist manner, I wished my father well, and all of us gathered there well. The two blessings gave voice to all I wished for my father and for all of us in our family. This leave taking was a part of his life and of ours. There was no resistance to the moment, no picking and choosing, no suffering. Just commending him and each other on the great way. And gratitude for his life well lived.

The Five Remembrances

The recitation of the Five Remembrances offers an embodied way to "teach us to count our days that we may gain a wise heart," as the psalmist puts it (90:12). The intention of this practice is to help you wake up to the significance of *this* moment, the impermanence of possessions and plans, and the significance of the actions you choose. Recited as a daily practice, the Five Remembrances bring relief to the suffering of loss by helping you hold these changes, without resistance, in mindful awareness. It is the dropping of resistance to these facts of life that brings relief from suffering.

Begin the practice by inviting your mind and body to be joined with awareness of your breath. After a few minutes of following the breath in silence, give voice to the Five Remembrances.[1]

Breathing in, I know that I am of the nature to grow old.

Breathing out, I know that I cannot escape growing old.

In-breath, "Growing old" ... *out-breath,* "No escape."

(Repeat "Growing old ... No escape" for a number of breaths)

Breathing in, I know that I am of the nature to grow ill.

Breathing out, I know that I cannot escape growing ill.

In-breath, "Growing ill" ... *out-breath,* "No escape."

(Repeat "Growing ill ... No escape" for a number of breaths)

Breathing in, I know that I am of the nature to die.

Breathing out, I know that I cannot escape dying.

In-breath, "Dying ... *out-breath,* "No escape."

(Repeat "Dying ... No escape" for a number of breaths)

Breathing in, I know that I will lose what is precious to me.

Breathing out, I know that there is no escape from losing what is precious to me.

In-breath, "Losing what is precious to me" ... *out-breath*, "No escape."

(Repeat "Losing what is precious ... No escape" for a number of breaths)

Breathing in, I know that the only thing I will leave behind is the results of my actions.

Breathing out, I know that there is no escape from leaving behind the results of my actions.

In-breath, "Results of my actions" ... *out-breath*, "No escape."

(Repeat "Results of my actions ... No escape" for a number of breaths)

A Healing Good-bye

Rabbi Elie Kaplan Spitz

As a rabbi performing life-cycle events ranging from baby namings to funerals, I regularly encounter others' emotional wounds. Life-cycle moments are family reunions that often bring suppressed feelings to the surface: memories of hurt and distrust, as well as yearnings for greater closeness and ease. By expressing gratitude and love and offering forgiveness, we enable healing and increase our emotional well-being.

With an approaching death, I witness how often relationships are incomplete, even in close, loving relationships. There is a quality of honesty that comes with this last phase of life, especially for the person who is dying. At the bedside of a dying person, life is quite real. Such moments are holy due to the transparency of emotions and the preciousness of limited time. Honest words in the final days and hours can allow for fuller acceptance of life's incompleteness, forgiveness, and the healing of relationships, enabling closure and enhanced ease in the last phase of life.

The five statements below provide a "healing hand."[1] They offer focus and concrete actions for meaningful, honest words, whether in bidding farewell or in living in closer relationship with loved ones now.

1. **Thank you.** Express gratitude personally, whether for something quite simple or more profound.

2. **Forgive me.** Ask your loved one to forgive you for your shortcomings or for a particular act that caused pain—the more specific, the more helpful. Sincerity is essential. The larger goal of reconciliation trumps who is right.

Rabbi Elie Kaplan Spitz is a spiritual leader, scholar, author, and speaker to a wide range of audiences. He is author of *Increasing Wholeness: Jewish Wisdom and Guided Meditations to Strengthen and Calm Body, Heart, Mind and Spirit* (Jewish Lights) and rabbi of Congregation B'nai Israel in Tustin, California.

3. **I forgive you.** Let the other person know that you forgive him or her for the specific ways that he or she has hurt or disappointed you. To forgive is not to condone hurtful behavior but to gain release from it. The work of forgiveness is to accept the other person and to embrace compassionately the whole person, including and despite shortcomings.

4. **I love you.** With forgiveness comes an opening of the heart and a larger capacity for compassion and love. Expressing love is a great gift. Nothing feels better than being told that we are loved. We should never assume that it is known. Putting our love into words makes an enormous impact on both the person to whom we say the words and ourselves.

5. **When you are ready, you can go.** In a deathbed situation, it helps to give the dying person permission to leave. Doing so conveys, "Do not worry; I can manage; I am willing to let go of holding on to you so that you can be released from pain." In other relationships, it is important that we let go and give our loved ones permission to choose their own path.

Even after our family members have passed, we can aid our own healing by writing a letter to the departed using the five statements of the healing hand. Furthermore, we need not wait until the end is near to do the courageous work of healing and expressing our love.

Don't Waste Your Sorrows

Linda Douty

Lora's simple words hinted at a much deeper reality. "I can go on," she said, "when I can see someone else who has gone on." No expert in an ivory tower has the credibility of a fellow sufferer in the trenches. Living through hardship confers an experiential PhD in Life, and those credentials call us to share what we have learned....

The sharing of pain doesn't remove the sting; it just makes it more bearable. Why? Because you can look into the eyes of someone who has been there and lived to tell it.

Marsha endured the unthinkable. After burying her first husband in 1973, she later endured the suicide of a son while caring for her terminally ill second husband. He died three months after that. The losses continued to multiply as her daughter moved seven hundred miles away and another son and daughter-in-law divorced. She found it necessary to relinquish her position as a church minister and went on a two-month sabbatical alone to bravely spend time in prayer. Though paralyzed with grief for a long time, some wise and faithful part of her knew she needed to enter God's healing process of grief with her whole heart. She didn't shrink from the unspeakable pain. She roamed the Cape Cod beaches, threw driftwood into the surf in a rage, shook her fist at God, and experienced the anger that is a normal response to loss. She offered these reflections on those first experiences of healing: "I didn't realize it took so much energy to grieve. I was too exhausted to pray like I normally did. I rested and slept for hours on end. It felt as if I had joined the angry confusion expressed in the book of Job. There was a growing certainty that God couldn't heal what I was unwilling to feel. It hurt, but I had to be real with God if I expected God to become real for me."

Linda Douty, a leading speaker on the topics of meaningful aging, personal growth, and spiritual formation, is author of *How Did I Get to Be 70 When I'm 35 Inside? Spiritual Surprises of Later Life* (SkyLight Paths), a spiritual director, and a contributor to *Presence* (the journal of Spiritual Directors International).

Several years after that life-changing time, I asked her to pass on the wisdom she gained from that experience. She was very specific:

- Don't avoid the pain; don't cover it up with busyness.

- Get much more rest than you normally require.

- Allow others to help you; ask for what you need. (Those who want to support you feel helpless, and your honesty gives them a way to express their support. Don't make them guess what you want, even if all you want is for them to sit with you silently.)

- Lean on the traditional liturgies of the church, especially those dealing with death.

- Read the Psalms daily.

- Don't force your prayers. Allow others to pray on your behalf and claim the truth of Romans 8:26: "Likewise the Spirit helps us in our weakness, for we do not know how to pray as we ought, but that very Spirit intercedes with sighs too deep for words."

Marsha eventually poured her energy and experience into action, founding a ministry for survivors of suicide, traveling far and wide with her message of hope and healing. She is also a gifted spiritual director with a special interest in bereavement counseling. She didn't waste her sorrows; she allowed God to use them to bring comfort and wisdom to the lives of others. In that process, she found surprising meaning in her own life.

Henry was a prominent retired professor of psychology who had wrestled for years with the chronic pain of neuropathy and then with cancer. Through doggedly discovering ways to manage his own pain, he was led to organize a support group for others suffering from the same condition. They exchanged medical information, swapped stories of their lives, and supported each other with strong bonds of friendship.

The challenge is this: be willing to offer your own experience of sorrow to God for the healing of others, and just watch what happens. People who need your hand of comfort and credibility will drift into your life. No matter how many helping hands are extended to hurting folks, the hand they will grasp is the one that has been there—hurting in the same ways, surviving in the same ways, and sharing that experience with grace and generosity.

Credits

The contents of this book originally appeared in materials published by SkyLight Paths and Jewish Lights and are reprinted with permission.

Swami Adiswarananda, "Tagore on Beauty and Tragedy," is excerpted from *Tagore: The Mystic Poets* (SkyLight Paths, 2004).

Marjory Zoet Bankson, "Reclaiming Riches from the Past When You Retire," is excerpted from *Creative Aging: Rethinking Retirement and Non-Retirement in a Changing World* (SkyLight Paths, 2010).

Peter Bankson and Deborah Sokolove, "Prayer for Trust and Healing," is excerpted from *Calling on God: Inclusive Christian Prayers for Three Years of Sundays* (SkyLight Paths, 2014).

Nancy L. Bieber, "Opening Our Hearts to Change" and "This Season of Life," are excerpted from *Decision Making and Spiritual Discernment: The Sacred Art of Finding Your Way* (SkyLight Paths, 2010).

Carolyn Jane Bohler, "Seeing God in Memories and Lasting Love," is excerpted from *God the What? What Metaphors for God Reveal about Our Beliefs in God* (SkyLight Paths, 2008).

Edith R. Brotman, "The Yoga of Courage," is excerpted from *Mussar Yoga: Blending an Ancient Jewish Spiritual Practice with Yoga to Transform Body and Soul* (Jewish Lights, 2014).

Michael J. Caduto, "The Circle of Life," is excerpted from *Everyday Herbs in Spiritual Life: A Guide to Many Practices* (SkyLight Paths, 2007).

Carolyne Call, "Recognizing and Honoring Grief after Divorce," is excerpted from *Spiritually Healthy Divorce: Navigating Disruption with Insight and Hope* (SkyLight Paths, 2010).

Carole Ann Camp, "Walking a Labyrinth for Healing and Connection," is excerpted from *Labyrinths from the Outside In*, 2nd Ed.: *Walking to Spiritual Insight—A Beginner's Guide* (SkyLight Paths, 2013).

Lynn L. Caruso, "Partingway Blessing for a Pet," is excerpted from *Blessing the Animals: Prayers and Ceremonies to Celebrate God's Creatures, Wild and Tame* (SkyLight Paths, 2008).

William Cleary, "Losses in Life—When Saddened by Failure," "Your Unfolding Forces—In Times of Disappointment," and "With Me in Pain—In Times of Anguish," are excerpted from *Prayers to an Evolutionary God* (SkyLight Paths, 2004).

Nancy Barrett Chickerneo, "The Wellspring of Life," is excerpted from *Woman Spirit Awakening in Nature: Growing into the Fullness of Who You Are* (SkyLight Paths, 2008).

Paul Wesley Chilcote, "Life and Death Are in Thine Hand," is excerpted from *John & Charles Wesley: Selections from Their Writings and Hymns—Annotated & Explained* (SkyLight Paths, 2011).

Nancy Copeland-Payton, "Losing Security, Beliefs, Identity," "Mourning the Loss of Physical Well-Being," and "Valley Journeys," are excerpted from *The Losses of Our Lives: The Sacred Gifts of Renewal in Everyday Loss* (SkyLight Paths, 2011).

Linda Douty, "Don't Waste Your Sorrows" and "Honoring Memories," are excerpted from *How Did I Get to Be 70 When I'm 35 Inside? Spiritual Surprises of Later Life* (SkyLight Paths, 2011).

Marica Ford, "Hope in Spite of Uncertainty," is excerpted from *Finding Hope: Cultivating God's Gift of a Hopeful Spirit* (SkyLight Paths, 2006). "Raging at God," is excerpted from *The Sacred Art of Forgiveness: Forgiving Ourselves and Others through God's Grace* (SkyLight Paths, 2006).

Monica Furlong, "Finding Healing and New Perspectives Through Prayer," is excerpted from *Women Pray: Voices Through the Ages, from Many Faiths, Cultures and Traditions* (SkyLight Paths, 2004).

Caren Goldman, "Childhood Losses," is excerpted from *Restoring Life's Missing Pieces: The Spiritual Power of Remembering and Reuniting with People, Places, Things and Self* (SkyLight Paths, 2011).

Kent Ira Groff, "Living Awake to What Is," is excerpted from *Honest to God Prayer: Spirituality as Awareness, Empowerment, Relinquishment and Paradox* (SkyLight Paths, 2012).

Steven Greenebaum, "Interfaith Prayers for Grieving and Healing Together," is excerpted from *Practical Interfaith: How to Find Our Common Humanity as We Celebrate Diversity* (SkyLight Paths, 2014).

Yusuf Hasan and George Handzo, "Anniversaries and Holidays after a Disaster," is excerpted from *Disaster Spiritual Care: Practical Clergy Responses to Community, Regional and National Tragedy*, edited by Rabbi Stephen B. Roberts, BCJC, and Rev. Willard W. C. Ashley Sr., DMIN, DH (SkyLight Paths, 2008).

Ana Hernández, "The Chant of the Heart," is excerpted from *The Sacred Art of Chant: Preparing to Practice* (SkyLight Paths, 2004).

Cait Johnson, "Grieving with Water" and "Sound Prayer," are excerpted from *Earth, Water, Fire and Air: Essential Ways of Connecting to Spirit* (SkyLight Paths, 2003).

Dr. Warren A. Kay, "Running as Sanctuary," is excerpted from *Running—The Sacred Art: Preparing to Practice* (SkyLight Paths, 2007).

Karyn D. Kedar, "Change for the Sake of Transformation," is excerpted from *Our Dance with God: Finding Prayer, Perspective and Meaning in the Stories of Our Lives* (Jewish Lights, 2004). "Waiting for Light" is excerpted from *God Whispers: Stories of the Soul, Lessons of the Heart* (Jewish Lights, 2000).

Kay Lindahl, "Listening for a Still Point," is excerpted from *The Sacred Art of Listening: Forty Reflections for Cultivating a Spiritual Practice* (SkyLight Paths, 2001).

Jay Marshall, "Speaking Love and Healing," is excerpted from *Thanking & Blessing—The Sacred Art: Spiritual Vitality Through Gratefulness* (SkyLight Paths, 2007).

Margaret D. McGee, "The Heart of a Moment," is excerpted from *Haiku—The Sacred Art: A Spiritual Practice in Three Lines* (SkyLight Paths, 2009). "Joy in the Memories," is excerpted from *Sacred Attention: A Spiritual Practice for Finding God in the Moment* (SkyLight Paths, 2010).

Ron Miller, "Being a Healing Presence," is excerpted from *The Gospel of Thomas: A Guidebook for Spiritual Practice* (SkyLight Paths, 2004).

Diane M. Millis, "Listening to Your Life," is excerpted from *Conversation—The Sacred Art: Practicing Presence in an Age of Distraction* (SkyLight Paths, 2013). "Tending Your Grief-Seeds," is excerpted from *Deepening Engagement: Essential Wisdom for Listening and Leading with Purpose, Meaning and Joy* (SkyLight Paths, 2015).

Timothy J. Mooney, "Becoming Whole," is excerpted from *Like a Child: Restoring the Awe, Wonder, Joy and Resiliency of the Human Spirit* (SkyLight Paths, 2014).

Linda Novick, "Still Life: Stepping Back," is excerpted from *The Painting Path: Embodying Spiritual Discovery Through Yoga, Brush and Color* (SkyLight Paths, 2007).

Christine Valters Paintner, "The Gift of Tears" and "Surrendering to the Desert," are excerpted from *Desert Fathers and Mothers: Early Christian Wisdom Sayings—Annotated & Explained* (SkyLight Paths, 2012); "Heart-Centered Prayer" and "Welcoming and Lamenting with Our Inner Witness" are excerpted from *Lectio Divina—The Sacred Art: Transforming Words & Images into Heart-Centered Prayer* (SkyLight Paths, 2011).

Gordon Peerman, "The Dharma of Dying," is excerpted from *Blessed Relief: What Christians Can Learn from Buddhists about Suffering* (SkyLight Paths, 2008).

M. Basil Pennington, "Give Ear to My Prayer," is excerpted from *Psalms: A Spiritual Commentary* (SkyLight Paths, 2008).

Jan Phillips, "No Holding Back," is excerpted from *Divining the Body: Reclaim the Holiness of Your Physical Self* (SkyLight Paths, 2005).

Jamal Rahman, "The Healing Art of Living in the Present," is excerpted from *Spiritual Gems of Islam: Insights & Practices from the Qur'an, Hadith, Rumi & Muslim Teaching Stories to Enlighten the Heart & Mind* (SkyLight Paths, 2013). "Not All Tears Are Equal" is excerpted from *Sacred Laughter of the Sufis: Awakening the Soul with the Mulla's Comic Teaching Stories & Other Islamic Wisdom* (SkyLight Paths, 2014).

Cory Richardson-Lauve, "Finding Your Focal Point Through Scrapbooking," is excerpted from *The Scrapbooking Journey: A Hands-On Guide to Spiritual Discovery* (SkyLight Paths, 2007).

Tom Stella, "Discovering God in the Midst of Evil," is excerpted from *Finding God Beyond Religion: A Guide for Skeptics, Agnostics & Unorthodox Believers Inside & Outside the Church* (SkyLight Paths, 2013).

Lori Joan Swick, "Dreaming as a Means of Spiritual Healing," is excerpted from *Dreaming—The Sacred Art: Incubating, Navigating and Interpreting Sacred Dreams for Spiritual and Personal Growth* (SkyLight Paths, 2014).

Rabindranath Tagore, "Into a Larger Existence," is excerpted from *Tagore: The Mystic Poets* (SkyLight Paths, 2004).

Rodney L. Taylor, "Confucius on True Expression in Mourning," is excerpted from *Confucius, the Analects: The Path of the Sage—Selections Annotated & Explained* (SkyLight Paths, 2011).

Terry Taylor, "A Pilgrimage for Brokenness," is excerpted from *A Spirituality for Brokenness: Discovering Your Deepest Self in Difficult Times* (SkyLight Paths, 2009).

Jane E. Vennard, "Accepting the Life That Awaits You" and "From Deserts of Loneliness to Gardens of Solitude," are excerpted from *Fully Awake and Truly Alive: Spiritual Practices to Nurture Your Soul* (SkyLight Paths, 2013).

Cynthia Winton-Henry, "Dancing with Our Shadows," is excerpted from *Dance—The Sacred Art: The Joy of Movement as a Spiritual Practice* (SkyLight Paths, 2009).

Andi Young, "Intimate with Suffering," is excerpted from *The Sacred Art of Bowing: Preparing to Practice* (SkyLight Paths, 2003).

Notes

Preface: Surrendering to the Desert

1. *The Sayings of the Desert Fathers: The Alphabetical Collection*, trans. Benedicta Ward (Collegeville, MN: Cistercian Publications, 1975), Alonius 2.
2. Ibid., Nilus 2, 5.

Welcoming and Lamenting with Our Inner Witness

1. Editor's note: *Meditatio* is the second step in a contemplative practice known as *lectio divina* (holy reading), practiced widely in the desert monastic tradition and, later, in the Benedictine order. *Lectio divina* is a process of prayer that involves savoring a sacred text through four steps or movements, which are often summarized as reading (*lectio*), reflecting (*meditatio*), responding (*oratio*), and resting (*contemplatio*).
2. See Naomi Shihab Nye, "Kindness," in *Words Under the Words: Selected Poems* (Portland, OR: Far Corner Books, 1995).

Acknowledging Large and Little Losses in Caregiving

1. Editor's note: See "Leaving a Legacy of Love" on pp. 231–234 for more about writing an ethical will.

Tagore on Beauty and Tragedy

1. Rabindranath Tagore, chapter 1 in *The Home and the World* (New York: Penguin Books, 2005).
2. Krishna Kripalani, *Tagore: A Biography* (New York: Grove Press, 1962), 204.

Becoming Whole

1. Gerald May, *Will and Spirit: A Contemplative Psychology* (San Francisco: HarperOne, 1987), 214.

Not All Tears Are Equal

1. Editor's note: The mythical Mulla Nasruddin is a village simpleton and sage rolled into one. His wisdom stories are treasured by the Sufis for their insight and humor. The Mulla is timeless and placeless. The earliest written accounts of him appeared in the thirteenth century, but oral stories of him were being told as early as the eighth century. He is a Muslim of Middle Eastern origin, but because his insights are universal, he is accepted as a citizen of the world. The Mulla is a popular figure, for example, in contemporary China. Most of the Mulla stories are fictional but are rooted in metaphors and images of the Qur'an and sayings of the Prophet Muhammad.

From Deserts of Loneliness to Gardens of Solitude

1. Paul Tillich, *The Eternal Now* (New York: Charles Scribner's Sons, 1963), 17–18.
2. Henri J. M. Nouwen, *Reaching Out: The Three Movements of the Spiritual Life* (Garden City, NY: Doubleday, 1966), 22.
3. John Chryssavgis, *In the Heart of the Desert: The Spirituality of the Desert Fathers and Mothers* (Bloomington, IN: World Wisdom, 2008), 49–51.

The Chant of the Heart

1. William Sloane Coffin, interview by Bill Moyers, *Bill Moyers on Faith & Reason*, PBS, March 5, 2004, www.pbs.org/moyers/faithandreason/print/coffin_print.html.

Running as Sanctuary

1. This quotation is the title of one of George Sheehan's essays and can be found at www.georgesheehan.com/essays/essay46.html.
2. Author's note: This account and the two quotations are taken from a paper written by one of my students for the course I teach, "The Spirituality of Running," and is used by permission.
3. Alfred North Whitehead, *Religion in the Making* (Cambridge, UK: Cambridge University Press, 1927), 6.
4. Abraham Joshua Heschel, *Man's Quest for God: Studies in Prayer and Symbolism* (New York: Charles Scribner's Sons, 1954), xiv.
5. George Sheehan, *Running and Being: The Total Experience* (New York: Simon and Schuster, 1978), 229.

The Circle of Life

1. Editor's note: Lustral water is used for sacred or purifying purposes ("lustral" meaning having purifying properties). In the Catholic church, it is synonymous with holy water, though many other religions have practices that use lustral water in rituals and ceremonies.

Seeing God in Memories and Lasting Love

1. Thornton Wilder, *The Bridge of San Luis Rey*, repr. (New York: HarperCollins, 2004), 123.

Childhood Losses

1. Arthur Schopenhauer, *The Essays of Arthur Schopenhauer: Studies in Pessimism*, trans. T. Bailey Saunders (Boston: Indiepublish.com, 2004), 54.
2. Akiko Busch, *Geography of Home: Writings on Where We Live* (Princeton, NJ: Princeton Architectural Press, 2003), 20–21.
3. Lawrence Kushner, *Invisible Lines of Connection: Sacred Stories of the Ordinary* (Woodstock, VT: Jewish Lights, 1996), 54.
4. Bruce Chatwin, *The Songlines* (New York: Penguin Books, 1987), 2.

Honoring Memories

1. Editor's note: See "Leaving a Legacy of Love" on pp. 231–234 for more about writing an ethical will.

Tending Your Grief-Seeds

1. "Gathering Blossoms," from *Beyond Bulrush* (Lit Fest Press, 2015), © Jeannie E. Roberts, used with permission of the poet, Jeannie E. Roberts; for more information, visit www.jrcreative.biz.
2. Author's note: One of the dominant frameworks for understanding grief has been, and continues to be, that of Elisabeth Kübler-Ross. Kübler-Ross identified an understanding of the stages of grief based on her experience of listening to and observing people with terminal diagnoses. Later in life, she conveyed that her conceptualization of the emotions that accompanied dying was never intended as a way to strategize grief. She clarified that, rather than put forth a stage theory—denial, anger, bargaining, depression, acceptance—her intent was to identify the features of the terrain. There is no template for grieving. Just as two persons who share the same experience may construct very different narratives about their experience, no two people experience the same loss (for example, the loss of a loved one) in the same way.
3. Angeles Arrien, *The Second Half of Life: Opening the Eight Gates of Wisdom* (Boulder, CO: Sounds True, 2005), 146–147.

Valley Journeys

1. C. S. Lewis, *A Grief Observed* (New York: HarperCollins, 1989), 60.

The Gift of Tears

1. Rule of St. Benedict, 20:3.
2. John Chryssavgis, *In the Heart of the Desert: The Spirituality of the Desert Fathers and Mothers* (Bloomington, IN: World Wisdom, 2003), 48.
3. Irenee Hausherr, *Penthos: The Doctrine of Compunction in the Christian East* (Kalamazoo, MI: Cistercian Publications, 1982), 8.
4. Hausherr, *Penthos*, 29.

Dreaming as a Means of Spiritual Healing

1. Robert Moss, *Dreaming the Soul Back Home: Shamanic Dreaming for Healing and Becoming Whole* (Novato, CA: New World Library, 2012), 62–63.

Finding Healing and New Perspectives Through Prayer

1. Mechthild of Magdeburg, quoted in *Beguine Spirituality* by Fiona Bowie, trans. Oliver Davies (London: SPCK, 1989).

The Wellspring of Life

1. Editor's note: SPA Sisters (Spirit, Place, and Authentic Self) is a nonprofit organization whose mission is to awaken women to their true selves through interaction with nature, creative expression, and connection with other women.

Change for the Sake of Transformation

1. Ralph Waldo Emerson, *Self-Reliance* (New York: Peter Pauper, 1967), 21.

Hope in Spite of Uncertainty

1. Eugene Robinson, "Nation of Fear," *Washington Post*, May 16, 2006, www.washingtonpost.com/wp-dyn/content/article/2006/05/15/AR2006051501187_pf.html.
2. Bernie S. Siegel, *Love, Medicine and Miracles: Lessons Learned about Self-Healing from a Surgeon's Experience with Exceptional Patients* (New York: HarperCollins, 2011), 28.

Discovering God in the Midst of Evil

1. Robert Farrar Capon, *The Third Peacock* (Minneapolis, MN: Winston Press, 1986).

Why? Perennial Wisdom on a Perennial Question

1. Stephen Mitchell, *The Book of Job* (San Francisco: North Point Press, 1987), xxviii.
2. Marcus Aurelius, *The Meditations of Marcus Aurelius: Selections Annotated & Explained*, annotation by Russell McNeil; translation by George Long, revised by Russell McNeil (Woodstock, VT: SkyLight Paths, 2007), 203.

Anniversaries and Holidays after a Disaster

1. Editor's note: The family experience described here is that of the first author, Imam Yusuf Hasan.

Listening to Your Life

1. John O'Donohue, *To Bless the Space Between Us: A Book of Blessings* (New York: Doubleday, 2008), 49.
2. Jill Freedman and Gene Combs, *Narrative Therapy: The Social Construction of Preferred Realities* (New York: W.W. Norton, 1996), 98.
3. Dave Isay, *Listening Is an Act of Love: A Celebration of American Life from the StoryCorps Project* (New York: Penguin, 2007), 1.
4. See Freedman and Combs, *Narrative Therapy*, 42–76, for more information on deconstructive listening and questioning and opening space for new stories.
5. Richard L. Hester and Kelli Walker-Jones, *Know Your Story and Lead with It: The Power of Narrative in Clergy Leadership* (Herndon, VA: Alban Institute, 2009), 35.

Leaving a Legacy of Love

1. Author's note: A "living will" is one that provides for those medical measures one wishes to be taken or not taken on his or her behalf if physicians declare him or her to be in a persistent vegetative state with no likelihood of regaining consciousness.

The Dharma of Dying

1. This is the form of the Five Remembrances practice given by Thich Nhat Hanh in *The Blooming of a Lotus*, trans. Annabel Laity, rev. ed. (Boston: Beacon Press, 2009).

A Healing Good-bye

1. Author's note: I learned this from Cantor Susan Deutsch as "the healing hand," now further developed in her book *The Healing Hand: Five Discussions to Have with the Dying Who Are Living* (Mission Viejo, CA: Handutch Press, 2014). The steps of saying good-bye to a loved one are well presented in palliative physician Ira Byock's *The Four Things That Matter Most: A Book About Living*, 10th anniv. ed. (New York: Atria Books, 2014).

Inspiration

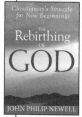

The Rebirthing of God
Christianity's Struggle for New Beginnings
By John Philip Newell
Drawing on modern prophets from East and West, and using the holy island of Iona as an icon of new beginnings, Celtic poet, peacemaker and scholar John Philip Newell dares us to imagine a new birth from deep within Christianity, a fresh stirring of the Spirit.
6 x 9, 160 pp, HC, 978-1-59473-542-4 **$19.99**

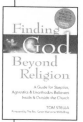

Finding God Beyond Religion: A Guide for Skeptics, Agnostics & Unorthodox Believers Inside & Outside the Church
By Tom Stella; Foreword by The Rev. Canon Marianne Wells Borg
Reinterprets traditional religious teachings central to the Christian faith for people who have outgrown the beliefs and devotional practices that once made sense to them.
6 x 9, 160 pp, Quality PB, 978-1-59473-485-4 **$16.99**

Deepening Engagement
Essential Wisdom for Listening and Leading with Purpose, Meaning and Joy
By Diane M. Millis, PhD; Foreword by Rob Lehman
A toolkit for community building as well as a resource for personal growth and small group enrichment.
5 x 7¼, 176 pp, Quality PB, 978-1-59473-584-4 **$14.99**

Fully Awake and Truly Alive: Spiritual Practices to Nurture Your Soul
By Rev. Jane E. Vennard; Foreword by Rami Shapiro
Illustrates the joys and frustrations of spiritual practice, offers insights from various religious traditions and provides exercises and meditations to help us become more fully alive.
6 x 9, 208 pp, Quality PB, 978-1-59473-473-1 **$16.99**

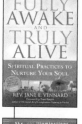

Perennial Wisdom for the Spiritually Independent
Sacred Teachings—Annotated & Explained
Annotation by Rami Shapiro; Foreword by Richard Rohr
Weaves sacred texts and teachings from the world's major religions into a coherent exploration of the five core questions at the heart of every religion's search.
5½ x 8½, 336 pp, Quality PB, 978-1-59473-515-8 **$16.99**

Journeys of Simplicity: Traveling Light with Thomas Merton, Bashō, Edward Abbey, Annie Dillard & Others *By Philip Harnden*
5 x 7¼, 144 pp, Quality PB, 978-1-59473-181-5 **$12.99**

Saving Civility: 52 Ways to Tame Rude, Crude & Attitude for a Polite Planet
By Sara Hacala 6 x 9, 240 pp, Quality PB, 978-1-59473-314-7 **$16.99**

Spiritually Healthy Divorce: Navigating Disruption with Insight & Hope
By Carolyne Call 6 x 9, 224 pp, Quality PB, 978-1-59473-288-1 **$16.99**

Or phone, fax, mail or email to: SKYLIGHT PATHS Publishing
Sunset Farm Offices, Route 4 • P.O. Box 237 • Woodstock, Vermont 05091
Tel: (802) 457-4000 • Fax: (802) 457-4004 • www.skylightpaths.com
Credit card orders: (800) 962-4544 (8:30AM–5:30PM EST Monday–Friday)
Generous discounts on quantity orders. SATISFACTION GUARANTEED. Prices subject to change.

Personal Growth

Deepening Engagement
Essential Wisdom for Listening and Leading with Purpose, Meaning and Joy
By Diane M. Millis, PhD; Foreword by Rob Lehman
A toolkit for community building as well as a resource for personal growth and small group enrichment.
5 x 7¼, 176 pp, Quality PB, 978-1-59473-584-4 **$14.99**

The Forgiveness Handbook
Spiritual Wisdom and Practice for the Journey to Freedom, Healing and Peace
Created by the Editors at SkyLight Paths; Introduction by The Rev. Canon Marianne Wells Borg
Offers inspiration, encouragement and spiritual practice from across faith traditions for all who seek hope, wholeness and the freedom that comes from true forgiveness. 6 x 9, 256 pp, Quality PB, 978-1-59473-577-6 **$18.99**

Decision Making & Spiritual Discernment: The Sacred Art of
Finding Your Way *By Nancy L. Bieber*
Presents three essential aspects of Spirit-led decision making: willingness, attentiveness and responsiveness.
5½ x 8½, 208 pp, Quality PB, 978-1-59473-289-8 **$16.99**

Like a Child
Restoring the Awe, Wonder, Joy and Resiliency of the Human Spirit
By Rev. Timothy J. Mooney
Explores Jesus's counsel to become like children in order to enter the kingdom of God. 6 x 9, 160 pp, Quality PB, 978-1-59473-543-1 **$16.99**

Secrets of a Soulful Marriage
Creating & Sustaining a Loving, Sacred Relationship
By Jim Sharon, EdD, and Ruth Sharon, MS
An innovative, hope-filled resource for developing soulful, mature love for committed couples who are looking to create, maintain and glorify the sacred in their relationship. Offers a banquet of practical tools, inspirational real-life stories and spiritual practices for couples of all faiths, or none.
6 x 9, 192 pp, Quality PB, 978-1-59473-554-7 **$16.99**

A Spirituality for Brokenness
Discovering Your Deepest Self in Difficult Times
By Terry Taylor
Compassionately guides you through the practicalities of facing and finally accepting brokenness in your life—a process that can ultimately bring mending.
6 x 9, 176 pp, Quality PB, 978-1-59473-229-4 **$16.99**

The Bridge to Forgiveness
Stories and Prayers for Finding God and Restoring Wholeness
By Karyn D. Kedar
6 x 9, 176 pp, Quality PB, 978-1-58023-451-1 **$16.99***

Conversation—The Sacred Art
Practicing Presence in an Age of Distraction
By Diane M. Millis, PhD; Foreword by Rev. Tilden Edwards, PhD
5½ x 8½, 192 pp, Quality PB, 978-1-59473-474-8 **$16.99**

Hospitality—The Sacred Art
Discovering the Hidden Spiritual Power of Invitation and Welcome
By Rev. Nanette Sawyer; Foreword by Rev. Dirk Ficca
5½ x 8½, 208 pp, Quality PB, 978-1-59473-228-7 **$16.99**

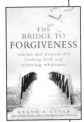

The Losses of Our Lives
The Sacred Gifts of Renewal in Everyday Loss
By Dr. Nancy Copeland-Payton
6 x 9, 192 pp, Quality PB, 978-1-59473-307-9 **$16.99**; HC, 978-1-59473-271-3 **$19.99**

*A book from Jewish Lights, SkyLight Paths' sister imprint

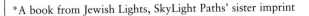

About SKYLIGHT PATHS Publishing

SkyLight Paths Publishing is creating a place where people of different spiritual traditions come together for challenge and inspiration, a place where we can help each other understand the mystery that lies at the heart of our existence.

Through spirituality, our religious beliefs are increasingly becoming a part of our lives—rather than *apart* from our lives. While many of us may be more interested than ever in spiritual growth, we may be less firmly planted in traditional religion. Yet, we do want to deepen our relationship to the sacred, to learn from our own as well as from other faith traditions, and to practice in new ways.

SkyLight Paths sees both believers and seekers as a community that increasingly transcends traditional boundaries of religion and denomination—people wanting to learn from each other, *walking together, finding the way.*

For your information and convenience, at the back of this book we have provided a list of other SkyLight Paths books you might find interesting and useful. They cover the following subjects:

Buddhism / Zen	Gnosticism	Poetry
Catholicism	Hinduism / Vedanta	Prayer
Chaplaincy		Religious Etiquette
Children's Books	Inspiration	Retirement & Later-Life Spirituality
Christianity	Islam / Sufism	
Comparative Religion	Judaism	Spiritual Biography
	Meditation	Spiritual Direction
Earth-Based Spirituality	Mindfulness	Spirituality
	Monasticism	Women's Interest
Enneagram	Mysticism	Worship
Global Spiritual Perspectives	Personal Growth	

Or phone, fax, mail or email to: SKYLIGHT PATHS Publishing
Sunset Farm Offices, Route 4 • P.O. Box 237 • Woodstock, Vermont 05091
Tel: (802) 457-4000 • Fax: (802) 457-4004 • www.skylightpaths.com
Credit card orders: (800) 962-4544 (8:30AM–5:30PM EST Monday–Friday)
Generous discounts on quantity orders. SATISFACTION GUARANTEED. Prices subject to change.